The Bird-Friendly Backyard™

NATURAL GARDENING FOR BIRDS

The Bird-Friendly Backyard™

Natural Gardening for Birds

Simple Ways to Create a Bird Haven

Julie Zickefoose and the Editors and Writers of *Bird Watcher's Digest*

Illustrations by Julie Zickefoose

RODALE

RODALE

WE **INSPIRE** AND **ENABLE** PEOPLE TO IMPROVE
THEIR LIVES AND THE WORLD AROUND THEM

The information in this book has been carefully researched, and all efforts have been made to ensure accuracy. Rodale Inc. assumes no responsibility for any injuries suffered or for damages or losses incurred during the use of or as a result of following this information. It is important to study all directions carefully before taking any action based on the information and advice presented in this book. When using any commercial product, *always* read and follow label directions. Where trade names are used, no discrimination is intended and no endorsement by Rodale Inc. is implied.

Printed in the United States of America on acid-free (∞), recycled (♻) paper

We're always happy to hear from you. For questions or comments concerning the editorial content of this book, please write to:

Rodale Book Readers' Service
33 East Minor Street
Emmaus, PA 18098

Look for other Rodale books wherever books are sold. Or call us at (800) 848-4735.

For more information about Rodale Organic Living magazines and books, visit us at
www.organicgardening.com

On the cover: The peppery red fruits of spicebush (*Lindera benzoin*) are irresistable to eastern bluebirds, and they provide a feast for the gardener's eye as well.

Editor: Karen Bolesta
Contributing Editor: Susan B. Burton
Cover and Interior Book Designer: Nancy Smola Biltcliff
Cover and Interior Illustrator: Julie Zickefoose
Layout Designer: Faith Hague
Researchers: Diana Erney and Sarah Wolfgang Heffner
Copy Editor: Linda Brunner
Product Specialist: Brenda Miller
Indexer: Lina Burton
Editorial Assistance: Susan L. Nickol and Megan O'Connell

Rodale Organic Living Books

Editorial Director: Christopher Hirsheimer
Executive Creative Director: Christin Gangi
Executive Editor: Kathleen DeVanna Fish
Art Director: Patricia Field
Content Assembly Manager: Robert V. Anderson Jr.
Studio Manager: Leslie M. Keefe
Copy Manager: Nancy N. Bailey
Projects Coordinator: Kerrie A. Cadden

Library of Congress Cataloging-in-Publication Data

Zickefoose, Julie.
  The bird-friendly backyard : natural gardening for birds : simple ways to create a bird haven / Julie Zickefoose and the editors and writers of Bird Watcher's Digest ; illustrations by Julie Zickefoose.
      p. cm.
Includes bibliographical references (p.   ) and index.
  ISBN 0–87596–873–2 (hardcover : alk. paper)
  ISBN 0–87596–883–X (pbk. : alk. paper)
  1. Gardening to attract birds—United States. I. Bird Watcher's Digest
(Firm) II. Title.
  QL676.55 .Z53 2001
  639.9'78—dc21   2001004819

Distributed in the book trade by St. Martin's Press

2 4 6 8 10 9 7 5 3 1   hardcover

2 4 6 8 10 9 7 5 3 1   paperback

Kay Saunders

For DOD, who always said
I'd forget about chasing birds when
I discovered horticulture. You were
right—now I let them come to me!

Rodale
Organic Gardening Starts Here!

HERE at Rodale, we've been gardening organically for more than 60 years—ever since my grandfather J. I. Rodale learned about composting and decided that healthy living starts with healthy soil. In 1940 J. I. started the Rodale Organic Farm to test his theories, and today the nonprofit Rodale Institute Experimental Farm is still at the forefront of organic gardening and farming research. In 1942 J. I. founded *Organic Gardening* magazine to share his discoveries with gardeners everywhere. His son, my father, Robert Rodale, headed *Organic Gardening* until 1990, and today a third generation of Rodales is growing up with the magazine. Over the years we've shown millions of readers how to grow bountiful crops and beautiful flowers using nature's own techniques.

In this book, you'll find the latest organic methods and the best gardening advice. We know—because all our authors and editors are passionate about gardening! We feel strongly that our gardens should be safe for our children, pets, and the birds and butterflies that add beauty and delight to our lives and landscapes. Our gardens should provide us with fresh, flavorful vegetables, delightful herbs, and gorgeous flowers. And they should be a pleasure to work in as well as to view.

Sharing the secrets of safe, successful gardening is why we publish books. So come visit us at www.organicgardening.com, where you can tour the world of organic gardening all day, every day. And use this book to create your best garden ever.

Happy gardening!

Maria Rodale
Rodale Organic Living Books

Contents

Plant It, and They Will Come

A weekend in May, and I find myself in Chicago. It's high migration time, and as I explore the city on foot and by bus, I find warblers everywhere, sitting dazed and confused on the hard sidewalks of the concrete canyons. Other people don't seem to notice this phenomenon; they step over the tiny birds as they would candy wrappers, but I'm scurrying everywhere, trying to help. These avian migrants have arrived here at night, having been drawn in by the skyscrapers' lights. They've bumbled about in confusion, and daylight has found them in unfriendly territory. I see a tiny yellowthroat being blown about in the backdraft of a city bus, and I pick it up; it's exhausted but unhurt, its eyes bright and defiant in its black bandit mask. Smiling, I slip the little bird into a coat pocket. I've got a plan.

THE MAGIC HEDGE

There's a park on a little peninsula that juts out into Lake Michigan, and in that park is a row of bushes that's called the Magic Hedge. Bird watchers have given it this name because any species is likely to turn up in it at any time. It's nothing special botanically, mostly privet, but it's the last real cover migrant birds can use to feed and rest before they make the great flight across Lake Michigan on their way north in the spring. In the fall, exhausted migrants plummet into the hedge after they've flown the length of the lake on their way south. The hedge is essential, and it doubtless saves many small lives. I would hate to be a caterpillar in the Magic Hedge.

I disembark the bus and make my way to the lakefront and the hedge. I barely get my pocket open before the little yellowthroat slips out and dives into the hedge; he'll make it now. Glowing with satisfaction, I scan the privet bushes with my binoculars and see the first sedge wren of my life, as if in reward for the small service I've done. Other birders stand quietly, appreciating wave after wave of birds that pass through the hedge.

The Magic Hedge quietly gives its gift to birds and birders alike every season. I reflect on the interrelationship of this simple planting, intended merely as a windscreen, and the hoards of migrant birds and bird watchers who have learned to exploit it. Yes, its importance is en-hanced by its unique location, but there are Magic Hedges everywhere. We've only to plant them or to stand back and let them develop.

BIRDS: NATURAL GARDENERS

When my husband and I bought our 80-acre, southeast Ohio property in 1992, the grounds were devoid of trees, shrubs, or flowers. The big meadow, mown three times each summer, was mostly orchard grass and not very botanically interesting.

In the 8 years since then, we've done a dance with the property, planting here, mowing there, letting this and that go. We've planted butterfly gardens, hummingbird gardens, and seed gardens for the finches. Our efforts, while colorful and pleasing, pale in comparison to the intricate tapestry nature has woven around the edges of our lawn. Birds like edges; they perch a lot where woodland meets meadow, and they naturally sow the seeds of the fruits they enjoy there. Black raspberry, sumac, dogwood, sassafras, tupelo, aster, goldenrod, foxtail, deertongue, spicebush—it's a glorious tangle, one we could never dream of or plant ourselves.

A WEALTH OF HABITATS

This book is a celebration of gardens, planned and unplanned, and the myriad ways they enrich our lives. It sprang up when the editors at both *Bird Watcher's Digest* and Rodale decided to bring the wealth of natural gardening information in the magazine's features to a larger audience. Paging through the book, you'll find meadows and hedgerows, berry patches, ponds, and shrubby cover—the habitats that experienced birders know shelter the most birds. Why not bring one or more of them to your own backyard? Imitate nature with your plantings, and you'll welcome nature nearby. The dividends pay out in birds, small mammals, reptiles, amphibians, and insects, all riches beyond measure for the naturalist in each one of us.

Whether you're about to plant a hummingbird garden, install a water feature, create perches from dead snags, start a feeding station, or simply let a corner of your property run wild, you'll find inspiration and information on every page of *The Bird-Friendly Backyard: Natural Gardening for Birds*. Let it help you welcome nature, in all its carefree disorder, into your yard and your life, and forge a deep and joyous connection to all things wild and wonderful. The view from your windows will never be mundane again.

Julie Zickefoose
Whipple, Ohio

1

THE BEST PLANTS FOR BIRDS

Fruit, Nectar, Seeds, and Shelter

juniper berries evergreen penstemon columbine morning glory vine blossom foxglove **plants**

SOME OF THE LOVELIEST GARDENS to human eyes may not appeal to birds and beasts at all. Birds may shun a well-pruned garden of exotic plants and prefer to hang out in the overgrown and weedy abandoned lot down the street. How could they desert your lovely rose beds for what seems to be the low-rent district in the neighborhood? Simple. Birds need what nature produces—fruit, nectar, and seeds to sustain them, and overgrown tangles to provide shelter. If you want to live with the birds, let the plants they love thrive in your yard. Well-chosen plants will welcome the local birds and will signal to migrating birds that your gardens are bountiful and safe.

Guidelines for Great Gardens

CREATING gardens for birds takes a little thought and planning. You'll want to be sure to choose plants that will work well in your neck of the woods. As your imagination fires up and you plan new beds or revamp the old, consider what each plant provides for birds, how big each plant gets, how different plants can combine to add color and interest throughout the growing season, and how important foundation plantings are. If you keep these things in mind, you'll be set for success.

WHAT GOOD IS IT?

When considering any new plant addition, ask yourself what it's good for. Will it bear berries or seeds for birds? Does it have bright, tubular blossoms that will attract hummingbirds? Does it shine with flat clusters of tiny flowers for butterflies? As it grows, will it produce thick, dense foliage that will provide shelter for birds and insects? Most plants offer something for birds and insects but some are of more use than others are. The more perks a particular plant offers, the more it belongs in your landscape.

HOW BIG IS BIG ENOUGH?

Beware—some plants can really sneak up on you. Consider a plant's size when it is mature before you add it to your garden. That charming little buddleia in the ½-gallon pot could tower far above your head by summer's end, engulfing the Siberian iris at its feet. When shopping for plants, note the mature height and width of each selected plant so you can allot space for it in your garden design. A good rule of thumb—if a plant is happy where you've put it, it will probably use the space you've given it and then some.

PRETTY ALL YEAR LONG

You'll want color and interest in your garden year-round. Every garden book notes that anyone can have a beautiful garden in late June—it's having color in August that's the trick.

Don't succumb to spring fever and buy everything that's blooming at the nursery in mid-May. Space out your gardening efforts through the dog days of summer and early autumn, so you'll always have something nice to look at, and the birds and insects will have nectar and fruit throughout the growing season.

A FIRM FOUNDATION

Don't neglect foundation plantings for the showier bloomers. Set aside space for junipers, arborvitaes, rhododendrons, and dwarf spruces. Song sparrows will soon be snooping around these shrubs. When winter comes, you'll be mighty glad to look at something green and know that birds can tuck themselves into a thick juniper for the night (and get a late-night snack of juniper fruits to boot!).

FITTING IT IN

Be aware of your garden conditions as you choose your plants. How much sun does the spot get? Do you need to choose plants that do well in partial shade or full sun? Is your soil acidic? Can the plants you'd like to add to your garden survive in your climate's extremes? Don't try to grow plants that aren't suited to your backyard or you and the birds will be disappointed.

Just Say No!

MANY of the plants that gardeners have propagated have jumped beyond defined boundaries and continue to spread across the continent. They compete with (and even destroy) native plant communities. In many cases, birds quicken the spread of invasive plants by gobbling up the palatable fruit and dispersing seed through their droppings or even dropping fruits as they fly.

Exercise self-control when you are tempted to add these plants to your backyard garden. They may look like quick fixes for erosion problems or trouble spots and birds may enjoy their fruit, but they quickly become uncontrollable marauders in the landscape. To find out about invasive species in your specific area, ask your state or provincial natural heritage officer, or contact the Nature Conservancy. (See "Resources and Supplies" on page 232.)

Mimosa
  (*Albizia julibrissin*)

Giant reed
  (*Arundo donax*)

Japanese barberry
  (*Berberis thunbergii*)

Asiatic bittersweet
  (*Celastrus orbiculatus*)

Crown vetch
  (*Coronilla varia*)

Queen Anne's lace
  (*Daucus carota*)

Russian olive
  (*Elaeagnus angustifolia*)

Climbing euonymus
  (*Euonymus fortunei*)

Dame's rocket
  (*Hesperis matronalis*)

Perennial pea
  (*Lathyrus latifolius*)

Japanese honeysuckle
  (*Lonicera japonica*)

Double bird's foot trefoil
  (*Lotus corniculatus*)

Purple loosestrife
  (*Lythrum salicaria*)

Sweet clovers
  (*Melilotus* spp.)

Fountain grass
  (*Pennisetum setaceum*)

Reed canary grass
  (*Phalaris arundinacea*)

Buckthorn
  (*Rhamnus frangula*)

Planting for Birds and Butterflies

WHAT are birds looking for in your yard that you can supply? Whenever you ponder such questions, seek answers that also attract butterflies. Since birds and butterflies share the same habitats, there are many plants that cater to both.

Birds are not as picky about plant species as they are about habitat structure and type of food. If the nesting site suits or the seed tastes good, they don't fuss about whether it's "natural" or not. Butterflies, on the other hand, are notoriously provincial. Although they'll favor some exotic varieties on occasion, they definitely prefer native plants. Your job as a gardener is to strike a balance between foreign and native species and, at the same time, lay out the welcome mat to both birds and butterflies.

SEEDS AND SWEET NECTAR

Fields of mixed native grasses and wildflowers not only provide seeds and nesting habitats for grassland birds but they also provide the vegetation local butterflies feed upon both as caterpillars and adults. Some wildflowers are excellent sources of food for seed-eating

---

Quick Reference | **BE FRUITFUL**

CERTAIN native shrubs and trees provide threefold service: leaves (and sometimes buds and blossoms) to feed caterpillars, flower nectar to nourish adult butterflies, and fruits to fill birds' bellies.

THREEFOLD NATIVE PLANTS	BUTTERFLIES THEY NOURISH
Hawthorns (*Crataegus* spp.)	Several swallowtails and admirals
Cherries (*Prunus* spp.)	Several swallowtails and admirals
Sumacs (*Rhus* spp.)	Red-banded hairstreaks
Blueberries (*Vaccinium* spp.)	Pink-edged sulphurs and brown elfins

Quick Reference	NESTING AND NECTAR

SHRUBS and trees that provide nesting for birds also attract lovely butter-flies. Try these in your garden if they are suited to your region's climate.

NESTING TREES AND SHRUBS	BUTTERFLIES THEY SUPPORT
Catclaw acacia (*Acacia greggii*)	Marine blues
Wild lilacs (*Ceanothus* spp.)	California tortoiseshells
Hackberries (*Celtis* spp.)	Hackberry emperors
Ashes (*Fraxinus* spp.)	Eastern tiger and two-tailed swallowtails
Locusts (*Gleditsia* spp. and *Robinia* spp.)	Silver-spotted skippers
Spicebush (*Lindera benzoin*)	Spicebush swallowtails
Red bay (*Persea borbonia*)	Palamedes swallowtails
Poplars and willows (*Populus* spp. and *Salix* spp.)	Canadian and western tiger swallowtails, mourning cloaks, viceroys, and admirals such as the white, Weidemeyer's, and Lorquin's
Mesquite (*Prosopis juliflora*)	Leda hairstreaks and Reakirts's blues
Sassafras (*Sassafras albidum*)	Spicebush swallowtails

birds such as finches and sparrows, and some also serve as nectar flowers for adult butterflies. These double-duty plants include blanket flowers (*Gaillardia* spp.), rough gayfeather (*Liatris aspera*), and thistles (*Cirsium* spp.). Be cautious when choosing or planting thistles, though: Some alien thistle species are widespread, noxious weeds that invasively displace native plants. Check your local weed ordinances before planting any type of thistle.

NESTING HABITAT

"The more the merrier" should be your goal when you are planting your bird-friendly backyard. Look to deciduous shrubs and trees to provide nesting locations for many bird species. Tall shrubs and trees are ideal because they offer birds a safe respite from predators, such as cats and raccoons, who can reach their nests in lower-growing woody plants. If you want to play host to both birds and butterflies, choose shrubs and trees that also provide caterpillars with food; if you do, you'll be host to both birds and butterflies with the same plant. The adult butterflies that you attract will fly around your yard in search of food and each other, while the caterpillars will stay close to the plants that provide food. Looking for them is part of the fun, but keep a distance from active bird nests, and wait until summertime for all-out caterpillar searches.

A hackberry emperor lays its eggs on its chosen food plant. Birds also relish hackberry fruits.

Flying or Fluttering, Welcome It

IF you want to encourage butterflies as well as birds to your yard, tempt butterflies that are already nearby. Instead of planting something different, try a plant or two that is attracting butterflies in the field down the road. The butterflies using those plants may expand their range to use your offerings, too. Use a field guide to determine which species of butterflies live in your area.

Insects are a vital part of a healthy and hospitable garden. Most birds include insects as a major portion of their diet. Although you may not want to attract some types of pests, a healthy garden will (and should) have many insects. While butterflies, bees, and other pollinators fly or flutter in to your yard to visit your flowers, innumerable tiny insects actually live on the stems and leaves of your plants. Many of these are beneficial, like the lady beetles and lacewings that eat aphids. Most insects rarely do permanent damage to plants, and nature can usually keep their numbers in check—partly due to the vigilance of the birds. It's great fun to watch the wrens and flycatchers feed their way through the yard every day, keeping insect numbers down.

plants

juniper berries evergreen penstemon columbine morning glory vine blossom foxglove

The Importance of Junipers

WHEN you plan and plant a bird garden, you'll need to incorporate a variety of shrubs and trees into the design. But this emphasis on trees and shrubs may conflict with your desire for a refined, beautiful ornamental garden. Don't despair! One group of plants—the junipers—can satisfy both needs. Birds love them (and the habitat they provide), yet their good looks will certainly gratify your aesthetic nature.

Junipers are suitable for practically any planting scheme. Juniper varieties run the range of color— light to dark green, gray-green, bluish green, steel blue, and even gold. Being evergreen, many of these plants retain their hues throughout winter, although some turn shades of purple. The reddish bark of many junipers only adds to their attractiveness.

GROW 'EM ANYWHERE

Junipers are a hit with gardeners because they tolerate a variety of light conditions, soil conditions, and

A chipping sparrow feeds her brood in a columnar juniper. Shrubby and prostrate junipers also afford cover and food for birds.

Warblers living in the fine-needled evergreen canopy have very high-pitched songs with a frequency that carries the farthest in this dense environment.

temperatures. Ideally, they should have full sun, but they can take partial to light shade in stride. As long as your soil has good drainage, junipers will do well in it.

They need water, like all plants do, but they can often be found growing in dry, stony, and sandy soils. And they can even survive droughts. Most junipers will withstand salt spray and ocean winds, making them prized plants for seaside gardens. They are also among the hardiest of the evergreens.

A few junipers grow in parts of Alaska and Canada where the temperatures are frigid in winter, while others grow throughout the United States, as far south as Florida, California, Texas, and on into Mexico. There are about 15 species native to North America and some 50 other species worldwide.

ALL SHAPES AND SIZES

Junipers fall into three basic categories—prostrate, bushy, and columnar. Prostrate, or creeping, junipers are low-growing plants, reaching 1 to 4 feet (0.3 to 1.2 m) in height, and spreading 4 to 8 feet (1.2 to 2.4 m) wide. They provide excellent cover for ground birds. Although they are less likely than other junipers to produce fruitlike cones, some still supply an adequate amount of food. *Juniperus horizontalis*, a creeping juniper with at least 20 different varieties, is native to North America, as is the common juniper, *J. communis*.

The bushy junipers come in a variety of sizes ranging from 2 to 15 feet (0.6 to 4.5 m) tall and from 3 to 10 feet (0.9 to 3 m) wide. The *Pfitzeriana* hybrids are often seen growing around buildings, both commercial and residential. Varieties of *J. sabina* and *J. squamata* are other shrubby junipers.

By far the best-known junipers are the ones that have columnar shapes, which include many native species, most notably the eastern red cedar (*J. virginiana*). It's the perfect choice for bird watchers who garden in the Northeast. Its western counterpart is the Rocky Mountain juniper (*J. scopulorum*), which grows throughout the West. Both trees can reach 30 feet (9 m) or more in height and 20 feet (6 m) wide. Many varieties of *J. chinensis* fall into this category as well.

Other junipers that grow well in the West include the western (*J. occidentalis*), the one-seed (*J. monosperma*), the Utah (*J. osteosperma*), the alligator (*J. deppeana*), and the pinchot (*J. pinchotii*). If you live in the Southeast, try planting southern red cedar (*J. silicicola*), and you won't be disappointed.

Junipers are adaptable and hardy, and they will make a great addition to your bird garden no matter where you live.

An Audubon's warbler weathers a cold snap with oil-rich juniper fruits.

NATURAL · GARDENING

GO NATIVE!

PLANTS or seeds that originate in your climate will be more successful in your backyard than plants or seeds that come to you from more extreme areas. It's not difficult to choose native plants for your yard, and the birds and butterflies will appreciate it.

Look for regional seed suppliers and nurseries that offer varieties particularly suited to your area. Many garden centers can easily point out the native plants that they have for sale. Or you can check your local library for the *Andersen Horticultural Library's Source List of Plants and Seeds*; it contains information on mail-order cata-

JUNIPER BUFFET

Like other conifers, junipers provide bird food in the form of cones. However, junipers are unique because the cones have a waxy covering that makes them look like berries; that's why they're known as "juniper berries." The berrylike cones of most junipers are blue, although those of the native redberry junipers are red.

For the most part, junipers have male and female flowers that are borne on separate plants. Only those junipers with female flowers will produce berries, and a male plant, needed for pollination, must be growing nearby.

Juniper berries are an important source of food for birds in the winter. When winter snows hit, they can be a lifesaver for many bird species. The fruits are hardy, and they are produced high enough on the plant to be seen above the snow.

A wide variety of birds compete for juniper berries. For example, the berries of the eastern red cedar may attract as many as 90 different species of birds. The fruitlike cones entice bobwhites, turkeys, bluebirds, robins and other thrushes, thrashers, catbirds, mockingbirds, warblers, phoebes, juncos, sparrows, grosbeaks, cardinals, nutcrackers, pinyon jays, mourning doves, tree swallows, pine siskins, flickers, and red-bellied woodpeckers. Cedar waxwings are so fond of juniper berries that they were named after

logs and seed suppliers in your area. You can also look around and simply sow or transplant what nature offers. It only takes a little effort to collect seeds from local plants, and it's great fun. (Of course, always ask permission to gather if you're not the landowner.) Transplanting volunteers from one place to another on your property works well, too. Often the plant you'd like to grow outside the picture window sprouts enthusiastically somewhere else.

Then there's good, old-fashioned bartering with fellow plant lovers. When your wild columbines produce a bumper crop of seeds, swap a few spoonfuls of your seeds for your neighbor's jewelweed seeds.

the plants. Yellow-bellied and red-naped sapsuckers not only eat the fruitlike cones but they also drill into the woody plants for sap.

PLANTING JUNIPERS

Plant junipers in clumps, groupings, or as a hedge to increase their usefulness to birds for nesting and cover. You can use them for screens, windbreaks, foundation plantings, and groundcovers.

Junipers make great container plants as well since they can tolerate the extremes of both hot and cold temperatures. The prostrate varieties can even be grown in hanging baskets because they will spill beautifully over the container edges. When used in hanging baskets, creeping juniper (*J. horizontalis*, especially 'Bar Harbor' and 'Wiltonii'), *J. procumbens*, and *J. conferta* may provide nesting and roosting sites for house finches or Carolina wrens.

Keep junipers away from apples, crabapples, or other closely related plants, though, because they are alternate hosts for a fungal disease called cedar-apple rust. Junipers usually suffer less damage from the oozing, fleshy growths of the rust than do the apples, though. Eastern red cedar and Rocky Mountain juniper seem to be more susceptible to this disease than other junipers.

Juniper Claim Jumpers

BECAUSE of their evergreen foliage, junipers provide birds with protective shelter year-round—blocking the cold winds in winter and the hot sun in the summer. These birds use junipers for shelter and may also find favorable nesting sites among the dense branches.

Northern mockingbirds	Juncos
Brown thrashers	Northern cardinals
Robins	Evening grosbeaks
Cedar waxwings	Chipping sparrows
Warblers	Song sparrows

Birds Love Winding, Twining Vines

DON'T overlook vines when planning a garden because vines supply food, nesting sites, and cover for your birds. During the growing season, the luscious foliage and pretty blossoms of vines provide beauty and habitat, and during colder weather, the evergreen varieties add interest to your winter landscape while providing protection from the cold for the birds.

If you have limited space for a bird garden, vines are just about the perfect plants. They can cover large areas of a fence or wall in a short time yet only take up about a foot or two (30 to 60 cm) of space in front of these structures.

THE WELL-ATTACHED VINE

Vines use several devices to attach themselves, with most vines falling into four basic categories—the clingers, the grabbers, the twiners, and the sprawlers.

The clingers, such as Virginia creeper, trumpet vine, Boston ivy, and wintercreeper, affix themselves to objects by rootlets or tendrils with adhesive disks. (Be aware that Boston ivy and wintercreeper are invasive in some areas.) Clingers work the best on rough-textured, broad surfaces such as brick, block, or stone walls, and wooden fences and tree trunks. Although clinging vines look attractive on buildings, their rootlets can damage bricks and mortar; do not allow them to grow on framed buildings because they can damage the wood.

The grabbers use either their tendrils or their leaf stems to grab on and wind around supports. Grapes, greenbriers, and porcelain berries are some of the common grabbers that climb well on chain-link fences, lattices, or shrubs. Be cautious with porcelain berry because it is invasive in some areas.

Chain-link fences, lattices, arbors, and shrubs also provide ideal supports for the twiners, which climb by twisting their stems around these types of underpinnings. Honeysuckles, American

plants

Quick Reference | GRAND AND GLORIOUS VINES

SOME vines do double or even triple duty in your bird-friendly yard, providing cover, fruit, and nesting opportunities. Try some of these beauties to see who comes calling! Before you plant, though, check to see if any of these vines are invasive in your area.

VINES	BIRD-FRIENDLY FEATURES				
	COVER	FRUIT	NECTAR	NESTING	SEEDS
Porcelain berry (*Ampelopsis brevipedunculata*)	✓	✓			
Rattan vine (*Berchemia scandens*)		✓			
Trumpet creeper (*Campsis radicans*)	✓		✓		✓
American bittersweet (*Celastrus scandens*)	✓				✓
Morning glories (*Ipomoea* spp.)	✓		✓		
Cardinal climber (*I.* × *multifida*)	✓		✓		
Coral honeysuckle (*Lonicera sempervirens*)	✓		✓		
Moonseeds (*Menispermum* spp.)	✓	✓			
Virginia creeper (*Parthenocissus quinquefolia*)	✓			✓	
Boston ivy (*P. tricuspidata*)	✓			✓	
Climbing roses (*Rosa* spp.)	✓			✓	
Greenbriers (*Smilax* spp.)		✓			
Grapes (*Vitus* spp.)	✓	✓			✓

bittersweets, silver-lace vines, and morning glories are some of the more typical examples of twining vines.

Climbing roses are members of the group of vining plants known as sprawlers because they lie on their supports, sending up progressively longer shoots. They easily scramble through shrubs and trees and can be used on fences, trellises, arbors, and even deck railings. You may need to tie them to their supports, however, in order to keep them growing in the direction you want.

VINE SWEET VINE

Grapes, wintercreepers, Virginia creepers, honeysuckles, and other perennial vines supply long-lasting nesting and cover sites for a variety of birds, especially when allowed to grow thickly. Gray catbirds, northern mockingbirds, American robins, house finches, northern cardinals, and chipping sparrows are some of the birds that are known to nest in vines. (Climbing roses make particularly attractive nesting sites for mockingbirds.)

Almost hidden by foliage, a house finch weaves her basketlike nest in the shelter of a Virginia creeper.

plants

shine morning glory vine blossom foxglove

VINES FILL THE BILL

Besides cover and nesting, vines are also excellent sources of food for birds, offering nectar, seeds, and berries. Various vines offer flowers that are virtual magnets for hummingbirds, orioles, and other nectar-sipping birds.

Members of the morning glory family, which includes cardinal climber, scarlet creeper, and common morning glory, readily attract these birds, as do the numerous varieties of honeysuckle and the trumpet vines.

The trumpet vine's flowers give way to seeds that are eaten by chickadees, finches, and sparrows. These birds, as well as cardinals, towhees, juncos, buntings, blackbirds, pheasants, and quail, eat the seeds of the silver-lace vine. The seeds of the American bittersweet vine are enclosed in a bright red covering. You'll find that bluebirds, robins, cardinals, pheasants, quail, and turkeys consume these seeds voraciously.

By far, berries are the most abundant food source vines have to offer. Grapevine, porcelain berry, Virginia creeper, Boston ivy, honeysuckle, greenbrier, and even poison ivy produce fruits that are eaten by a whole host of backyard birds, including cardinals, catbirds, mockingbirds, thrashers, robins, thrushes, grouse, turkeys, waxwings, woodpeckers, and many others.

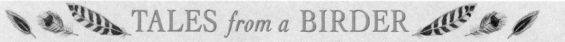

TALES *from a* BIRDER

FOR several years after I moved into my home, a pair of house finches tried to make their nests on the L-shaped ledge of a pillar on my porch. Each time, they were unsuccessful, either because the ledge was too narrow to support the nest or because their efforts were sabotaged by house sparrows. Then one year I planted a Virginia creeper in front of the pillar. By the following spring, the vine had grown up to and around the ledge, providing enough support for the finches to successfully build a nest. The vine also camouflaged the nest from other prying avian eyes.

That was my introduction to growing vines for birds. Now vines are an integral part of my landscape and the birds delight in every addition I make.

—Kathy Piper

AS THE VINE TWINES

You can add climbing plants to your yard for texture, variety, height, and most important of all, habitat. Virginia creeper or Boston ivy grown around a dead tree or tree stump can enhance its appearance and at the same time increase its value to birds. "You can...make an old tree stump into a great cover for birds," writes George Adams in his book *Birdscaping Your Garden*, "by planting ivy plants around the base and training them over the trunk. Smaller birds, such as wrens and chickadees, will roost and find shelter in the foliage, and birds will nest in the network of thick ivy branches."

If you don't like the look of a rock or brush pile, then let a wintercreeper, grapevine, or trumpet vine clamber over it. Vines not only improve the pile's attractiveness for you, but they also make it more alluring to birds by affording them extra cover. Similarly, vines add appeal to fences, trellises, house walls, and stone walls in the garden.

Anchor your Christmas tree in the ground near a feeder after the holidays are over to provide extra

> **As nesting season approaches in late winter, cardinals may be seen "kissing." This is actually ritualistic courtship feeding in which the male feeds the female before mating.**

shelter for the birds. When all of the needles fall off and you are left with a bare tree, plant a perennial vine at the base of the tree in spring; it will soon be covered by that vine, adding a permanent source of bird food and shelter to your yard. If you use an evergreen vine, such as wintercreeper or some varieties of greenbrier, the cover will be available all year long.

You can also allow certain vines to make their way up through the branches of shrubs and trees, and intertwine with hedges and hedgerows. When allowed to grow this way, many become perfect guests, their flowers, fruits, and leaves complementing that of their hosts.

There are some vines, however, that are like visitors who never know when to leave — they take over everything and do far more

foxglove **plants**

than just make themselves at home. Asiatic bittersweet, wild grape, and Japanese honeysuckle are so invasive that they can completely engulf other plants in a short time. The resulting tangle becomes a haven for birds, but it ultimately kills the host plant—something you may not appreciate.

Annual vines, such as morning glory and cardinal climber, grow quickly, their foliage producing seasonal cover for their supports. Since they last only from spring to frost, annual climbers are invaluable for bird watchers who are renting and therefore can't plant anything permanent.

Birds Love Vines

GROWING vines in your backyard will help attract many species of birds because vines offer a wealth of food, safe shelter, and ideal nesting space. Annual vines, such as morning glories and scarlet runner beans, grow quickly; Virginia creeper, trumpet creeper, and other perennial vines may creep upward more slowly, but they'll provide you with year after year of attractive cover and habitat for birds. Birds flock to vines for various reasons, so browse this list to see which birds may find their way to the vines in your backyard.

Birds That Eat Fruits from Vines
Wild turkeys

Grouse

Waxwings

American robins

Thrushes

Thrashers

Northern mockingbirds

Gray catbirds

Woodpeckers

Northern cardinals

Grosbeaks

Birds That Eat Seeds from Vines
Wild turkeys

Ring-necked pheasants

Quail

Chickadees

Blackbirds

Juncos

Northern cardinals

Finches

Buntings

Towhees

Sparrows

Birds That Nest in Vines
Carolina wrens

American robins

Gray catbirds

Northern mockingbirds

Northern cardinals

House finches

Birds That Sip Nectar from Vines
Hummingbirds

Orioles

REGION-BY-REGION PLANTING

Each ecoregion of North America supports different bird species (see page 244 to identify your ecoregion). Your bird-friendly backyard should include plants that are suited to your climate and are also attractive to birds that live in your neighborhood. These plant suggestions are just a starting point; ask your local garden or wild-bird center for advice on plants that thrive in your area *and* attract throngs of birds.

PACIFIC COAST/NORTHWEST

The abundant moisture and rich soils of the Pacific Northwest support a great diversity of bird-friendly plants. This list is just a small sampling.

PLANT NAME	TYPE OF PLANT
Agapanthus (*Agapanthus* spp.)	Perennials
Barberries (*Berberis* spp.)	Shrubs
Deodar cedar (*Cedrus deodara*)	Tree
Hinoki false cypress (*Chamaecyparis obtusa*)	Tree
Crocosmias (*Crocosmia* spp.)	Perennials
Daphnes (*Daphne* spp.)	Shrubs
Hardy fuchsia (*Fuchsia magellanica*)	Shrub
Witch hazels (*Hamamelis* spp.)	Shrubs
Hollies (*Ilex* spp.)	Shrubs, trees
Cherries (*Prunus* spp.)	Trees
Rhododendrons (*Rhododendron* spp.)	Shrubs
Currant (*Ribes sanguineum*)	Shrub
Hemlocks (*Tsuga* spp.)	Trees
Blueberries (*Vaccinium* spp.)	Shrubs

REGION-BY-REGION PLANTING

PACIFIC COAST/CALIFORNIA

Tough seaside plants and self-sowing annuals and perennials dominate this list of seed and berry producers. By using well-adapted, native, or naturalized plants, you can ensure that your garden will continue to attract and provide habitat for visiting birds year after year—with minimal work.

PLANT NAME	TYPE OF PLANT
Columbines (*Aquilegia* spp.)	Perennials
Calendula (*Calendula officinalis*)	Annual
Blueblossom (*Ceanothus thyrsiflorus*)	Shrub
Pacific dogwood (*Cornus nuttalii*)	Tree
Purple coneflowers (*Echinacea* spp.)	Perennials
Wild buckwheats (*Eriogonum* spp.)	Annuals, perennials, shrubs
Golden yarrow (*Eriphyllum lanatum*)	Perennial
California poppy (*Eschscholzia californica*)	Annual
Toyon (*Heteromeles arbutifolia*)	Shrub
Shore juniper (*Juniperus conferta*)	Shrub
Lupines (*Lupinus* spp.)	Annuals, perennials
Indian plum (*Oemleria cerasiformis*)	Shrub
Poppies (*Papaver* spp.)	Annuals, perennials
Penstemons (*Penstemon* spp.)	Perennials
Holly-leaved cherry (*Prunus ilicifolia*)	Shrub
Coffeeberry (*Rhamnus californica*)	Shrub
Salvias (*Salvia* spp.)	Annuals, perennials
Elderberries (*Sambucus* spp.)	Shrubs

MOUNTAIN WEST

In the Mountain West region, look for varieties with shorter growing seasons and for plants with fruit or seedheads that will provide birds with sustenance through the long dormant period. Both the native and the introduced plants listed here are adapted to the extremes of mountainous climates.

PLANT NAME	TYPE OF PLANT
Serviceberries (*Amelanchier* spp.)	Shrubs
Columbines (*Aquilegia* spp.)	Perennials
Trumpet vine (*Campsis radicans*)	Perennial vine
Common hackberry (*Celtis laevigata*)	Tree
Red-osier dogwood (*Cornus stolonifera*)	Shrub
Rocky Mountain juniper (*Juniperus scopulorum*)	Tree
Cardinal flower (*Lobelia cardinalis*)	Perennial
Oregon grapeholly (*Mahonia aquifolium*)	Shrub
Four o'clocks (*Mirabilis jalapa*)	Annual
Bee balm (*Monarda didyma*)	Perennial
Nicotiana (*Nicotiana* spp.)	Annuals
Penstemons (*Penstemon* spp.)	Perennials
Garden phlox (*Phlox paniculata*)	Perennial
Golden currant (*Ribes aureum*)	Shrub
Elderberries (*Sambucus* spp.)	Shrubs
Coralberry (*Symphoricarpos orbiculatus*)	Shrub
European cranberry bush (*Viburnum opulus*)	Shrub
Weigelas (*Weigela* spp.)	Shrubs

REGION-BY-REGION PLANTING

DESERT SOUTHWEST

In the desert, every drop of water is essential to preserving life. These drought-tolerant species provide a source of food or water for visiting birds. Most have water-retaining adaptations, such as hairy or succulent leaves that allow them to survive in the harsh desert environment.

PLANT NAME	TYPE OF PLANT
Acacias (*Acacia* spp.)	Shrubs, trees
Agaves (*Agave* spp.)	Perennials
Saguaro (*Carnegiea gigantea*)	Cactus
Hop bush (*Dodonaea viscosa*)	Shrub
Ocotillo (*Fouquieria splendens*)	Shrub
Blanket flowers (*Gaillardia* spp.)	Annuals, perennials
Chuparosa honeysuckle (*Justicia californica*)	Shrub
Silverleaf (*Leucophyllum frutescens*)	Shrub
Chollas (*Opuntia* spp.)	Cactuses
Palo verde (*Parkinsonia florida*)	Tree
Beardlip penstemon (*Penstemon barbatus*)	Perennial
Mesquites (*Prosopis* spp.)	Shrubs, trees
Texas sage (*Salvia coccinea*)	Annual
Autumn sage (*S. greggii*)	Perennial
Texas betony (*Stachys coccinea*)	Perennial
Cape honeysuckle (*Tecoma capensis*)	Shrub
Yellow bells (*T. stans*)	Shrub
Yuccas (*Yucca* spp.)	Perennials

MIDWEST/GREAT PLAINS

It's only natural that the native species of the prairies that once dominated the central United States are the plants of choice for birds in this ecoregion. Whether you use these plants in a meadow garden or in a designed landscape, birds will flock to feed on their seeds and fruits.

PLANT NAME	TYPE OF PLANT
Purple giant hyssop (*Agastache scrophulariifolia*)	Perennial
Bluestems (*Andropogon* spp.)	Perennials
Pennsylvania sedge (*Carex pensylvania*)	Perennial
Purple coneflowers (*Echinacea* spp.)	Perennials
Strawberries (*Fragaria* spp.)	Perennials
Prairie smoke (*Geum triflorum*)	Perennial
Eastern red cedar (*Juniperus virginiana*)	Tree
Lupines (*Lupinus* spp.)	Annuals, perennials
Virginia creeper (*Parthenocissus quinquefolia*)	Vine
Jacob's ladders (*Polemonium* spp.)	Perennials
White oak (*Quercus alba*)	Tree
Bur oak (*Q. macrocarpa*)	Tree
Buffalo currant (*Ribes odoratum*)	Shrub
Compass plant (*Silphium laciniatum*)	Perennial
Blue-eyed grass (*Sisyrinchium graminoides*)	Perennial
Goldenrods (*Solidago* spp.)	Perennials
Indian grass (*Sorghastrum nutans*)	Perennial
Birdsfoot violet (*Viola pedata*)	Perennial

CONTINENTAL EAST

Many garden staples provide food and habitat for birds. By combining trees, shrubs, and perennials or annuals in a single planting, you can create a layered landscape that will pay homage to the deciduous forest that once occupied most of this region of the country.

PLANT NAME	TYPE OF PLANT
Maples (*Acer* spp.)	Trees
Canada columbine (*Aquilegia canadensis*)	Perennial
Trumpet creeper (*Campsis radicans*)	Vine
Gray dogwood (*Cornus racemosa*)	Shrub
Red-osier dogwood (*C. stolonifera*)	Shrub
Sunflower (*Helianthus annus*)	Annual
American holly (*Ilex opaca*)	Shrub, tree
Jewelweeds (*Impatiens* spp.)	Annuals
Impatiens (*I. walleriana*)	Annual
Cardinal flower (*Lobelia cardinalis*)	Perennial
Black gum (*Nyssa sylvatica*)	Tree
Spruces (*Picea* spp.)	Shrubs, trees
Pines (*Pinus* spp.)	Shrubs, trees
Azaleas (*Rhododendron* spp.)	Shrubs
Arrow-wood (*Viburnum dentatum*)	Shrub
European cranberry bush (*V. opulus*)	Shrub
Blackhaw viburnum (*V. prunifolium*)	Shrub
American cranberry bush (*V. trilobum*)	Shrub

HUMID SOUTH

In a region where many plants go dormant to cope with summer heat, be sure to give your bird garden a structure of heat-tolerant trees and shrubs. Trellised vines are also real garden assets in the Humid South, shading your patio while attracting hummingbirds to their nectar-filled blossoms.

PLANT NAME	TYPE OF PLANT
Red maple (*Acer rubrum*)	Tree
Red buckeye (*Aesculus pavia*)	Shrub, tree
Ginger lilies (*Alpina* spp.)	Perennials
Cross vine (*Bignonia capreolata*)	Vine
Cigar flower (*Cuphea ignea*)	Shrub
Carolina jessamine (*Gelsemium sempervirens*)	Vine
Yaupon (*Ilex cassine*)	Tree
American holly (*I. opaca*)	Shrub, tree
Cypress vine (*Ipomoea quamoclit*)	Vine
Shrimp plant (*Justicia brandegeeana*)	Shrub
Coral honeysuckle (*Lonicera sempervirens*)	Vine
Red mulberry (*Morus rubra*)	Tree
Southern waxmyrtle (*Myrica cerifera*)	Tree
Pentas (*Pentas* spp.)	Perennials, shrubs
Pines (*Pinus* spp.)	Trees
Oaks (*Quercus* spp.)	Trees
Pineapple sage (*Salvia rutilans*)	Annual
Mapleleaf viburnum (*Viburnum acerifolium*)	Shrub

CANADIAN NORTH

The reliable snow cover of this ecoregion provides trees and shrubs with winter protection, and it may allow you to grow bird-friendly perennials that are not, according to their normal growing zones, supposed to be hardy. Experimenting with plants one zone south of yours is often a good gamble.

PLANT NAME	TYPE OF PLANT
Juneberries (*Amelanchier* spp.)	Shrubs, trees
Gray birch (*Betula populifolia*)	Tree
Pagoda dogwood (*Cornus alternifolia*)	Shrub, tree
Red-osier dogwood (*C. stolonifera*)	Shrub
White ash (*Fraxinus americana*)	Tree
Winterberry (*Ilex verticillata*)	Shrub
Eastern red cedar (*Juniperus virginiana*)	Tree
Larches (*Larix* spp.)	Trees
Trumpet honeysuckle (*Lonicera sempervirens*)	Vine
Flowering crabapples (*Malus* spp.)	Trees
Blackberries (*Rubus allegheniensis, R. canadensis*)	Brambles
Red raspberry (*R. idaeus*)	Bramble
Black raspberry (*R. occidentalis*)	Bramble
Snowberry (*Symphoricarpos albus* var. *laevigatus*)	Shrub
Highbush blueberry (*Vaccinium corymbosum*)	Shrub
Nannyberry (*Viburnum lentago*)	Shrub, tree
American cranberry bush (*V. trilobum*)	Shrub
Old fashioned weigela (*Weigela florida*)	Shrub

Gardening for Hummers

HUMMINGBIRDS hold a special place in the hearts of many birding enthusiasts. Many gardeners make a special effort to tempt these tiny treasures to their backyard gardens with flowering plants, bright red blooms, and nectar-filled feeders.

Gardening for hummingbirds can be as simple or as complex as you like. First, of course, you need a patch of ground within the breeding or migratory range of one or more hummingbird species. Throughout the eastern United States, the ruby-throated hummingbird is the species you'll see nesting in trees and passing through town during spring and fall migrations. Western folks see a variety of species, and in the southeastern United States, the ruby-throat and the rufous may both wander by. Canadians may catch a glimpse of ruby-throats in the East and Anna's and rufous out West.

To draw hummingbirds to a new garden, tie red ribbons or cloth strips in the area. If hummers are buzzing around the neighborhood, they'll notice the colors and zoom in to investigate.

plants

columbine morning glory vine blossom foxglove

If you're within hummingbird range, plant the right flowers and they will come. Some wildflowers and flowering shrubs and trees are irresistible to hummingbirds, and including them in the garden is like hanging a welcome sign on your door for these glorious creatures.

OFF TO THE RIGHT START

The bright reds, oranges, and yellows that hummingbirds use as guides to food and drink are delightful for the hummingbird gardener, too. Every plant that attracts hummingbirds produces gorgeous blossoms, so if you provide food for the birds, you will also create a garden you can revel in.

A simple hummingbird garden might consist of a few plants of one or two species—just enough to bring hummers close for a look during the growing season. Of course, if you like your gardens grand and want to keep hummingbirds visiting you throughout the season, you'll need to cultivate a variety of plants.

Some hummingbird flowers can also appeal to hungry butterflies. Double-duty nectar sources include plants such as bee balm, penstemon, phlox, and sage.

The best plants for hummingbirds vary from region to region. If possible, it's always best to choose native plants rather than exotic ones. Ecologists are increasingly aware of the havoc alien plants are wreaking in environments around

TALES *from a* BIRDER

MY first attempt at cultivating plants for hummers was wildly successful, and it consisted simply of transplanting a perennial herb called wild bergamot from a meadow where it was abundant. The plants were ready to bloom, and I loved the idea of seeing the buds open outside a picture window I had recently installed. By careful digging and frequent watering after the plants were relocated, I kept all of them alive. They flowered magnificently, attracting several hummingbirds. Fourteen years later, the wild bergamot and its offspring still thrive outside my window, as do the hummers, which may be descendants of the bergamots' first visitors.

—*Edward Kanze*

the world. The beauty of gardening with indigenous plants is that it's a win-win-win situation. You can conserve natural resources, minimize your workload (natives, when planted in the right place, require little care), and grow a beautiful garden all at the same time.

Hummingbirds don't limit their feeding preferences just to native plants, however. These little nectar drinkers, with their enormous thirst and the high caloric cost of keeping themselves airborne, will come readily to clematis, eucalyptuses, foxgloves, fuchsias, horse chestnuts, lantanas, lilacs, morning glories, nasturtiums, petunias, and snapdragons.

SCENTLESS BUT SHAPELY

Hummingbird flowers generally have little odor, but no matter—most hummers have little or no sense of smell anyway. But what hummingbird blossoms lack in scent, they make up for in pleasing shapes and colors.

Hummingbird flowers are usually trumpet-shaped, with the long tube or throat of the trumpet drooping downward. This shape and its downward orientation help to deter would-be nectar robbers such as bees and butterflies. For the hummingbird, though, the trumpet, or tubular corolla, guides the bird's bill to its sweet reward.

Having both hummingbird feeders and hummingbird flowers will help attract customers to your nectar and keep them coming back for more.

GREAT HUMMINGBIRD PLANTS

WESTERN NORTH AMERICA

Western gardeners can attract such beauty-pageant winners as rufous, broad-tailed, black-chinned, Calliope, and Anna's hummingbirds. In the West, native hummingbird plants are as diverse as the birds that sip from them.

KEY **A** Annual **C** Cactus **P** Perennial **S** Shrub **T** Tree **V** Vine

PLANT NAME	HEIGHT	SPREAD	FLOWER COLOR
T California buckeye (*Aesculus california*)	25 feet (7.5 m)	30 feet (9 m)	White, pink
P Columbines (*Aquilegia* spp.)	1 to 2 feet (30 to 60 cm)	1 to 2 feet (30 to 60 cm)	Red, pink, blue, purple
P Scarlet delphinium (*Delphinium cardinale*)	6 feet (1.8 m)	18 inches (45 cm)	Scarlet
C Claret cup cactus (*Echinocereus triglochidiatus*)	1 foot (30 cm)	6 inches (15 cm)	Red
C Ocotillo (*Fouquieria splendens*)	30 feet (9 m)	6 feet (1.8 m)	Red
A Texas bluebonnet (*Lupinus texensis*)	1 foot (30 cm)	9 inches (23 cm)	Blue
P Scarlet monkey flower (*Mimulus cardinalis*)	3 feet (90 cm)	2 feet (60 cm)	Scarlet
P Firecracker penstemon (*Penstemon eatonii*)	2 feet (60 cm)	1 foot (30 cm)	Scarlet
P Obedient plant (*Physostegia virginiana*)	2 feet (60 cm)	1 foot (30 cm)	White
T New Mexico locust (*Robinia neomexicana*)	20 feet (6 m)	15 feet (4.5 m)	Pink
S Jim sage (*Salvia clevelandii*)	2 feet (60 cm)	2 feet (60 cm)	White, blue, purple
P Indian pink (*Spigelia mariandica*)	1 foot (30 cm)	1 foot (30 cm)	Scarlet

NORTH AMERICAN PRAIRIE

Plant a red or nearly red flower in your backyard on the prairie, and you'll attract plenty of hummingbird traffic. And once that hummer is in your garden, it will flit from blossom to blossom, no matter what the flower color.

KEY **A** Annual **C** Cactus **P** Perennial **S** Shrub **T** Tree **V** Vine

PLANT NAME	HEIGHT	SPREAD	FLOWER COLOR
P Butterfly weed (*Asclepias tuberosa*)	3 feet (90 cm)	1 foot (30 cm)	Orange
V Trumpet creeper (*Campsis radicans*)	30 feet (9 m)	Vertical habit	Orange, red
S Desert willow (*Chilopsis linearis*)	6 to 25 feet (1.8 to 7.5 m)	6 to 25 feet (1.8 to 7.5 m)	Pink
P Turk's-cap lily (*Lilium michiganense*)	2 to 5 feet (60 cm to 1.5 m)	1 foot (30 cm)	Orange
P Cardinal flower (*Lobelia cardinalis*)	3 feet (90 cm)	1 foot (30 cm)	Red
P Great lobelia (*L. siphilitica*)	2 feet (60 cm)	1 foot (30 cm)	Blue
P Wild bee balm (*Monarda fistulosa*)	4 feet (1.2 m)	18 inches (45 cm)	Pink, purple
P Ozark sundrop (*Oenothera macrocarpa*)	6 inches (15 cm)	20 inches (50 cm)	Yellow
P Foxglove penstemon (*Penstemon cobaea*)	1 to 2 feet (30 to 60 cm)	12 to 18 inches (30 to 45 cm)	White, pink, violet
P Smooth phlox (*Phlox glaberrima*)	2 to 3 feet (60 to 90 cm)	18 inches (45 cm)	Purple
S Flowering currant (*Ribes sanguineum*)	6 feet (1.8 m)	6 feet (1.8 m)	Red
P Blue sage (*Salvia azurea*)	5 feet (1.5 m)	2 to 3 feet (60 to 90 cm)	Blue, white

GREAT HUMMINGBIRD PLANTS

NORTHEASTERN NORTH AMERICA

If you grow any of these plants in the Northeast and not a single ruby-throat ever appears, you will be satisfied with the beauty of the flowers alone. When hummers do appear, they are the icing on a brightly colored cake.

KEY   A Annual   C Cactus   P Perennial   S Shrub   T Tree   V Vine

PLANT NAME	HEIGHT	SPREAD	FLOWER COLOR
P Canada columbine (*Aquilegia canadensis*)	2 feet (60 cm)	1 foot (30 cm)	Scarlet with yellow
P Indian paintbrush (*Castilleja coccinea*)	2 feet (60 cm)	1 foot (30 cm)	Red
T Turtlehead (*Chelone obliqua*)	2 feet (60 cm)	1 foot (30 cm)	Pink, purple
P Fringed bleeding heart (*Dicentra eximia*)	2 feet (60 cm)	18 inches (45 cm)	Pink, purple
A Fireweed (*Epilobium angustifolium*)	2 feet (60 cm)	1 foot (30 cm)	Pink
A Jewelweed (*Impatiens capensis, I. pallida*)	2 to 5 feet (60 cm to 1.5 m)	1 foot (30 cm)	Orange, yellow
P Cardinal flower (*Lobelia cardinalis*)	3 feet (90 cm)	1 foot (30 cm)	Scarlet
P Virginia bluebells (*Mertensia virginica*)	1 foot (30 cm)	1 foot (30 cm)	Blue
P Bee balm (*Monarda didyma*)	3 feet (90 cm)	2 feet (60 cm)	Pink, red, purple
P Wild bee balm (*M. fistulosa*)	4 feet (1.2 m)	1 foot (30 cm)	Pink, purple
S Pinxterbloom azalea (*Rhododendron periclymenoides*)	5 feet (1.5 m)	9 feet (2.7 m)	White, pink, purple
T Basswood (*Tilia americana*)	80 feet (24 m)	50 feet (15 m)	Yellow

SOUTHEASTERN NORTH AMERICA

If you live in the lower portion of the Southeast, you've probably seen hummingbirds engaging in a feeding frenzy to gather strength for their flight across the Gulf. Do your part by offering sustenance with blossom-heavy flower gardens and landscape shrubs.

KEY   A Annual   C Cactus   P Perennial   S Shrub   T Tree   V Vine

PLANT NAME	HEIGHT	SPREAD	FLOWER COLOR
T Red buckeye (*Aesculus pavia*)	15 feet (4.5 m)	10 feet (3 m)	Red
S Scarlet trompetilla (*Bouvardia ternifolia*)	2 to 3 feet (60 to 90 cm)	1 to 2 feet (30 to 60 cm)	Scarlet
P Cannas (*Canna* spp. and hybrids)	Varies	Varies	Red, yellow, orange
S Japanese flowering quince (*Chaenomeles japonica*)	3 feet (90 cm)	6 feet (1.8 m)	Red
P Coral bells (*Heuchera sanguinea*)	1 to 2 feet (30 to 60 cm)	1 foot (30 cm)	Pink
S Rose of Sharon (*Hibiscus syriacus*)	10 feet (3 m)	6 feet (1.8 m)	Pink, red
T Tulip tree (*Liriodendron tulipifera*)	100 feet (30 m)	50 feet (15 m)	Yellow
V Coral honeysuckle (*Lonicera sempervirens*)	12 feet (3.6 m)	Vertical habit	Scarlet
P Four o'clocks (*Mirabilis jalapa*)	2 feet (60 cm)	2 feet (60 cm)	Red, pink, yellow
S Azalea (*Rhododendron* spp.)	Varies	Varies	Pink, red, orange
P Wine sage (*Salvia van houttii*)	3 feet (90 cm)	3 feet (90 cm)	Red
A Mexican sunflower (*Tithonia rotundifolia*)	6 feet (1.8 m)	1 foot (30 cm)	Orange

plants

juniper berries evergreen penstemon columbine morning glory vine blossom foxglove

DISTRIBUTING YOUR DINERS

Just providing the proper plants isn't enough to pull in hordes of hummers. As a gardener and air-traffic controller, your choice of planting locations may have an important effect on the number of hummers you can attract and the amount of time they spend battling each other. Distributing plants around the four sides of a house, for example, will help ensure that more than one hummingbird enjoys your floral smorgasbord. Both male and female hummingbirds will defend their favorite feeding grounds, but there is a limit to just how much area one bird can survey and defend. You can also promote peace among hummers by choosing plants with modest numbers of blossoms and growing many of them. This will allow several hummers to co-exist in an area that otherwise might support only one.

OFFER FEEDERS *AND* FLOWERS

Hanging a few nectar feeders in or near your garden will surely bring hummingbirds to your yard, but even a small planting of hummer-friendly flowers near those feeders will ensure that the birds stick around for a while when they come to visit. Hummers benefit by having a variety of nectar sources.

If you have hummingbird feeders in your garden, don't rush out to buy commercial nectar formulas. You can make your own in a jiffy. Simply boil 4 parts of water, stir in 1 part table sugar by volume, and cool to fill your feeders. Be sure to keep unused solution in the refrigerator, and to keep your feeders clean.

Don't worry that you'll keep hummingbirds from migrating by

HOMEMADE NECTAR
at a glance

- 4 parts water
- 1 part white table sugar

Add sugar to water, stir, bring to a boil, then cool before filling feeders. Refrigerate extra.

leaving your feeders up in the fall. Migratory birds are genetically programmed to migrate when their internal "clocks" tell them that they have to go, and the presence of your feeder won't impede that need. On the contrary, by leaving feeders hanging in the garden, you may be helping early or late migrants along their way.

A concern many people have is the supposedly dangerous red dye that is found in premixed hummingbird foods. No conclusive scientific evidence exists showing that red food dye is harmful to hummingbirds. However, the red dye in the premixed nectar solutions just isn't necessary because the bright red parts on hummingbird feeders do just as much to attract the birds as the colored solution does. So,

what's your best bet? Make your own sugar solution and omit the red dye (as well as the powdered sugar, honey, and molasses!).

Even if you have regular visitors at your feeders, take the time to add the plants that hummingbirds like the best. Remember, flowers provide most of their nectar needs. Besides, wouldn't you rather see hummers flitting back and forth from flower to flower than seeing them land again and again in the same manner on a factory-made feeder? These hot-blooded helicopters hover, advance, retreat, and drive off their competitors as conditions necessitate, and watching them sip nectar from your long, tubular flowers will provide a delightful course in civil and not-so-civil aeronautics.

TALES *from a* BIRDER

IN positioning a hummingbird feeder in your backyard, I recommend that you keep it within view of hummingbird-friendly plants and well away from your other ordinary bird feeders. Once, my wife and I hung a hummingbird feeder a few inches from a feeding shelf frequented by a male cardinal, and the result was ugly. A male hummer zoomed in, jabbed the much larger red bird several times in the belly, and backed off, hovering. The cardinal, meanwhile, either terrorized or affronted, fled the scene and never appeared again at the feeder.

—*Edward Kanze*

Catalog Dreams

An Essay by Lynn Hassler Kaufman

IN many parts of North America, cold weather prohibits outdoor gardening activities during the winter months. Gardeners suffer from what I like to call "green" deficiencies as they struggle to remember what it's like to dig in the dirt, to tend their flowers, and to nurture their stock. But then those plant and seed catalogs start arriving in the mailbox with the promise of another spring to come. Gardeners feast upon these catalogs and imagine warmer days and gardens of grandeur.

Buying for the Birds

Winter is the perfect time for planning a bird garden. All you need is a comfortable chair, pencil and paper, and a variety of plant and seed catalogs. Many catalogs carry unusual or hard-to-find plants (notably many native species) that are not available at local nurseries. You could probably spend hours leafing through catalogs, gasping and exclaiming with delight at the photos of floriferous plants, imagining hummingbirds swarming around. Or you daydream when you see shots of dense, fruit-bearing shrubs that might be covered with cedar waxwings in your yard. Could your garden really look that good? Which plants should you get? Will the birds like them? Maybe you can't get everything, but you can imagine the magnificence of it all.

When catalogs arrive in my mailbox, I curl up in my easy chair and start turning pages slowly and expectantly. Now, here's something with an intriguing name—great bladdery milkvetch. I wonder what the heck that is? The description looks interesting, but there's no photograph. Better do some research on that one.

As I look through my catalogs, I begin planning. First, I'll need flowering plants for the nectar sippers, maybe hot pink and scarlet red penstemons. Since I live in Tucson and have hummingbirds year-round, I'll need plants that flower at different seasons. How about Mexican honeysuckle? It blooms on and off all year. For summer, let's try Baja fairy duster with its red powder-puff blooms—rich in nectar and insect life and a favorite with hummers.

For the quail, doves, finches, and sparrows, I'll need members of the composite (daisy) family since these plants tend to be prolific producers of seed. I know brittle bush (with its masses of bright yellow flowers) works well in my climate and produces a profusion of seeds. Goldfinches love the globular seedheads of blanket flower or firewheel. Ornamental grasses also produce great seeds and provide nesting material to boot.

Mockingbirds and thrashers like fruit-bearing plants. How about a desert hackberry? It provides good cover and shelter in addition to having tasty berries. Native plants generally attract native birds, so maybe I should stick with this theme. The wolfberry looks good for cover, plus it has short, lavender, tubular flowers for the hummers and bright red berries for the phainopeplas, mockers, and thrashers. The berries may even tempt robins and waxwings, if these birds stage a winter invasion.

I'll need trees to provide roosting sites, song perches, and food, either directly through seeds, flowers, or fruit, or indirectly through the insects they attract. The photograph of this desert willow looks inviting.

White-crowned sparrow

The Dream Continues

I've covered the basics—tubular flowers for the hummers, flowering plants in the composite family for the seed-eating birds, shrubs for the fruit and berry eaters, and trees for shelter. Now, have I forgotten anything? Perhaps something specific for the insect eaters. Maybe I need a shrubby groundcover. I'll plant a Texas ranger and leave the leaf litter beneath this flowering shrub to attract more insects for the birds.

Now for the fluff—the plants that look interesting, but I have yet to try. Here are a few that may work in my climate, but wait! I have a small yard that's already overflowing, and anything I plant must be able to survive 100°F (38°C) temperatures in the summer and freezing weather during the winter.

I guess I'll reluctantly end my plant and seed catalog perusal for this year. It's given me hours of entertainment and stirred my imagination, and I think the birds will be happy. Unfortunately, it looks like I won't be able to fit in the great bladdery milkvetch. Well, there's always next year.

Plants

Q **I planted a trumpet vine next to my little fishpond, and it's popping up everywhere! I thought this was a native plant. What should I do?**

A In horticulture, the term "native" doesn't necessarily mean well behaved. Some native species, such as trumpet vine (*Campsis radicans*), can be very invasive. It's a vigorous vine that can grow to 30 feet (9 m), so you need to be careful where you plant it in your home landscape. You'll need patience and diligence to remove it; a well-established trumpet vine sends roots several feet down and transversely, so you're in for some digging if you truly wish to eradicate this vine.

Q **Should I use seeds or transplants in my garden?**

A Growing your own plants from seed can be economical and rewarding, and can allow you to be more selective about the varieties you wish to plant. You can get a head start on the season by starting seedlings indoors for crops that require a long growing season to bloom or bear fruit. Indoor seedlings do best with 12 to 14 hours of light and consistent watering. Gradually acclimate your seedlings to outdoor conditions. You can also plant seeds of many flowers, herbs, and vegetables directly into the garden, particularly if you live where summers are long and winters are mild.

Q **What's the best organic fertilizer for my plants?**

A Apply 1 to 2 inches (2.5 to 5 cm) of compost annually to give your plants the nutrients they need and to improve soil structure and moisture retention. Make your own compost by layering shredded leaves and grass clippings with garden debris and kitchen wastes (excluding meat, dairy products, and grease). Turn the pile several times monthly, adding water periodically if it doesn't rain to keep the pile "cooking," and you'll have finished compost in about 8 weeks.

Making Plants Grow

THE gardens you grow in your imagination can't flourish in reality without a little work from you. If you choose lots of native plants for your garden, you're already well on your way to success because natives are already adapted to your region and local conditions and will need little coaxing to thrive. Site selection and planting, however, shouldn't be haphazard. These seven steps will help you get those bird-friendly plants started right.

1 Prepping the Site. After removing existing weeds, test your soil for pH, micronutrients, and organic matter. Your local cooperative extension office or garden center can help you conduct a soil test and interpret the results. If you have extremely poor soil with low levels of organic matter, you'll probably be advised to add large quantities of well-composted material such as aged manure, leaves, or organic refuse to the top 1 to 2 feet (30 to 60 cm) of soil. Organic matter increases the water-holding capacity of sandy soils and improves the water and air circulation of heavy clays. This helps the roots develop and plants grow. Even if your soil is in fairly good health, adding aged compost to a new planting site is almost always beneficial.

2 Getting the Right Number of the Right Plants. One plant per 1 to 2 square feet (30 to 60 cm) is a good starting point, but check out seed packages and information tags on transplants to determine how much room your plants will need. Choose plants that will brighten your yard, and feed and shelter birds all year-round. Mix in grasses for the seeds they produce and the support they can give to the taller flowering plants that may have a tendency to flop.

Add organic matter, such as aged compost and shredded leaves, to improve the quality of your soil.

plants — *juniper berries evergreen penstemon columbine morning glory vine blossom foxglove*

3 Planting. Give the roots plenty of room. For most plants, dig down about a foot (30 cm) and loosen the soil well. Dig a hole large enough to spread out the root structure of each plant, and then after planting tamp the soil around the roots to prevent air pockets. Shrubs and trees can be cumbersome to plant, even if they're only moderately sized. Your local garden or nursery center may offer planting services when you buy and can save you hours of hard labor.

4 Mulching. Mulch around, not over, each transplant with 2 inches (5 cm) of weed-free straw or bark mulch. Mulch helps keep plants moist and weeds out.

5 Marking. Don't forget to mark the locations of your plants so that you don't pull them up in a spell of absent-minded weeding. Writing each plant's name on a garden marker, Popsicle stick, or a disposable plastic fork with a permanent marking pen, and sticking it firmly in the ground near the plant will do the trick. Be careful, though, not to injure the plant or its roots when you insert the marker into the soil.

6 Watering. During the first 4 to 6 weeks after planting trees, shrubs, or perennials, water thoroughly once a week, soaking the plant's root zone, especially if you plant in late spring or in sandy or clay soils. After this, only water during prolonged dry periods. Be careful not to overwater any new plants, and avoid watering at night because fungi could attack transplants under cool, damp conditions.

7 Weeding. Yes, it's a necessary chore. Weeds will compete with your new transplants for water, light, and space, and there's really no sense in planting a new garden if it's just going to become a weed patch. Of course, it's true that birds do love weeds because of their tasty seeds, but you'll want to keep weeds under control in most areas of your garden. Using an organic mulch, such as aged compost or shredded bark, can stop weeds dead in their tracks.

THE NEW LAGOON

Bringing Water to Your Backyard Habitat

FROM LAKES AND SHORES to rivers and ponds, the shimmery elixir known as water draws both birds and bird watchers alike. Add water to your backyard habitat and you'll be rewarded with a steady stream of avian guests, while discovering a new way to interact (from a distance!) with birds of many species. A simple birdbath can create a noteworthy splash in your landscape, and a well-designed, in-ground water garden can provide food, drink, bathing facilities, and cover for both regular and migrant bird visitors.

Water — Essential for Life

WHETHER it drips, puddles, flows, or splashes, the sound and sight of water is irresistible to birds. They depend on water for hydration and temperature control, and surprisingly, for flight. Birds use water to clean their feathers, and clean feathers are essential for efficient flying. Whether they want to bathe, drink, or cool off, birds seek out sources of water on a daily basis and will only live within flying distance of a water source. Bird enthusiasts can entice birds into their bird-friendly backyards by providing access to wet, wild, and wonderful water.

THE BASIC BIOLOGY

Water plays an important role in the health and well-being of a bird, and it is as necessary as food, vitamins, and minerals. The amount of water a given bird species needs daily depends on a wide range of environmental and physiological variables. The smaller a bird is, the more water it loses through skin and respiratory system evaporation. For example, a house wren weighing about ½ ounce can lose 37 percent of its body weight in water daily in this manner. On the other hand, some birds can supply up to 80 percent of their water needs from chemical processes in their own bodies.

Many birds, such as raptors, use the bodily fluids of their prey to provide an important source of water. Similarly, insect-eating birds get most of their water from the juices of their insect prey. Swallows are an exception, though. They often dip down to lakes and streams during flight to drink surface water, helping to replace the rapid water loss that occurs during their long flights. Seed-eating birds, with their dry diet, have the greatest need for water, and they actively seek it out from streams, ponds, water holes, dew, raindrops, puddles, and even snow.

THIRSTY BIRDS

Birds fall into two categories of drinkers—gulpers and slurpers. Land birds use the most commonly seen drinking method. They immerse their beak in water, tip their head up, and allow the water to trickle into their throat so they can swallow it. Pigeons and doves, in equine style, just hold their beaks in the water and suck it up through pumping motions in the throat. Pelicans simply open their huge beaks during a rainfall.

A number of shorebird species wet their food before they eat it, providing another source of water in the diet. While many species have been observed wetting their food, ornithologists haven't determined why they do it. Is it to make swallowing easier, or is it to simply clean the food? Regardless of the reason, shorebirds depend heavily on the water supply they find in their habitat for their existence.

THE ART OF THE BATH

You probably know that birds use water bathing as a way to cool themselves off on a hot and sultry summer day, but *water* bathing also helps with *water*proofing, surprisingly enough. After birds clean their feathers, they oil, preen, and run their feathers through their beaks to realign the hooks (also called barbs) that give the feathers the structural integrity needed for successful flight.

Contrary to what some might think, birds are not completely covered in feathers from head to toe. The feathers actually grow in tracts known as *pterylae* that generally cover only 30 percent of the body, at least for land birds. The spaces in between are referred to as *apteria*. When birds bathe, they open and close certain feather tracts to expose those parts to the water. The trapped water is next forced into the *apteria* and then squeezed through the *pterylae* to rinse and bathe the base of the feathers. This activity generally results in a thoroughly soaked and waterlogged bird. Since waterlogged birds cannot escape predators easily, they seek out bathing opportunities in safe conditions so there is time for grooming. For most birds, though, the goal in bathing is to dampen the plumage evenly, not soak it, to help with the oiling and preening process.

Feather tracts, or pterylae, are easily seen on this fledgling American robin.

KNEE DEEP

Just about all songbirds (jays, titmice, blackbirds, finches, thrushes, warblers, and sparrows) and most large land birds (eagles, hawks, crows, and owls) engage in the practice of "stand-in" bathing. This generally consists of wading into a body of water, usually between 1 to 3 inches (2.5 to 8 cm) deep, according to the bird's need. The raptors often lie right in the water when bathing, partly submerged and motionless in between bouts of violent splashing.

Bathing is a bit more exciting for swifts and swallows. Their short, weak legs and narrow, pointed wings make standing in water difficult, so they simply dive into water during flight. They submerge just long enough and deeply enough to create a spray that is scooped over their backs. A raised tail slows their velocity and catches the spray of water, while vibrating feathers help break it up into tiny bubbles.

The arboreal flycatchers and kingfishers perform a variation on this theme by diving (often up to 50 feet/15 m) from a favorite perch into water below. After a quick dousing, they return to their perches and vibrate their wet feathers to dry off.

Awesome Antics

Just as humans enter the waves at the beach in various manners (from the one-toe-at-a-time folks to the dive-right-in crowd), birds perform a variety of stunts to get wet. For instance, vireos and buntings sometimes perform a combination of both "stand" and "dive" bathing. After standing for a few seconds beside a shallow stream (or by a puddle in the case of buntings), vireos perform a short dip and roll, and then return to a perch to vibrate their feathers. Livelier, active birds, like yellowthroats, wrens, and Carolina chickadees, quickly dive, dart, or leap into the water, roll around and flick their wings, and then head off to a bank or branch briefly to dry out.

If there is no stream, rain, birdbath, or sprinkler handy, some birds, such as hornbills, commonly resort to seeking out and rubbing against vegetation that is wet with rain or dew. A number of North American species, such as vireos, warblers, and dark-eyed juncos, have also been observed "leaf bathing" or fluttering about on wet plant surfaces.

Birds in playful moods might "test the waters" if a bathing situation presents itself and looks just too enticing to resist. A branch conveniently located above the eddying water in a crystal clear stream can serve as a bathing, diving, or preening perch if the moment is right. On other occasions, a bird may be forced to use bathing methods that are not especially well suited to it. For example, flickers prefer rain baths, so they can look somewhat clumsy and off balance bathing in a stream when there's been a dry spell.

SINGING IN THE RAIN

There are still other ways for birds to bathe. Parrots, woodpeckers, nuthatches, and larks love a good soaking from drizzling rain. They adopt special postures, similar to those used in sunbathing, to make the most of it.

Sometimes birds actually lie down in the rain. During sudden downpours in England, flocks of feral pigeons have been observed lying on the grass on one side while raising the other wing vertically. Larks often bathe in the rain by lying down with both their wings outstretched. Robins regularly hop across a lawn under the spray of a water sprinkler. And hummingbirds are well known for flying through the moving fine spray or mist of a sprinkler or garden hose.

The sound of moving water is very enticing to robins, flickers, and even hummingbirds. Robins love the steady shower of water that a lawn sprinkler provides.

Birdbath Bonanza

WATCHING an American robin wade breast deep into a standing pool of water on a hot summer's day and then vigorously dousing itself over and over is almost as refreshing as the sight of a clear mountain lake after a long, arduous hike. Yet, few homeowners pay as much attention to providing water for birds as they pay to providing birdseed in their backyard, and water is as much of a life-giving commodity as food is.

NEW DIRECTIONS

Fortunately, interest in birdbaths and water features in the backyard landscape is growing. Many birders say that it is much more fun to watch birds bathe than it is to watch them sit on a feeder and stuff their beaks.

Think of birdbaths, and the conventional pedestal-style staple comes to mind. Though recent versions may be plastic, resin, or metal instead of concrete, the pedestal bath has been around and unchanged for a century or more. Pedestal birdbaths are simple in design, usually consisting of an upper basin and a lower pedestal. With more stores selling birdbaths, designs have become more ornate and geared to buyers than to users—the birds. Many birdbaths on the market have drawbacks, which lessen their attractiveness to would-be bathers.

When shopping for a birdbath, look for three key features: First, the bathing basin should be less than 3 inches (8 cm) deep—and you should fill it with only 2 inches (5 cm) of water. Most songbirds won't

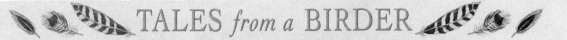

TALES *from a* BIRDER

I recall a summer when the captive kestrels at my avian research facility had a blast after I had strung a garden hose with evenly spaced holes over the roof of their breeding cages. The kestrels ran excitedly back and forth along their perches with wings outspread, chirping like children out playing in the rain.

—*Dr. David Bird*

bathe in water that's any deeper than that; they prefer to hunker down in a depth that barely reaches the bottoms of their bellies.

Second, make sure the bottom of the bathing basin has a rough surface. Many birdbath bottoms are often too slick to provide secure footing for birds, especially when a coat of algae forms on submerged surfaces. If you can find only a smooth surface basin, rough it up with sandpaper or the claws of a

No need to get fancy when you buy a birdbath. The simple, old-fashioned pedestal style attracts bathers from far and wide.

hammer (for plastic basins only!) before filling it with water.

Third, make sure the basin fits securely on the pedestal and won't be subject to tipping by thirsty dogs, raccoons, deer, or, in wilder reaches, bears. No one wants to pick up an overturned birdbath every morning, and few folks want to replace a broken basin every time a thirsty critter tries to scale the pedestal. You can search for a one-piece birdbath, or you could use a waterproof adhesive to attach the basin to the pedestal. Also, weight the base or sink it in the ground to minimize tipping over.

OLD IS NEW

If your pedestal birdbath doesn't feature these bird-friendly features, you can retrofit it to heighten its appeal to would-be bathers. If the bath is too deep or too slippery, pile thin, flat rocks in the deepest part of the bath to create ledges and small pools for bathing birds. Avoid using gravel or sand—both of these are easily dirtied and impossible to scrub clean. Adding rocks to your bath will solve both depth and footing problems.

BIRDBATHS
at a glance

BUYING a birdbath is for the birds, and that's the most important thing to remember! Look for these bird-friendly features when shopping:

- Shallow basin, less than 3 inches (8 cm) deep
- Rough, nonslip basin surface
- Steady, well-balanced pedestal and basin that won't easily tip

If your birdbath has a tendency to tip when it's crowded with birds or when thirsty critters come for a sip, remove the basin from the pedestal and place it directly on the ground. Be sure to site it at least 10 feet (3 m) from shrubbery, but not too much farther. Birds prefer to approach a water source in stages, checking to see that the coast is clear.

When birds are waterlogged, they fly poorly, and they'll need a perch close by to flutter to. Create shelter around a bath by pushing branches into the ground around the bath, making sure that the branches don't overhang the bath (to prevent perching birds from fouling the water).

DRIP, DRIP, DRIP

You can hike your birdbath's attractiveness another notch with the sound and sight of moving water. The simplest way to do this is with a dripper. Birds cue into a water source by sound as well as by sight, and dripping water is completely irresistible to a thirsty bird. The simplest dripper can be made with a gallon plastic milk jug. Punch a very small hole in the bottom and one near the top to vent air. Hang the jug from a pole or a shepherd's crook (used to hang bird feeders) a few feet above your bath. The water should last a day or so before needing to be refilled. If you find that the jug is collapsing, you'll need to make a larger vent hole in the top.

If you prefer a more permanent setup, there are some good drippers on the market. They have a generous length (usually 50 feet/15 m) of miniature plastic tubing that you

can connect directly to one of your outside spigots. Some models have a pedestal that sits in the bath to support the dripper tubing, but if the one you buy doesn't, just use a staked support to hold the tubing up over the side wall of the bird-bath. A small petcock, or valve, on the side of the support controls the drip rate. Add a two-way adapter to the spigot if you plan to use a garden hose, so you'll be unhampered by the dripper's operation.

Make your own dripper by filling a milk jug with water and punching a very small hole in the bottom, plus a larger vent hole in the top.

PUMP IT UP

Another way to add moving water to the birdbath is with a recirculating pump. Thanks to the water-gardening craze, recirculating pumps are available in a wide array of sizes and prices. Most will last for years without maintenance. For folks with limited water resources, a recirculating pump may be the best option for creating the sound and sight of splashing water in the confines of a backyard bird garden. You will have lots of fun setting up small waterfalls and fountains using flat rocks, and your bird visitors will be just as enthralled with the tumbling water as you are.

In any setup, hygiene is an important consideration. Be sure to flush and scrub your birdbath as often as necessary. This can be a daily operation for a heavily used bath in the summer months, and a once-a-week task in the winter. It helps to keep a plastic scrub brush hidden near the bath and to situate your water feature within easy reach of the garden hose. Remember, the more elaborate the setup, the more difficult it will be to clean, so keep that in mind when you add bird-baths to your landscape.

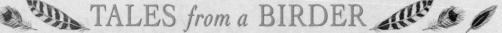

LIKE most backyard bird watchers, I feel that keeping a supply of fresh water on hand is a year-round commitment. But in the summer months this commitment carries a few extra challenges. With a constant progression of birds taking baths, their splashing can deplete the water level in no time, and in 90°F (32°C)–plus heat, it doesn't take long for water temperatures to become quite uncomfortable, even in the shade.

During the heat wave last summer, I began replenishing my birdbaths with ice cubes. How time-consuming! It was then that I realized that my air conditioner, with its constant supply of cool water accumulating from the condensation coils, offered me a better solution.

Not all air conditioners are alike, but mine provided a steady source of condensation drips. For years, this condensation had dripped from a foot-long (30 cm) plastic tube onto the ground, right next to the foundation of the house. Using an inexpensive coupling and 10 feet (3 m) of extra tubing, I extended this line out into my yard on a slightly downward plane. To keep the tube from curling, I secured it to the ground with a couple of U-shaped pieces of coat-hanger wire.

I placed a large dish under the tube to collect the dripping water, elevating one end of the dish with a small rock so that the overflow would drip into a smaller dish wedged just below it. The final overflow from this bi-level birdbath seeps into the ground and waters my dogwood tree.

At first I worried that the water might include some harmful substance (such as the freon that is used to help cool the air), but both my air-conditioner repairman and the unit's manufacturer assured me that the water created by condensation does not come into contact with any coolant inside the unit.

It took only a day for the birds to discover this new oasis, and they soon competed for the chance to refresh themselves on hot summer days. To my pleasant surprise, the damp ground below the dishes also provides butterflies with a "puddling" area during times of drought. As long as my air conditioner is running, I can now offer my birds a self-replenishing supply of cool water, and it's absolutely free!

When your air conditioner clicks on this spring, remember the birds, and put that waste water to good use!

—Sandra Stephens

water
birdbath cool mist splash waterfall pools bathing puddles streams rain sprinkles oasis

Water in Winter

BIRDS drink water all year, and it's important to try to maintain a water source during the cold winter months. As a good bird host, you'll need to pay special attention to keeping extra water sources unfrozen. It helps if the water you provide is located where it can receive a good dose of sunshine to keep it from icing over. If that's not possible, there are a number of other options such as heaters that are readily available from garden, nature, and wild-bird centers.

SITING THE BATH

Maintaining a winter birdbath is an excellent way to attract birds to your backyard when cold winds blow, but it's important to choose the location of the birdbath carefully. Above all, place the bath where you

Birds will return to a water source in any weather. On cold days, birds may not be interested in bathing, but they may come for a drink. When there's ice outside, provide drinking water by setting out a shallow pan of warm water at least once a day.

can see it from inside your house because bathing birds are great fun to watch. Bird photographer Susan Day vividly recalls watching a family of seven bluebirds using her birdbath every day one winter when there were 2 inches (5 cm) of ice and snow. Every evening the energetic group would spend several minutes splashing together in the water before making a beeline to one of her nest boxes to roost for the night.

You might also want to consider placing the bath on the south side of the house and out of the wind. It should also be near electricity if you plan to use a heater or pump.

Remember that you'll need to walk to your bath to fill it when the snow is deep, so choose a spot with easy access. Garden hoses are out of the question in winter, and unless you have a water faucet next to your bath, you probably won't enjoy trudging through deep snow toting a bucket of water.

KEEPING IT OPEN

Naturally, the biggest challenge to supplying water in winter is avoiding the deep freeze. There are many types of baths and deicers available. You can buy self-

TALES *from a* BIRDER

WE keep our feeders full during the winter months, and they're as busy as the best restaurant in town on a Saturday night. With the perches full of hungry diners, the cardinals, goldfinches, and chickadees wait in a nearby elm tree for the next available seat. Since we provide water for the birds during the summer, we decided to add a heater to our backyard pond so that birds would have access to water all winter. Once we added the heater, we noticed a steady stream of birds checking out the local watering hole after filling their bellies at the feeders.

All the seed-eating birds at the feeders, including titmice, blue jays, juncos, and cardinals, became regulars at the water, stopping by for a sip or splash. Fruit-eating birds like bluebirds and mockingbirds often join them for a drink. Adding a heater to the pond was one of the best things we've done to attract birds to our southern Illinois backyard in the wintertime.

—*Susan Day*

water

> **Most young birds migrate to the appropriate wintering grounds for their species without following older birds. Knowledge of the route appears to be part of the genetic inheritance of the bird.**

contained birdbath models with built-in heaters; all you need to do is add water and plug it in. Some of these models clamp onto deck or porch rails, others sit on top of pedestals, and some are placed directly on the ground. The built-in heater may be a fuss-free way to offer year-round water for birds.

Other heaters or deicers attach to baths or are the floating types used in pet or cattle watering tanks. Know your weather patterns and keep them in mind as you shop for winter equipment; ask for advice from local wild-bird stores, as well. It's important to buy what will work best for your situation. In milder climates, a recirculating pump or aerator may be enough to keep the water moving. Many pumps and aerators designed for fish tanks can be used outdoors.

If you're technically challenged or prefer a less expensive way to provide water in winter, simply fill your regular birdbath with hot water. You may have to change it several times a day, depending on outdoor temperatures, but bird visitors will appreciate your watering efforts. Some people use black birdbaths in winter because the sun warms them up faster than lighter-colored baths.

Other bird watchers cover their baths with pieces of swimming-pool solar covers at night to help prevent heat loss. You can also put a moving float in your birdbath; a plastic milk jug tied to a rock for an anchor will bob around in the water and keep it open, in the same way a duck paddling atop icy water keeps the water from freezing.

SHIVERY DIPS

In places with very cold winters, you may need both a heater and a moving float to keep the water open for the birds. If your winter weather conditions are extremely harsh, it's best to prevent birds from bathing altogether because their feathers might freeze before they

Bathing Birds

Q How often do birds bathe?

A A bird changes its bathing routine depending on the weather and the season of the year. On a sunny summer day, a chickadee or titmouse might bathe five times a day but not at all on a cold, windy one. While some birds bathe in the afternoon, other birds start bathing a few hours after sunrise and often end the day with a late evening bath.

Q How often should I clean my birdbath, and how should I do it?

A A heavily used birdbath should be flushed out daily in midsummer, or whenever it becomes visibly fouled. It should be scrubbed weekly with a weak solution of chlorine bleach (1 part bleach to 9 parts water), and rinsed thoroughly before being refilled. It's a good idea to keep an old scrub brush near the birdbath to make it more convenient to keep up with this chore.

Q We've seen several birds use our birdbath and become so waterlogged they were unable to fly for some time. Is this unusual?

A Some birds, especially recently fledged youngsters, bathe so enthusiastically that they temporarily rob themselves of the all-important power of flight. For this reason, it's a good idea to offer some get-away perches near your birdbath, in the form of small trees, shrubs, or even branches pushed into the ground, so that bathing beauties can have temporary, safe shelter among the branches when they're soaked. With some vigorous flapping and preening, the birds will soon be able to regain the air. Make sure, however, that nearby shrubbery does not harbor lurking cats. Siting your bath at least 15 feet (4.5 m) from dense cover will help prevent sneak attacks by predators.

pools bathing puddles streams rain sprinkles oasis

Discourage birds from bathing in cold weather by covering your birdbath with a plywood platform. Cut out a small hole for drinking.

can dry. Your goal then should be to provide water for drinking only.

There are several ways you can keep birds from dousing themselves by reducing the open area of your bath: Place a board or flat rock over open water to block off most of the bath, leaving a muffin-sized opening where birds can drink. Or, place a section of a pool liner or other cover over part of your bath to create a smaller opening; add weights to the edges of the cover or tie it on securely so it won't blow or flap in the wind.

No Shocks

When you install a water feature, consider hiring an electrician to add an underground line to the

BUILDING A BIRD CREEK

IN-GROUND water gardens allow lots of opportunities to attract birds with drips, trickles, and splashes. Most feature a deeper area for water-loving plants, but you should consider adding bird-friendly extras to the water garden, such as waterfalls, shallow pools, and small creek beds.

If you haven't embarked on a project like this before, you may want to consult a water-garden designer, or if you're experienced, you can plan your own water feature. Using a recirculating pump, create a waterfall that trickles to a creek area, letting the water splash from rock to rock as it makes its way down the falls. Use a

Submersible birdbath heaters and deicers cost about $25. You'll get your investment back threefold when birds flock to your backyard in icy weather.

birdbath. When using electricity near water, you should use a ground fault circuit interrupter (GFCI) to break the electric circuit if water enters the system. An electrician can install an outdoor outlet where you can plug in a timer for the pump and a heater in winter.

Look for a submersible heater with, at least, a 3-foot (90 cm)-long, all-weather cord. Your electrician can adjust the cord to the correct length for your pool. One thing you don't want to worry about is electrocuting the birds or yourself when you add water to your pool.

heavy-duty PVC liner for the creek bed that drops away from the falls, then cover the bed with pea gravel. Line the creek edges with rocks, and create shallow pools to serve as bathing areas. Design the creek bed to be about 1 inch (2.5 cm) deep, and it will become the center of bird activity, especially on cold days.

As warmer weather turns to winter, you'll notice birds busying themselves at the water. When all the other puddles and water sources are covered with ice, the birds know they can sip and dip at your bird creek. One advantage of keeping water in winter is seeing the winter migrants visit it as well.

water   *birdbath cool mist splash waterfall pools bathing puddles streams rain sprinkles oasis*

If you live in an area where winters are mild, you can keep water open by allowing a pump to recirculate the water; even slight movement may be enough to keep the water from freezing. But if it gets very cold even occasionally (with some snow and ice possible), you'll need to consider buying a heater. Look for one with a thermostat that turns the unit on when the water temperature drops near freezing. This type of heater will also automatically shut off if the pond should run dry.

DRY ICE

During extreme cold snaps, a heater will keep water open under a layer of ice in your water feature. But heat may also cause that water to evaporate, so watch for this and fill the pond as needed.

You can also heat a pedestal-style birdbath. Look for one that is constructed of freeze-proof plastic since ceramic and concrete may crack in winter. You can buy clamp-on heaters for your bath that are thermostatically controlled and will shut off if the bath runs out of water. Use an all-weather exten-sion cord for the heater and plug it into an outdoor outlet .

ROUTINE MAINTENANCE

Maintaining water for birds in winter takes a bit more attention than in summer. Check the water level daily and keep it clean, not only for the birds, but to prevent clogged pumps and filters. If air temperatures are below freezing, avoid getting your hands wet when cleaning and refilling your bath, and use a net to clean out debris.

The extra effort you'll need to make to provide water in winter will pay off by an increase in the number of birds you'll attract in nasty weather. When you have water at the ready for thirsty birds, you'll find your feeders crowded with hungry birds chattering among themselves and gulping down your offerings. You might even see a covey of quail or a group of mourning doves trundling over to the water after having their meal of cracked corn. And what better sight could brighten a drab winter day than cardinals and bluebirds sharing some bubbly at your watering hole?

3

SETTING THE TABLE

Outside Offerings That Attract Birds

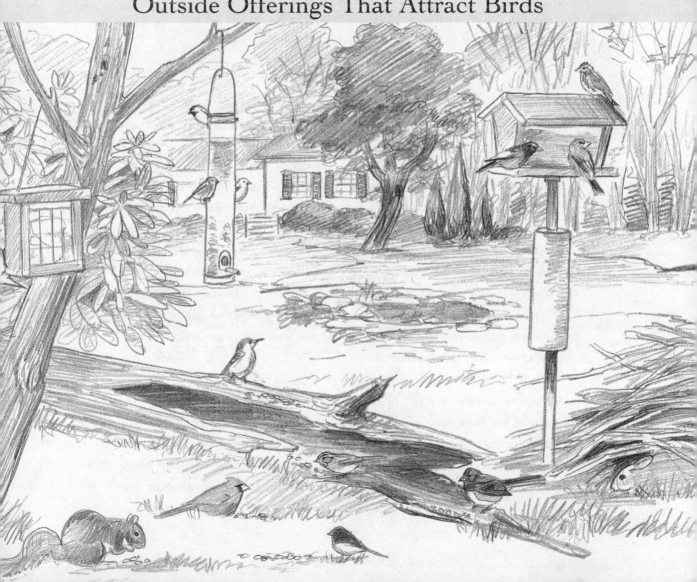

HAVING A BIRD-FRIENDLY YARD, with plenty of cover and natural food, will ensure that you'll always have something delightful to observe from every window. You'll need to decide for yourself whether or not you want to augment these natural offerings with a feeder. Feeding birds is optional, though, and not necessary for their winter survival. A feeding program is enjoyable, brings nature into your everyday life, and can encourage compassion for all wild creatures—and that is surely a good thing on the grander scale.

Ideal Feeding Stations

IF you decide to add a feeder or two, be forewarned—bird feeding can be an addictive hobby. The birds will make your bird-friendly backyard one of the stops on their daily feeding rounds. Successful bird feeding can be as simple or complex as you wish to make it.

One Connecticut woman I know has fed birds for 50 years by simply flinging a coffee can full of seeds out of her back door twice a day. She has wonderful birds, too, including a couple of titmice who peek in the windows, locate her— whatever room she's in—and tap on the window until she gets up to replenish their food. You may not relish that much of a routine, but you will surely enjoy seeing birds gathered at your feeders.

To build a feeding station, consider the different kinds of birds you want to attract and what they might need. If you provide a variety of feeder styles at different heights, you will encourage the greatest diversity of birds. The ideal feeding station offers shelter from both wind and predators with either established plantings or with the "instant habitat" of brush.

Construct your own bird habitat with all or some of the following elements and you'll have a constant stream of feathered visitors. Here's a rundown on the feeding stations you might choose when setting the table for birds.

THE OLD HOLLOW LOG

A hollow log can serve as a natural ground-level feeder and may be near your back door in the woodpile. The majority of species that frequent feeders find all or part of their natural food on the ground, and some, such as sparrows, doves, towhees, and juncos, rarely forage anywhere else. Scatter seed in and on the log and you'll delight in the scene—cardinals, juncos, Carolina wrens, and song sparrows will peck at and scratch the dark, weathered wood as they forage for seed.

Old fence rails make great feeders, too. Pile them up randomly and high enough to give the birds a little shelter and to get the seed up off the wet ground. To make sparrows feel at home, cut and bundle dry bluestem grass, asters, and goldenrod, and push the stems down into the cracks to create shelter.

Sparrows, doves, and other ground-feeding birds will flock to a hollow-log feeder. Place a fallen tree or stump in an out-of-the way corner, and as the wood weathers, you'll find more and more crevices to hold seeds.

food

BRUSH PILE HABITAT

It's great fun to create an "instant habitat" out of an otherwise dull landscape. Build a brush pile behind your feeding station by collecting branches and pushing or digging them into the ground in twisted, pleasing shapes to create a shelter. Come New Year's Day, add your Christmas tree to the brush pile and watch as the birds immediately adopt it as a haven from attacks by sharp-shinned or Cooper's hawks.

Such creations are like a living sculpture, decked with the color and motion of dozens of birds. Best of all, they provide shelter, one of a wild bird's three basic needs (food and water are the other two). If you have neighborhood cats on the prowl, keep the brush pile small so it doesn't become a spot for predators to ambush birds.

Allow your creative impulses to keep your landscape changing and growing. Move your brush pile and re-create it in a new design each year. You may want to dismantle your pile every spring to allow the trampled, hull-covered grass to recover. Rebuild it in the fall with an entirely new look.

BIRD TABLES at a glance

WHEN making a bird table or purchasing one, consider these pointers for the best design and installation:

- Long and narrow design, 8 inches (20 cm) wide at most
- Wood strips around the edges of the box for perching and containing seed
- Good drainage for rainwater, with either drilled holes or screening attached
- Mounted on a pole, with a squirrel baffle if necessary

THE BIRD TABLE

Bird tables—also called platform feeders—have the advantage that birds of different species may feed together, without the jostling for position and bickering engendered by hanging feeders. Tables are the most readily accepted and conspicuous feeders, and certain bird species, like evening grosbeaks, prefer them to any other kind.

A bird table is just a sheet of plywood on cinder blocks turned on their sides. The table should be long and narrow—8 inches (20 cm) wide at most. This encourages birds to perch around the edges rather than walking on it and fouling the seed.

Tack strips of wood around the edges to give birds a place to perch and to keep seed from blowing off the table. Drill ½-inch (1.25 cm) holes at intervals in the bottom of the table to help drain off rainwater, or consider using weatherproof screening for the bottom of the feeder to allow water to drain out.

Put your bird table on the ground or mount it on a pole. Or, better yet, you can make two poles—one low and one high—and draw both ground feeders and those that like a slightly higher perch. If you have a problem with squirrels raiding your feeding station, you'll need to take extra care to protect the bird table from the hungry mammals. Mount your table feeder on a post with a baffle, or guard, to frustrate squirrels.

Scatter seed on top of the table and into the compartments of the blocks to take advantage of all the surfaces. Clean your feeder of bird droppings and old seed regularly. Scrape the debris from the feeder, and wipe it clean or scrub and dry it before refilling.

A simple plywood-and-cinder-block bird table can be added to your natural landscape in a jiffy. Bird tables allow birds of different species to feed together.

Seed Feeders: The Three Types

ANY bird-feeding program will benefit from having hanging or post-mounted feeders. Feeders cater to woodland birds that prefer to feed above the ground, such as chickadees, titmice, nuthatches, and woodpeckers. Hanging feeders keep seed clean, dry, and constantly available in case of heavy snow. Suspend them from a wire to safeguard them from squirrels, raccoons, and other mammals that cheerfully vacuum up food on the ground or on low tables.

Elevated seed feeders fall into three main categories: hopper, tube, and globe. Each type has its strengths and can encourage certain birds to repeatedly visit your backyard. Consider these things before you buy: Is the feeder easy to fill and clean? (Keep this foremost in mind as you shop.) Is the filling hole wide enough to accommodate a scoop or coffee can lip without spilling most of the seed? Can the feeder be taken apart easily or opened for rinsing and scrubbing?

Hopper feeder

If you prefer a wood feeder, look for weather-resistant cedar. Plastic feeders should be reinforced with metal on parts that squirrels may chew. Perches should be metal or replaceable wooden dowels. Since you may be using a feeder for a decade or more, it pays to buy the sturdiest and most easily maintained one you can afford.

Hopper feeders are usually mounted on posts and are the most user friendly from a bird's standpoint.

They can resemble small barns or gazebos and are also often equipped with a catch tray and perches, where even ground feeders like doves and sparrows feel comfortable. Hoppers also entice the birds that are generally more reluctant to perch on tube feeders, such as rose-breasted and black-headed grosbeaks, indigo and painted buntings, and ground-feeding birds.

Tube feeders are long cylinders with perches at several feeding ports. These are perhaps the most popular feeder style, though their clientele is more limited than a hopper's. Tubes are used by small birds and are usually dominated by house finches, goldfinches, pine siskins, purple finches, chickadees, and titmice. Woodpeckers often learn to use them, but starlings, blackbirds, jays, and cardinals rarely succeed.

Tube feeder

Globe feeders are the most specialized of the feeders. These feeders, sometimes called satellite feeders, have seed holes but no perches. They attract birds that can cling upside down, chiefly chickadees, titmice, nuthatches, woodpeckers, and goldfinches. A feeder designed for these birds is a positive addition to any bird habitat. When ground, table, hopper, and tube feeders are overtaken by aggressive flocks of house finches or blackbirds, clinging birds can always find seed in a globe feeder.

Globe feeder

food

white proso millet cracked corn niger safflower suet peanuts apples egg-bells dogwood berries

When to Start Feeding and When to Stop Feeding

MANY people wonder what time of year to start feeding. If you enjoy bird feeding year-round, any month will do. If you'd prefer to feed only in winter, you should start in late summer or autumn. This way, you'll entice birds into including your feeder in their winter-feeding routes.

Come spring, should you wish to discontinue feeding, wait until you've noticed a drop-off in the number of birds coming and the amount of food consumed before tapering off your feeding routine. This is usually well into spring when leaves are unfurled and insect life is abundant. In some colder climates, this could be early summer.

Don't worry about getting the birds "addicted" to seed. By spring, the increasing energy demands of courtship, nest building, territorial defense, and egg laying dictate a shift in most birds' diets toward protein-rich insects. The birds will be only too happy to abandon your feeders. You may want to consider continuing your feeding efforts through the breeding season, though, because it can be the most rewarding birding experience of all.

KEEPING IT UP

Experts debate the question of how disruptive a break in feeding continuity can be for your bird population. Many people fear that missing a day or two in filling feeders, or taking a week's vacation, will mean the end of their feeder-dependent flocks. Most birds, however, visit a given feeding station as only part of a daily circuit, which may include neighbors' feeders as well as natural sources. Though you may feed only five chickadees at a time, as many as 60 could be using your feeders.

COLD WEATHER CONTINUITY

For bird species that keep to a winter territory, a stop-and-start feeding program can often be worse than none at all. If you're going away for a few days, fill up all of your feeders and scatter a good amount of seed on the ground under shrubbery. Large, hopper-style feeders are invaluable for this purpose, as long as they can be depended on to provide a free flow without clogging up. For longer vacations, pay a neighbor to fill your feeders.

IS FEEDING GOOD OR BAD?

Wisconsin researchers Margaret Brittingham and Stanley Temple did a study on the winter-feeding habits of black-capped chickadees. They discovered that black-capped chickadees, on average, take only from 20 to 25 per-

cent of their winter food requirements from bird feeders. However, they also found that those chickadees that used feeders had a better chance of surviving than the wild birds that had no access to feeders. While fully 69 percent of the feeder-using chickadees survived the winter, only 37 percent of the wild birds (without feeders) did.

While there aren't any similar studies on all of the other birds that visit feeders, we can only surmise that other species must enjoy a similar or even greater benefit from winter-feeding programs.

The sudden defection of birds from your feeders in spring, as soon as buds begin to swell and insects hatch, suggests that artificial feeding doesn't cause birds to lose their ability to find their own wild food.

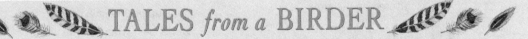

TALES *from a* BIRDER

WHEN I lived in rural Connecticut, I had an annoyingly huge flock of house finches—70 or more in number. They systematically emptied my feeders every day. A friend some 2 miles away often gloated that the house finches that once plagued her feeders had disappeared. Called away on business, I let my feeders go empty for 2 days, and guess where the finches went? After that, I'd sometimes wait to fill my feeders until midday and could barely suppress a cackle when Barbara would call to scold me for foisting the flock off on her.

—*Julie Zickefoose*

Feeding Birds

Q **We filled our tube feeder with wild birdseed, only to find that the birds empty it out, dumping all the seed on the ground without eating it. Why is this happening?**

A So-called wild birdseed is usually a millet-based mixture that contains some cracked corn, sunflower, and often wheat, milo, or other grains. The vast majority of birds that use tube feeders prefer sunflower seed. To get to the sunflower seed, the birds will rake out the mixed seed, which winds up all over the ground. It's best to offer straight sunflower seed in hanging feeders, and mixed seed on platform feeders, or scattered on the ground.

Q **Will the birds at my feeder become completely dependent on seed and lose the ability to forage naturally?**

A The food most birds eat at feeding stations is only a portion of their overall diet. Many seed-eating birds switch to an insect-based diet when the weather warms up in spring. Their numbers at your feeding station will naturally thin out as more attractive natural foods become available.

Q **Sunflower seed hulls are killing the grass under my feeders. What can I do?**

A Sunflower hulls in large quantities are indeed toxic to grass. There are several ways to avoid killing your lawn in exchange for your kindness to the birds. The nomadic approach is to simply move your feeding station when the hulls begin to build up. You can also rake the hulls up periodically (this works best when they're wet). Try spreading bark mulch under feeders, then raking it up and changing it periodically. Some bird-feeding catalogs offer a mesh-fabric mat for use under feeders that can be picked up, shaken out, and re-used.

The Scoop on Seed

IF you've ever driven across the upper Midwest in late summer, you were probably delighted by mile after mile of golden sunflowers nodding in the breeze, heralds of a quiet revolution in bird feeding. Years ago, the only sunflower seed available was the big, thick-shelled, gray-striped kind, accessible only to heavy-billed cardinals and grosbeaks or the resourceful chickadees and titmice that are able to hold and hammer the shell until it gives up its heart. Since then, black oil sunflower seed has almost completely overtaken gray-striped sunflower seed in sales.

There is a great variety of seeds available that you may wish to try to see which birds prefer which types of seeds. Some seeds may be less expensive, while others may create less mess in your yard. Experiment with the many different kinds available to learn which birds frequent your feeders, then make the seed choices suitable to you and your birds.

BLACK OIL SUNFLOWER SEED

 Black oil sunflower seed, so called because it has a higher oil (and thus, a higher caloric) content, is probably the universal favorite among North American birds. Much smaller than the gray-striped sunflower, black oil sunflower has a thin, papery shell that yields to the smaller bills of sparrows, juncos, and even goldfinches. It's a much better value since 70 percent of each seed is meat, compared to 57 percent for striped sunflower seed. Black oil sunflower is the heart of any feeding program because it is accepted by the greatest variety of birds. Offer sunflower seeds in tube, hopper, globe, or table feeders, and scatter it on the ground.

Buy your oil seed in bulk at a feed store or wild-bird supply store.

> Crows and jays cache, or store, food. They can remember the location of hundreds of different food caches in a single season and can use them in times of need.

food

white proso millet cracked corn niger safflower suet peanuts apples crabapples dogwood berries

Quick Reference · THE FOODS BIRDS PREFER

HERE are the general food preferences for the most common feeder birds of North America. Although there are no guaranteed methods for attracting certain birds to your feeders, the presence of water, adequate habitat or cover, and the birds' favorite foods will enhance the attractiveness of your yard. Foods are listed in approximate order of preference.

PIGEONS, DOVES
Millet, cracked corn, wheat, milo, thistle, buckwheat, sunflower seed, baked goods

HUMMINGBIRDS
Plant nectar, small insects, sugar solution

WOODPECKERS
Suet, meat scraps, sunflower hearts and seed, cracked corn, peanuts, fruits

JAYS
Peanuts, sunflower seed, suet, meat scraps, cracked corn, baked goods

CROWS, MAGPIES, NUTCRACKERS
Meat scraps, suet, cracked corn, peanuts, baked goods, leftovers, dog food

TITMICE, CHICKADEES
Peanut kernels, sunflower, suet

NUTHATCHES
Suet, suet mixes, sunflower hearts and seed, peanut kernels, peanut butter

WRENS, CREEPERS
Suet, suet mixes, peanut butter, peanut kernels, bread, fruit, millet (wrens)

MOCKINGBIRDS, THRASHERS, CATBIRDS
Halved apples, chopped fruits, baked goods, suet, nutmeats, millet (thrashers), soaked raisins and currants, sunflower hearts

ROBINS, BLUEBIRDS, OTHER THRUSHES
Suet, suet mixes, mealworms, berries, chopped fruits, soaked raisins and currants, nutmeats, and sunflower hearts

KINGLETS
Suet, suet mixes, baked goods

WAXWINGS
Berries, chopped fruits, canned peas, currants, raisins

WARBLERS
Suet, suet mixes, fruits, baked goods, sugar solution, chopped nutmeats

TANAGERS
Suet, fruits, sugar solution, mealworms, baked goods

CARDINALS, GROSBEAKS, PYRRHULOXIAS
Sunflower seed, safflower seed, cracked corn, millet, fruit

TOWHEES, JUNCOS
Millet, sunflower seed, cracked corn, peanuts, baked goods, nutmeats

SPARROWS, BUNTINGS
Millet, sunflower hearts, black oil sunflower seed, cracked corn, baked goods

ORIOLES
Halved oranges, apples, berries, sugar solution, grape jelly, suet, suet mixes, soaked raisins and currants

FINCHES, SISKINS
Thistle (niger), sunflower hearts, black oil sunflower seed, millet, canary seed, fruits, peanut kernels, suet mixes

Avoid seed that appears clumped by the webs of Indian meal moth larvae, looks shriveled, or has holes drilled through the shell by insects. Crack several seeds before buying to see that the shells are well filled and free of insects. Store your seed in tight-lidded garbage cans to keep it fresh and to keep rodents from moving in for a free meal.

If you'd like to reduce feeder waste and hull buildup, try offering small amounts of hulled sunflower seed, also called sunflower hearts. Virtually every bird that visits a feeder likes hulled sunflower. There's almost no waste produced, so cleanup is nil. (But it's more expensive and can get waterlogged.)

SEED MIXES

 Mixed seed, sometimes referred to as wild-bird mix, is the second vital ingredient of a sound feeding program. However, all mixes are not created equal, and bird preferences differ across the country. What is eagerly accepted in Arizona may simply go to waste in New York. A prime example is milo, a round, reddish seed that is a little smaller than a BB. It frequently appears with wheat in the inexpensive, grocery-store mixes that so often find their way into shopping carts. In the East, only blackbirds and doves eat milo with any regularity. You'll find a different scenario in the West where bird watchers defend milo and wheat because quail, doves, towhees, and sparrows eagerly accept both at feeders.

Despite regional preferences, there are some foods that most birds will eat. A fail-safe method is to buy a mix that consists primarily of white proso millet, a tiny, round, cream-colored seed with a shiny shell. Species as diverse as doves, Carolina wrens, thrashers, and cardinals will eat white millet, and it is a staple for most sparrows and juncos. Finely cracked corn and black oil sunflower are two other foolproof ingredients in a good mix.

If you can't find a mix featuring white millet, cracked corn, and black oil sunflower, a good feed store will usually sell them separately, and you can mix your own.

Seed mixes should always be offered on low table feeders or scattered on the ground. If you use it in your hanging feeders, the finches, chickadees, and titmice will toss out the corn and millet to find the sunflower seeds, and the mix winds up on the ground anyway.

CRACKED CORN

Cracked corn is the cheapest and best offering for quail, pheasants, and doves; most ground-feeding sparrows, towhees, and juncos will eat it, too. Corn is irresistible to blackbirds, grackles, and house sparrows—you may wish to limit your offerings if too many of these birds take over your feeders and scare away less aggressive species.

SUNFLOWER HEARTS

Experiment with a few sunflower hearts (or hulled seeds of the sunflower), and they will inevitably become an indispensable part of a well-rounded feeding program. You'll find that almost any species that comes to your feeding station will eat sunflower hearts. Woodpeckers love them. Catbirds devour them, and some bird enthusiasts report that bluebirds like them, too. Having no hulls, hearts are accessible to the weaker-billed pine siskins, redpolls, and Carolina wrens that are ordinarily unable to shell even the black oil sunflower. Goldfinches,

OFFER A BOUNTIFUL FEAST

BIRD feeding at its best doesn't replace the role of nature in the lives of birds. Rather, it enhances it. Pull the natural world to your feeding stations by adding brush piles and logs for feeders. Offer foods that fill birds' natural needs—seeds for carbohydrates and fat, suet and nuts for protein, and eggshells for calcium.

By imitating the birds' natural habitats and catering to their nutritional needs in your backyard, you can tempt these lovely wild creatures to live in your landscape.

Follow nature's lead and you are on the road to success with your feeding program. The red on the hummingbird feeders is simply a great idea stolen from nature. Hummingbirds are attracted to the color

which shell sunflower seeds with varying degrees of success, eagerly accept sunflower hearts.

Hearts have the distinct advantage of being 100 percent edible. This means they last much longer in a feeder than black oil seeds. More important, they are free of the messy hulls that pile up to smother grass and rot decks.

Sunflower hearts are prohibitively expensive in small quantities, but if you purchase them in 50-pound (23 kg) bags, you can save money, eliminate waste, and cater to the most species per dollar. Feed sunflower hearts only in suspended feeders, or by the handful in open trays because they quickly become waterlogged in wet weather or if left on the ground. Once you start supplying sunflower hearts, you'll be surprised at how many species of birds you'll attract.

NIGER

Niger, often called thistle seed, is actually not a thistle. Instead, niger comes from a daisylike flower (*Guizotia abyssinica*). Many people swear by niger for attracting goldfinches, but it is equally attractive to pine siskins, house finches, and mourning doves. This oil-rich seed must be offered in special tube feeders with tiny slots through which the seeds can be extracted one by one.

red because it often denotes a good feeding source for them.

A look at the world around you will tell you why the best feeding stations offer food at different levels. In a natural environment, the birds seek their suppers at different heights—on the forest floor, high in the treetops, or at the tips of grasses in a rippling meadow. Seeing waxwings flock to a mulberry tree en masse and witnessing a full-scale attack by cardinals on your lovely sunflower border will easily convince you that offering different types of seeds will attract different kinds of birds for your viewing pleasure. And what better way to spend a glorious summer morning than by watching birds enjoying your backyard?

Niger can be subject to mold, especially in hot, damp weather (and perhaps due to the lack of air circulation in tube feeders). To avoid this problem, shake your thistle feeders daily to ensure that the seeds have not compacted in the holes. Remove moldy seeds and dispose of them where the birds will not find them. Wash and dry the feeder thoroughly before refilling it. You may also purchase fine-mesh nylon, cylindrical bags or thistle socks to offer niger seed, instead of offering it in a tube feeder. Niger seed is heat-treated so it won't germinate and become a troublesome weed if it falls to the ground.

SAFFLOWER SEED

Safflower is a white, shiny, conical seed that is gaining in popularity. Cardinals like safflower, but squirrels and grackles don't. You can usually buy it in bulk at better feed stores. Offer it on the ground, on low tables, or in hoppers, where cardinals prefer to feed.

You can encourage brightly colored goldfinches and discourage often-pesky house finches by hanging feeders that are designed for upside-down feeding. This position is a breeze for goldfinches but cumbersome for house finches.

Suet, Nuts, and Beyond

BY widening the scope of your offerings, you widen your birdwatching horizons. Suet and peanut feeders, baked goods and fruits, and various summer offerings, such as insects and sugar water, target birds that can't eat seed or prefer other food. They'll turn your kitchen window into an observatory.

SERVING UP SUET

Omnivores like chickadees, titmice, and nuthatches, and birds that normally eat insects—wrens, sapsuckers, warblers, creepers, orioles, and catbirds—will eagerly accept suet. Suet is the dense, white fat that collects around beef kidneys and loins. You can find it in most grocery stores—request it at the meat counter if you don't see it out on display.

A little goes a long way, but be sure not to mistake the inedible white rind left when all the fat is pecked away for edible suet; that rind is your key to knowing when you should toss the suet away. Good kidney fat will keep for weeks in cold weather, and you may not find it necessary to render it in winter. For tips on how to feed suet in the summer, see page 84.

Offer your suet in heavy-wire cages that you attach to posts or to the branches of trees (change the location if you notice any bark splitting, disease, or other ill effects on the tree).

If you prefer a natural feeder that will attract shyer woodpeckers, drill shallow, 1-inch (2.5 cm) holes in a small log and hang it from one end by suspending it from a wire. You can use a ball-peen hammer to pound fresh suet into the holes.

Should crows, jays, or starlings make short work of this feeder, try hanging the log horizontally from two wires, so that all of its holes face downward. This orientation poses no problem for woodpeckers, nuthatches, and chickadees but will effectively discourage the less acrobatic starlings.

Many seed-eating birds feed their young exclusively on insects.

food — white proso millet cracked corn niger safflower suet peanuts apples eggshells dogwood berries

A lucky bird watcher might find the hairy woodpecker sharing suet with its smaller cousin, the downy. Suet is the ideal food to feed in winter. A woodpecker's beak is strong enough to peck away at a frozen suet block.

NUTTY FOR NUTS

Jays and crows will take peanuts in the shell, but shelled peanuts offered in a peanut feeder will appeal to a greater variety of birds that can't deal with nuts still in the shell. Peanuts offer a terrific high-protein boost to winter-weary birds, and insect-eating birds like woodpeckers and wrens eagerly accept them as a welcome alternative to seed and suet. The birds that eat peanuts—woodpeckers, titmice, nuthatches, Carolina wrens, and yellow-bellied sapsuckers, among others—will stuff themselves. You may want to buy raw, shelled peanuts in bulk from a feed or wild-bird supply store. These are rejects from the candy and cocktail nut industries. Either roasted or raw peanuts will work, but watch to see that the nuts don't become dark, rancid, or moldy, especially when the weather is hot and humid.

You can use a nylon-mesh onion or garlic bag to hold the peanuts, or make your own feeder out of ¼-inch (6 mm)-mesh hardware cloth, which is sold in rolls at hardware stores. Simply roll the cloth into a cylinder, crimping the bottom shut; then cut and fold over a flap for the top; secure it with a twist tie; and hang it by a wire. Both types of peanut feeders will allow birds to peck small bits of the peanuts but will discourage them from carrying off whole nuts.

FROM THE BAKERY

Many backyard birders start out by feeding birds stale white bread. It's a beacon to house sparrows, starlings, grackles, robins, and mockingbirds. Birds in a yard invariably attract more birds, and with that humble beginning, a lifetime of bird feeding can begin. Have a couple of muffins gone

hard? Crumble them and offer them on a shelf or table. Many birds gobble up cornbread and crumbled doughnuts.

Don't be surprised if birds accustomed only to seed refuse your first few offerings. Keep offering crumbled baked goods in small amounts, and the birds will catch on to a good thing soon enough. Avoid offering moldy bread because it may hurt the birds that eat it. Like peanut butter and suet mixtures, baked goods can help attract insectivores through the winter and increase the diversity of species you may attract.

FAVORITE FRUITS

If you have fruit trees in your yard, you've probably already realized that birds like fruit. They'll often devour the very last shriveled apples or pears on a tree.

You can offer fruit, especially apples, in other ways, too. Cut a piece of fruit in half, then impale it on a short twig or in the branches around your feeders. (If you have a problem with deer, you may need to be creative in order to keep the fruit out of their reach.)

Experiment with different kinds of fruit, even trying different kinds of apples. Sapsuckers, red-bellied woodpeckers, house finches, and starlings may readily accept red apples and may leave the green ones untouched. Offer halved oranges and other fruits, such as peaches, berries, and cherries, in summer when they are cheap and abundant, and when the orioles and tanagers that prefer them have come back from the tropics.

For winter feeding, try offering raisins and currants. Many people chop them up or use hot water to soften them. Mockingbirds, catbirds, and thrashers seem to appreciate these most.

WINTER BERRIES

Entice wintering bluebirds to your feeders by draping branches laden with bittersweet berries (a natural food) over a table feeder.

Ripe fruit is a great enticement. Tempt sapsuckers to your feeders with fruit, or plant a variety of fruit trees so that birds can dine in nature's own cafeteria.

Once attracted to the bright red-orange berries, bluebirds may also sample your soaked or chopped raisins and currants.

Many people, especially in the South, gather and refrigerate the red fruits of dogwood, offering them in shallow dishes or on platform feeders. Stored in moist sawdust, in a covered container and refrigerated, dogwood fruits may keep for months. You could also try gathering clusters of pokeberry in the late summer and the fall, refrigerating them, and offering them throughout the cold winter months when food is scarce. Lucky is the backyard bird enthusiast who is able to invite bluebirds to the winter table! If you regularly see bluebirds in your vicinity in winter, it's worth a try.

MARVEL MEAL

If bluebirds overwinter in your area of the country, you may wish to entice them into your bird-friendly backyard with an easy-to-make homemade treat called Marvel Meal. Many different species of birds will learn to love it when you offer it regularly. Blue-

MARVEL MEAL at a glance

THIS simple suet mixture may help you lure bluebirds from far and wide:

- ■1 cup lard or melted suet
- ■4 cups yellow cornmeal
- ■1 cup all-purpose flour
- ■1 teaspoon corn oil
- ■Sunflower hearts, chopped peanuts or peanut hearts, and soaked, chopped raisins

1. Melt lard or suet and stir in cornmeal, flour, and oil.
2. Spike with sunflower hearts, peanuts, and raisins.
3. Let set until cool and hard, and then cut into chunks.
4. Offer chunks as you would suet—in a cage or in drilled holes in logs.

birds may follow the lead of the other birds, sample the offering, and become regular visitors to your suet feeders. You'll find the recipe in "Marvel Meal" above.

GRIT

Lacking teeth, birds must digest their hard seed diet with a muscular stomach called a gizzard. They ingest small quantities of grit, which remain in the gizzard for a short time, and which serve as grindstones for the seeds they eat. In periods of snow, when normal grit sources such as driveways and roadsides are covered, supply your birds with an offering of either coarse builder's sand or chicken grit, available at feed and farm-supply stores. Chicken grit is attractive to birds, and it includes crushed oyster shell, which has the bonus of adding calcium and minerals to birds' diets.

Female birds lose calcium during egg laying and will value lightly baked, broken eggshells if you provide them. The shells will attract females of a variety of species, depending on where you live. Rinse the eggshells, then lightly bake the shells at 250°F until they are dry and are just starting to turn brown. Break the shells into small pieces, and then scatter them in an obvious, open area.

AS THE WORM TURNS

Gardening is a great way to attract inquisitive birds. Curious robins, hungry catbirds, and opportunistic mockingbirds may stalk the gardener turning over garden beds before spring planting. Turn over some soil, exposing worms and grubs, and they will come. Meanwhile, your garden, especially when it's free of harmful pes-

---

OFFERING EGGSHELLS
at a glance

FEMALE birds will gobble up any eggshells you offer to them, especially during the egg-laying season. Here's what you'll need to do:

1. Rinse shells.

2. Bake them at 250°F until dry and just starting to brown.

3. Pound them into fragments.

4. Distribute shells in small amounts in an open area.

ticides, will provide safe cover and insect food for birds throughout the season, and even after, if you leave your garden standing for the birds into the fall.

Mealworms provide another interesting, and squirmy, food option. These smooth, dry, segmented beetle larvae are available from pet stores or by mail. Put them in a dish that's easily accessible to birds, yet prevents the mealworms from crawling out. Bluebirds, catbirds, and many other birds that don't normally come to feeders will join

Bluebirds hunt open fields and lawns for insects in summer but retreat to wooded swamps to find berries and fruit in winter.

the regulars in eagerly snapping up the twisty orange morsels.

Mealworms should be housed in an open, shallow container, in a bed of old-fashioned (but not quick-cooking) rolled oats. Add a few thin slices of carrot or apple for moisture.

Bluebirds are among the birds that will eagerly step up to the table when you're serving mealworms. These wiggly bits of protein can be fed throughout the year.

Summer Feeding

AS the days lengthen and temperatures rise, many bird watchers pack up their feeders and hit the road to bird watch. While they scour the shores for sandpipers, hike the hills for nesting warblers, or monitor migration hot spots, they sometimes miss some of the best finds — in their own backyards. Although it's true that winter is an important time to feed birds, the rest of the year holds too many pleasures to pass up. By providing food, water, and other accoutrement, your yard can become one of your favorite birding hot spots at any season.

THE JOYS OF SUMMER FEEDING

Feeding beyond the winter months can bring you new visitors or simply bring your old friends spruced up. For instance, you can enjoy canary yellow goldfinches instead of these same birds in their humble-looking, olive-drab winter garb. You may also get surprise feeder guests, such as migrating indigo or lazuli buntings. During spring, late summer, and early fall, warblers and other migrating birds will be drawn to your backyard, briefly investigating all that activity around your feeders and dropping in for a drink if you've set up a water station to their satisfaction.

In the midst of summer, when the migrants are gone and your neighborhood birds start raising their young, your yard can become a day-care center for birds. Adult birds will bring by recently fledged young for food and water. Soon, the juveniles will come on their own, sometimes loitering in gawky, mixed-species gangs. These young birds will provide you with unusual opportunities to study juvenile plumage up close before the birds molt into adult colors.

CLEANLINESS IS KEY

For the backyard wildlife custodian, the real concern for summer feeding is disease. Birds are like unsuspecting diners in a soon-to-be-condemned restaurant. They don't travel around with food-testing kits, so you must do your part to provide them with safe, dry food. Summer is the high season for diseases such as *Salmonella typhimurium*, which has hit house finches hard, especially when bird feeders are overcrowded.

To protect your avian visitors, be sure to clean your feeders once or twice a month. Soak them in a 9-parts-water, 1-part-chlorine-bleach solution, and use a bottlebrush to get at the hard-to-reach corners in your tube feeders. Be sure to rinse the feeders well and leave them out to dry before refilling them.

Another way to stave off disease is by feeding moderately and thoughtfully. Before you refill your feeder, shake it to dislodge trapped, soggy seeds. You can remove any lingering clumps of old seeds with a small implement, such as an old, plastic chopstick or spoon. When it's time to refill, put in only as much seed as you think the birds will eat in a day. This practice not only helps prevent sickness but also protects your feeders from raccoons and other nocturnal raiders.

Next, look to the ground. Avoid spreading much or any seed on the ground in the warm summer months. This practice will keep birds on your regularly cleaned feeders and away from accumulated droppings and old, wet, moldy seed hulls. The birds will also be safer from lurking feline predators.

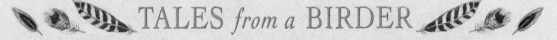

TALES *from a* BIRDER

SEEING migrants and juveniles is one of the greatest delights of spring and summer feeding. The most cherished migrant visitors to our small, suburban Maryland backyard include an immature, almost tailless mourning warbler; a northern waterthrush; one of the few black-billed cuckoos we've seen in the Washington, D.C., area; and a flock of five scarlet tanagers that dropped by for a drink one October morning. We're surprised anew each year by at least one exciting migrant.

I also look forward to the yearly arrival of the ragtag group of newcomers that hang around our pond. One late-July flock included 22 juveniles of six species—one mourning dove, two northern cardinals, one American robin, four gray catbirds, eight European starlings, and six house sparrows.

—*Howard Youth*

Areas directly beneath feeders and often-used perches accumulate the most droppings and can be the most dangerous areas for disease. Change feeder sites every once in a while since seeds invariably collect beneath them. When you rake up those old seed shells and droppings and move the feeders to new territory, put grass seed and mulch over the old bare spots so that they fill in by the end of the season.

SUMMER SUET TIPS

All winter long, you've enjoyed the parade of birds at your suet feeder. But now the hazy, hot days of summer are coming, and you don't fancy the thought of suet spoiling quietly in the sun's heat. If you want to feed suet in the hot summer months, you'll need to either purchase the prepackaged suet cakes or render your own suet to make it healthy for the birds. Rendering, or melting, turns the suet into a longer-lasting, harder product that has less tendency to liquefy and spoil in the heat.

The three Rs will make summer suet feeding more enjoyable!

Reduce. During the hot summer months, it's best to use smaller pieces of suet in a smaller feeder. Large feeders offer more surface area where a bird can soil its feathers on melting fat, which is a special problem for close-clinging woodpeckers. Put out only as much suet as the birds will clean up in 4 or 5 days.

Refrigerate. A small suet feeder can be dropped into a plastic bag and refrigerated or even frozen overnight to extend the life of the suet. This also helps to keep raccoons and other nocturnal robbers of summer bird feeders at bay.

Render. Rendering suet can be a messy proposition but with a little ingenuity and a microwave, or an outside outlet and an electric frying pan, you can minimize the mess. Whichever method you choose, take care! Don't leave the melting fat unattended, and be very careful not to spill the hot liquid on yourself! Try not to render suet indoors.

With a microwave, you can "nuke" small pieces of suet in minutes. Place a small amount of fat from your friendly butcher into a microwave-safe bowl, and cover it to prevent the melting fat from popping and spreading all over the inside of your oven. Microwave for a few minutes, checking about every 30 seconds to see if the fat has melted. Pour the melted fat into a shallow, heat-resistant container, and freeze it.

You can also render suet in an electric frying pan outdoors to keep the mess and the odor out of your kitchen. Pick a clear day with no threat of rain and set up your frying pan near an outdoor outlet and out of the reach of animals. Put a few chunks of fat into the skillet and turn it on low. As the fat liquefies, discard any rind or insoluble chunks, disposing of them in a place out of the reach of neighborhood dogs. For plain suet, pour the liquid fat into a container that won't melt, such as a small can or metal ice cube tray, and freeze it.

For fancier suet, pour the melted fat into a bowl and mix it with peanut butter, cornmeal, flour, or chopped peanuts and sunflower hearts. Don't mix in seed, even though commercial suet blocks often (and inexplicably) include millet, cracked corn, and even sunflower. The suet coating makes it

> **Flycatchers and tanagers, among others, eat stinging insects. First, they disable them by whacking them against a perch, then they remove the stingers before swallowing their meal.**

difficult for birds to shell the seeds, and they are only discarded. Pour the suet mixture into small plastic containers to create easy-to-use suet blocks, then freeze them.

BIRD FEEDER, BEWARE

You can feed birds the same things you put out in the winter, but again keep hygiene in mind; things go rancid much faster in summer. Suet feeders should be placed in the shade and cleaned and scrubbed more frequently. And if you feed your birds peanuts, consider chopping them into small pieces once young birds come around. Inexperienced birds might choke when they try to swallow pieces that are too large. If you

Cleaning Feeders 101

KEEPING bird feeders clean can be a tedious and difficult job, especially if you have post-mounted feeders that aren't easy to take apart for cleaning. But if you are going to feed the birds, you must do so responsibly. Try this cleaning method that's a favorite among backyard bird enthusiasts; it's quick and efficient, so you won't mind doing it each time you fill the feeders (or at least once a week in summer).

Your first step is to buy a small plastic bucket. Use the bucket to carry all your feeder-cleaning supplies as you go on your feeding and cleaning rounds.

Feeder Cleaning Supplies

Water bottle (especially useful in winter when outside spigots are frozen)

Another jug containing a bleach mixture (9 parts water to 1 part bleach)

Bottlebrush for cleaning tube feeders

Sponges

Rags

Two putty knives, one with a 1-inch (2.5 cm) blade and one with a 2-inch (5 cm) blade

Plastic bags, such as bread wrappers or newspaper delivery bags

A Cleaner Feeder in 5 Easy Steps

1. Remove old seeds and hulls, then put them in a plastic bag for disposal. This keeps the old seeds from being thrown on the ground where they become moldy.

2. Use the putty knives to scrape out any corners and crevices.

3. Dampen the sponge with water to wipe away remaining seed residue.

4. Use the bleach mixture to thoroughly wipe all surfaces with which the birds may come in contact. Then, rinse all surfaces with clean water.

5. Use another sponge or rag to dry the feeder as much as possible. Move on to the next feeder, leaving the first to air-dry before adding seed. Even if you have only a few feeders and it's a sunny or windy day, you can usually begin filling the dried feeders as soon as the cleaning round is completed.

don't want to chop your own peanuts, your local bird-food store might sell pieces, or you could substitute chunky peanut butter.

FRUIT TREATS

One of the treats of summer is offering exotic foods to exotic-looking birds. Some of the most colorful birds, including grosbeaks, tanagers, and orioles, often go for sliced oranges and other fruits. You can skewer halved fruit on branches, or purchase or build a special feeder with spikes for impaling fruit pieces. Catbirds, mockingbirds, and thrashers enjoy fruit, too, and are known to sample anything from raisins to bananas; woodpeckers will sometimes dine on apples and other fruits.

The produce you offer doesn't have to be in perfect condition. Windfalls and nonmoldy kitchen fruit kept past its prime are bonanzas at the feeding station. Fruit also attracts insects—the stingless varieties that birds relish. With fruit at your feeders, you may even see hummingbirds buzz by looking for fruit flies from time to time.

Skewer an orange half on a dowel, and stick it into the ground beneath low-hanging branches to bring in orioles. Many species of birds enjoy fruit so don't be shy about offering fruit on platform feeders or deck railings.

Hummers and Other Sugar Fiends

HUMMINGBIRDS—those minute and energetic dynamos—brighten up gardens throughout the continent. Each year, visiting hummers feed at salvias, bee balms, cardinal flowers, zinnias, and dozens of other easy-to-grow garden flowers. But for close views, nothing beats a hummingbird feeder.

THE FEEDERS

Generally, hummingbird feeders can range from having no perches at all to having as many as six perches. The simpler varieties have just a feeder tube. Your feeder will be attractive to hummingbirds if you do two things: have a red part somewhere on the feeder, and offer fresh sugar solution every couple of days (or daily if the feeder is in a very hot, sunny area).

While you can buy commercial varieties of hummingbird food, the cheapest, surest way to provide backyard hummers with sugar solution is to make it at home with a few simple ingredients; see the recipe in "Homemade Nectar" on page 34. There's no need to color your sugar water—the red part on your feeder is the only signal hummingbirds need to take notice.

Hummingbirds are territorial and appreciate an observational perch near the feeder so they can head off other hummers heading their way.

UNINVITED GUESTS

Dozens of other species also relish hummingbird solution, among them orioles, woodpeckers, grosbeaks, and unfortunately ants, bees, and wasps. Experiment with different locations if you are being "bugged." Water barriers that create little moats between the feeder's suspension wire and the ants' entry route can keep them at bay. Some feeders come with bee guards, little plastic grids that go over the feeder ports designed to prevent bees and wasps from reaching the sweet solution.

You can welcome larger birds, and perhaps distract them from your hummingbird feeder by putting out a jar of sugar water. A sugar-water jar is nothing fancy—simply a tilted jelly jar filled with sugar solution that is attached to a branch or clothesline by wire. The oriole, acorn woodpecker, or grosbeak just sidles up to the jar and leans in to get a high-powered drink. As with the hummingbird feeder, you can advertise your jar by attaching something bright red, perhaps a ribbon or an artificial flower spray, around its lip.

A small backyard may be home to a single hummingbird or maybe two, but if you live in more rural areas of the country, you may be hosting a dozen or more. If you have

TALES *from a* BIRDER

YOU might be surprised at how early in the season hummingbirds can show up. Depending on where you live, you can't put your feeder out soon enough. As we ate dinner on our friend's porch last year, a male ruby-throated hummingbird whizzed by us, then hovered at the spot where Bob had placed his feeder the year before. "I swear, I was going to put it up today!" he exclaimed. It was April 19.

The earliest date for Maryland, where we live, stands at March 27, but we usually don't start seeing ruby-throats until the first few days of May each year.

In the West, a staggered procession of hummingbird species passes through many areas starting in the early March. Of course, lucky West Coast backyards are host to Anna's hummingbirds year-round.

—*Howard Youth*

food white proso millet cracked corn niger safflower suet peanuts apples eggshells dogwood berries

many hummingbirds, you might want to put out several feeders.

Feisty by nature, hummingbirds will claim your feeders as their own and drive off others of their kind. A well-placed snag (a dead branch pushed into the ground) will provide your hummers with handy territorial perches that allow them to rest and watch for predators within sight of the feeder.

FEEDING EARLY AND LATE

Early migrating hummingbirds will be grateful for your feeder hung up early in the spring. As soon as the weather warms enough to keep the mixture from freezing, dig out the feeder.

As the season wanes, don't give up on feeding hummingbirds, though. Your neighborhood winged breeders may leave in late summer, but fall-migrating hummers are bound to show up. Later on, you may attract an unusual fall stray. For instance, in Maryland, most of the ruby-throats are gone before early October, while many of the rare sightings of the migrant rufous

hummingbirds, which are mostly feeder birds, occurred from late October through December.

BIRD BONDS

Feeding the birds can help them through inclement weather and the stresses of nesting. However, most ornithologists concur that it's of more benefit to the people doing the feeding than it is to the birds. Operating a clean, diverse feeding station can be a great source of relaxation and pleasure. It exposes you to countless opportunities to know your avian neighbors better, to witness their lives and their courtship rituals, and to learn how they care for and educate their young.

Bird feeding is the perfect first step to becoming a confident bird watcher. Whether or not it leads you beyond your own backyard, feeding birds will strengthen your connection to the out-of-doors, will make you more sensitive to the ways of the weather and the turning of the seasons, and will open your ears and your eyes to the grace that is all around, especially when you take the time to notice.

4
Making a Haven

Bird-Friendly Habitats for Your Backyard

BRING NATURAL ELEMENTS right to your doorstep, and you'll encourage the birds to come up close. Nature is always working to fill a void, create a tangle, and diversify a meadow. Meadows and hedgerows evolve and change year by year in fascinating ways. You can use dead plant material to create a bird-friendly landscape without adding maintenance work—brush piles, log feeders, and snags are all potent attractants for birds. And you'll derive great satisfaction by watching birds explore and inhabit the places you've made for them.

A Fresh Look

STEP to a window for a moment, and take a fresh look at your yard. Could your habitat be improved by creating a few shady spots, by providing some perches and sheltering corners, or by installing a flower and grass meadow? You bet!

After the initial work of planting your habitat, much of the upkeep of a more natural yard will be in the hands of nature. You may be pleasantly surprised to find that you're spending less time with the mower and more time with binoculars around your neck, watching your backyard visitors.

If you travel through most suburban developments, you will find yourself being impressed by one thing—the sameness of the landscaping. Only a few large shade trees and an occasional shrub may punctuate wide expanses of grass. Americans pride themselves on their flawless lawns, and they engage in chemical warfare to ensure that their grass is the greenest in the neighborhood. Hours are invested every summer mowing, fertilizing, applying chemical herbicides, and watering—all to maintain that golf-course–green look.

THE LOWDOWN ON LAWNS

To put the costs of achieving and maintaining all that carefully managed lawn in perspective, consider the following:

■ The suburban lawn is a wasteland for most wildlife because there are no seeds or fruits available to animals. Most grasses are cut down before they have the opportunity to flower and bear seed. Short grass provides no shelter for insects, birds, or small mammals.

■ Homeowners apply up to 10 times more toxic chemicals per acre than farmers do. The average homeowner applies 5 to 10 pounds (2.3 to 4.5 kg) of herbicides and pesticides per lawn per year, and an estimated 25 to 50 million pounds (11 to 23 million kg) of chemicals are introduced into yards in the United States in the name of green grass.

■ Grass clippings from mowing can make up 18 to 20 percent of solid waste produced in the summer. Clippings can be composted and used as natural mulch and fertilizer.

■ Americans overwater their lawns. Millions of gallons could be saved every year if lawns were watered more efficiently. Water evaporates less quickly in the early morning than in the afternoon.

It's time to rethink the goal of having acres of green lawn because of the enormous costs in dollars, energy, and time in trying to maintain a flawless field of green. And the birds will thank you for letting some of your yard go natural.

habitats

meadow environment prairie evergreen

Hospitable Habitat

A green thumb is not a prerequisite for creating your own backyard environment; what is needed is imagination, some manual labor, and, most important, a concept of how you would like to see your space eventually evolve.

Before you even sketch a plan, make a conscious effort to observe the local scenery. Take a walk on the wild side. See where and how specific trees, shrubs, and grasses occur naturally in your area. Think in terms of form, shapes, and textures rather than just planting everything in a row.

Consider how you want your habitat haven to feel. Perhaps you want to be drawn into a space by a

pathway. Or, perhaps you want to carve out bird-watching spots in various nooks around the yard. Each space in your yard should have its own character and feel, from the gurgling sounds of a water garden and the peace of a wildflower meadow to the shady spot beneath an oak tree and the sheltering tangle of a hedgerow.

Make lists of native plants and consider where they may fit into your scheme. Native plants make good gardening sense on many levels. Insects and native wildlife have evolved with native plant species and readily use them for food and cover. Native plants are apt to be hardier and more drought

KEEP IT NATURAL

THE U.S. Fish and Wildlife Service estimates that as many as 82 million Americans feed backyard birds, but many of the feeders we provide are a far cry from the natural environment that birds prefer and that keep them from danger when feeding.

When you decide to create a bird-friendly backyard, remember to incorporate elements that meet many of a bird's requirements for survival—food, shelter, water, and nesting sites. Include plants in your landscape that will provide the seeds, fruits, and nectar that birds and other wildlife want most. Select a variety

tolerant than most exotics. They also won't pose a threat if they "escape" from your garden. And they have a special beauty, a sort of rightness in the landscape that no exotic can match. Natives make your yard an extension of nature, brought up close for you to enjoy.

A main path through your backyard habitat invites close inspection of meadow wild-flowers and grasses and promises seclusion amidst evergreens.

of species that flower, set fruit, and produce seed, so birds can use the plants for food throughout the growing season.

Whenever possible, incorporate water into the landscape, whether it's a bird-bath, small pond, miniature marsh, bog, or water-filled container garden. When gathering brush, logs, and snags, don't scrape the platter clean—leave some scraps where they fell naturally.

You can also use branches, brambles, and snags, and add your Christmas tree to your feeding station to create a more developed habitat. After all, you are emulating one of the most important tenets of the natural world—waste not, want not.

habitat

sanctuary wildflowers diversity shelter meadow environment prairie evergreen

THE WILD CORNER

Set aside a "wild corner" in your yard to mimic the natural plant communities around you. Natural plant communities have layers of plants with tall trees and small understory trees and shrubs. Plant several clusters of trees and shrubs, then fill in with groundcovers, grasses, and flowering plants. Add vines like Virginia creeper after the trees and shrubs have become established.

Consider seasonal food choices when you choose your plants. Blackberries are summer treats while conifer, sumac, and crabapple trees provide winter fare. Even if you have a small yard, you can still have a wild corner by planting an area of wildflowers; see "Wonderful Meadows" on page 99. What looks like a lovely field of wildflowers can also be a secret sanctuary for foraging birds.

SHELTER FROM THE STORM

Many suburban yards are seas of grass, with few shrubs or low-lying vegetation to provide shelter for animals. If an animal ventured into the yard, it would run an increased risk of being preyed upon, particularly by the resident dog or cat. Trees, shrubs, and other expansive plant life provide ideal cover. Maintaining a brush pile along the yard perimeter can provide shelter for rabbits and birds. It's also a place to put your old Christmas tree. As the contents of the brush pile gradually decompose, the pile will offer shelter to small mammals, reptiles, and amphibians. A rock wall or rock pile provides nooks and crannies where snakes and toads may dwell.

DRAW IT UP

Sketch your habitat ideas on paper and ponder them for a bit, making changes here and there as the mood strikes you. Add some of the water features discussed in "The New Lagoon" on page 42 to provide that essential element for birds. Even after you begin to put your plan into action, you can change things and add elements that will enhance your habitat. You'll soon find that a flexible plan evolves—one that brings the best of the natural world to your doorstep.

GATHER YOUR PLANTS

Once you have a good idea of what you want to offer in your bird-friendly backyard, start collecting your plants. If you're unsure about which plants to buy, spend some time at a local nursery. Ask neighbors for plant recommendations, then go and browse through the stock. Chat with nursery personnel and ask their opinions. A plant that looks great on a paper plan may not work in your yard because of its size, soil and light preferences, or growing habit.

You may not want to buy all of your plants right away. Even though an instant landscape may bring gratification, it can be costly if plants are added in a less-than-thoughtful way. If you need to move plants, it's important to realize that many will not survive being transplanted a second time. If you're working on a budget, you can make great additions to your yard from root cuttings. These treasures will take time to become mature plants, but working slowly certainly has its advantages. As trees and shrubs grow, they dictate what your next move should be.

> **The chimney swift catches and stores flying insects in its throat for delivery to its young. It may take 150 to 700 insects to a single feeding.**

Working slowly may mean that your habitat won't resemble what you see in your mind's eye for several years, but, in the meantime, you can enjoy the work of planning and watch your property evolve. And you'll be delighted to see the steady increase in the number of creatures that come to enjoy your growing, thriving habitat.

HELP IS AT HAND

In addition to the staff at your local nursery, there are others who can give you advice in your bid to create a backyard wildlife sanctuary. The National Wildlife Federation (NWF) maintains a backyard habitat program that will certify yards in which the essential needs of wildlife have been met. The organization will supply lists of plantings that can serve both the needs

habitats

of wildlife and the aesthetic needs of the homeowner. They publish an informative packet that includes plastic templates for sketching scaled representations of your proposed backyard scheme. Your state division of wildlife or department of natural resources should have lists of plants to attract hummingbirds and butterflies. Your local office of the U.S. Department of Agriculture (USDA) is also a fine information source, and its employees can often help with any specific problems you may have once you are actually underway. (See "Resources and Supplies" on page 232 for NWF and USDA information.)

TALES *from a* BIRDER

IN just 3 short years my southeast Florida yard has transformed itself. It was a ⅓-acre grass wasteland, devoid of most of the regional creatures, and has now become a rather lush, semitropical haven for various birds, insects, and reptiles.

My plan called for choosing predominantly native trees and shrubs that would attract birds. The stopper, satin leaf, and southern red cedar trees I planted are all berry-producers; the geiger tree has flowers attractive to hummingbirds. I chose pyracantha, a nonnative shrub but an incredible berry manufacturer. I also planted native shrubs, such as waxmyrtle, coffee colubrina, and trumpet vine.

Perhaps the single most effective bird-luring addition to my backyard is the birdbath and waterfall I built just outside of our kitchen window. In this hot southern climate, fresh, cool water is as tempting as the best millet or sunflower seeds. At first, only blue jays, grackles, and doves (mourning and white-winged) would visit the birdbath, but the more recent visitors include painted buntings, cedar waxwings, red-bellied woodpeckers, northern and spot-breasted orioles, palm warblers, cardinals, and even an occasional snake. Earlier this morning a grackle was feeding parts of a tiny snake it had caught at the bath to its chick.

As time passes and my new trees and shrubs grow, they provide additional food and cover, encouraging more wildlife activity. Already I've had a dove nest in a tree and a family of red-bellied woodpeckers in a nest box. And all this in just 3 years!

—*Paul Ayick*

Wonderful Meadows

MEADOW gardening uses prairie wildflowers and grasses to create sustainable, low-maintenance landscapes. Wildflowers and grasses are beautiful, attractive to wildlife, and extremely durable—all thanks to their robust root systems and tolerance to severe drought and cold. A prairie garden is a long-term investment in your landscape, so plan carefully. Take care to select the site and plants, to prepare the site, and to maintain the planting until the plants become established. Establish your meadow from seeds, plants, or a mixture of the two.

SITE SELECTION

When siting your meadow, you need to keep two things in mind: the plants you want to use and your own convenience. As far as plants go, prairie wildflowers and grasses, both important players in a meadow, tolerate a variety of soils and moisture levels. You'll need to determine the general soil type and soil moisture of each area that you intend to plant so you can select the prairie wildflowers and grasses most adapted to your site and soil conditions.

Think about where you'll enjoy your meadow most, and especially the bird life that it will attract. Choose a sunny, open area that receives at least 5 hours of full sun per day during the growing season.

If possible, try to stay clear of weedy areas, such as old fields, when deciding where to put your meadow. Old fields contain perennial weeds, such as quack grass and bromegrass, which can spread into your newly planted area. To help prevent this invasion, maintain a 10-foot (3 m)-wide mown "buffer" between your new planting and the old field, and mow the adjacent field every summer in late July before the weeds set seed.

SITE PREP

To prepare your site for planting, you'll need to remove the existing vegetation first because it usually consists of perennial and annual weeds. Existing weeds will compete with prairie plants for nutrients, moisture, and sunlight.

Making a Haven

Q The brush pile I built last winter is a mess with bird droppings, and it's overgrown with weeds. What can I do about it?

A Check your local ordinances first, but the best way to dispose of your old brush pile is simply to burn it on the spot. Pick a damp, windless day, stuff some newspapers into it, light them, and guard it closely with a rake and shovel to prevent the fire from spreading. Or, turn the brush pile into a compost pile. Use a chipper shredder and run any branches through it so they can be composted. Layer shredded branches, dried weeds, and grass clippings with vegetable and fruit kitchen scraps (of course, no meat, fat, cat litter, or other pet feces).

Q I'm letting part of our large yard go as a meadow. There are wildflowers and grasses in it, but some trees and brambles are starting to invade. When and how often should I mow it to keep it as a meadow?

A Natural succession will do its best to turn your meadow into a bramble patch unless you intervene. However, you don't want to mow it too often. For much of the continent, late March is probably the best time to mow to control woody plants. Once every 1 or 2 years should suffice. Leave summer growth standing to provide seeds and cover for nesting and wintering birds.

Q I'd like to plant a wildflower meadow, but I've heard that some mixes contain invasive exotics, and I don't want to introduce them. Any advice?

A It is difficult to find a commercially packaged wildflower mix that consists only of native plants. In general, avoid the cheaper mixes that consist mostly of colored wood pulp or other filler. Check the ingredient list for plants like dame's rocket and cleome that can self-sow and take over in subsequent years, so that you can avoid mixes that include either of these seeds.

Although it is nearly impossible to remove all annual weed seeds, it is crucial to kill or remove perennial weeds, particularly those whose roots spread horizontally and send up shoots for new plants as they spread. The weeds with these types of roots, called rhizomes, can be powerful pests.

The type of prep work that you'll need to do to remove the existing vegetation is determined by what is growing on your site now. In general, you may need to till the soil, do some sod cutting, or cover the soil with clear plastic for several months to reduce or eliminate the existing perennial weed cover.

WHAT YOUR SOIL NEEDS

If you have poor, sandy soil or heavy clay soil with low levels of organic matter, add compost to the top 4 to 6 inches (10 to 15 cm) of soil. Organic matter increases the water-holding capacity of sandy soils and improves both the water and air circulation of heavy clays, enhancing root development and plant growth, and helping to ensure a plant's survival.

SELECTING MEADOW PLANTS

Once you have determined your soil type and soil moisture, start a list of all the meadow plants you want to include, focusing on those plants that are native to your area and right for your type of soil. Keep in mind that you'll need about one plant per square foot (30 cm) if you use transplants to start your meadow. Choose wildflower species with a variety of blooming times so that you will have bird cover, food sources, and landscape interest throughout the growing season.

Compass plant rises above smaller flowers and grasses in meadow plantings, and chickadees and sparrows flock to its large seeds.

Plan to evenly mix grasses with wildflowers. Prairie grasses, in addition to fall and winter colors, keep a garden relatively maintenance free by structurally supporting wildflowers and keeping out competing weeds with their fibrous root systems. Prairie grasses also produce nutritious seeds, which are coveted by sparrows, finches, juncos, and turkeys.

Wildflowers in the *Silphium* genus really seem to attract birds. These sunflower-like perennials are known by many common names, including compass plant, cup plant, prairie dock, and rosinweed.

STARTING FROM SCRATCH

Rather than use plants, you may choose to start your meadow from seeds. There are mixes available for every geographic location, as well as ones specifically for shady or sunny areas or for attracting butterflies. (See "Resources and Supplies" on page 232 for Prairie Moon Nursery and Prairie Nursery.) Not all the seeds in the mix will do well in your soil. To determine which wildflower species will do well, start with a mix and then resow with those plants that prove to be hardiest in your yard.

Your meadow may attract more than songbirds. You may even catch a glimpse of a wild turkey feasting on the nutritious seeds of prairie grasses.

Soil Sleuthing

BEFORE you dig into the soil to plant your meadow, find out a few things about your soil. Purchase a soil test kit from your local extension office, collect soil samples from several places in your yard, and send the samples to the lab for testing. The lab will analyze the soil for pH and nutrients, and you'll be able to determine which plants are most suitable for your soil type.

Another important piece of the soil puzzle is knowing whether your soil is mostly sand, clay, or loam because your soil type will also influence which plants you choose for your meadow.

■ Sandy or "light" soils are composed of large, loosely packed soil particles that drain easily and are easy to work. Sandy soils tend to be low in nutrients and are slightly acidic. Weeding is easier in sandy soils.

■ Clay or "heavy" soils consist of tightly packed soil particles that drain poorly and are difficult to work, but they can be rich in nutrients and very productive.

■ Loam, the intermediate soil type between sand and clay, is usually very fertile. It's composed of a variety of different-sized soil particles. This particle diversity provides good moisture-holding capacity and drainage, and an excellent medium for most prairie plants.

To determine whether your soil is sand, clay, or loam, rub a small amount of moist soil between your thumb and fingers. Sandy soil will be gritty and will fall apart easily, while clay soil will be slick and smooth and will bind together in a mass. Loamy soil will feel gritty, although not as gritty as sand, and will stick together more easily than sand but not as tenaciously as clay. In addition, if you think you have loamy soil but aren't completely sure, let your sample dry—it will have the texture of flour.

You should also identify whether your soil is moist or dry. Moist soils (whether they're clay or loam) hold water throughout the growing season. Dry soils (whether they're sand or soil mixed with gravel) rarely accumulate standing water, even after a heavy rain.

Knowing all that you can about your soil will help you make appropriate choices when deciding which plants to use in creating a meadow garden.

habitats

onment prairie evergreen

Prairie Wildflowers and Grasses

ESTABLISHING a meadow garden of prairie wildflowers and grasses will take some planning, but the results are well worth the effort. Model your garden after native prairies. A successful prairie plant mix combines 60 to 80 percent grass seeds along with 20 to 40 percent flower seeds; this combination provides food and shelter for birds and butterflies, as well as season-long beauty.

Starting a prairie garden from seeds is more economical than buying plants, but transplants will establish more quickly and give you a head start on controlling unwanted weeds. Prairie plants prefer full sun, but their soil needs can vary. Be sure to check on your soil type and drainage. Some native plants prefer well-drained, sandy soil, while others thrive in moist, poorly drained sites.

You may love the look of a prairie meadow, but your neighbors and local zoning board may not.

TALES *from a* BIRDER

AS an active and occasionally hyperactive member of working society, I seldom have time for scheduled bird-watching ventures into forests and wetlands. I enjoy birds on the fly: counting kestrels on power lines as I zoom down the highway, stopping for turkeys as they stroll across the road, and becoming distracted with a clay-colored sparrow's song while conducting a prairie plant tour. Some of my best bird observations occur in my gardens as I watch from the kitchen window while washing dishes or from the living room window as I drink my morning coffee.

I like to spend precious free moments watching my avian visitors, not maintaining a manicured garden full of plants that require constant attention to survive. My approach to gardening is one of somewhat organized chaos—my garden is full of perennial wildflowers and grasses that are tough enough to thrive through the Wisconsin elements on their own.

—*Jennifer L. Baker*

Some municipalities have strict ordinances about mowing, and what may look like a meadow to you may be perceived as a weedy field to someone else. Check local zoning regulations before investing time and money in planting a meadow; gardeners in dry areas may be advised to leave a minimum of 20 feet (6 m) of mowed lawn between a prairie garden and buildings to minimize any fire hazard, and you'll need to know this as you plan.

When starting a meadow garden with transplants, it's important to observe a few basic principles. The following guidelines should give you an overview of what you'll need to do to succeed.

1 Remove weeds from the planting site before setting out your transplants. Smother persistent weeds by spreading black plastic or a thick layer of newspapers topped with several inches of mulch or compost for several months prior to planting. You could also till the soil in late summer or fall the year before and plant a cover crop like annual rye grass or oats. These annuals will die over winter and the residue can be tilled under in the spring.

2 Till the planting area to a depth of 1 foot (30 cm) to create an easy-to-work planting bed that will accommodate the root length of the plants you're working with.

3 Following your design plan, set the transplants about 1 foot (30 cm) apart on center.

4 Dig each hole large enough to be able to spread out the root structure of each plant.

5 Place the plant in the hole and tamp the soil to prevent air pockets. Water thoroughly.

6 Mulch around each transplant with 3 to 4 inches (8 to 10 cm) of weed-free straw, such as winter wheat or marsh hay. Mulch will help retain moisture in the soil and will reduce weed invasion between the young plants.

7 Write the name of the transplant on a plant marker (a Popsicle stick will do nicely), then insert the marker into the soil next to the plant. The marker will help you identify which plants are meadow plants and which are weeds.

habitats

sanctuary wildflowers diversity shelter meadow environment prairie evergreen

POST-PLANTING MAINTENANCE

Water your transplants every other morning for 15 to 30 minutes during the first 4 to 6 weeks after planting, especially if you planted in late spring or in sandy or clay soils. Watering during the first growing season is essential to establishing the root systems of new transplants.

Watering. Although most prairie plantings need relatively little maintenance, you can give your newly introduced plants a helping hand in getting established in the neighborhood. After 6 weeks you shouldn't need to continue watering unless you are experiencing prolonged dry periods. Be careful not to overwater or to water at night because fungus could attack transplants under cool, damp conditions.

Weeding. During the first year, you'll need to do a little weeding to reduce the competition between weeds and prairie transplants for

Let milkweed linger in your meadow. Not only will monarch butterflies lay eggs among its leaves and small birds nip at the seeds, but orioles and other birds will also use the fibrous stalks for nest making.

water, light, and space. Pull out any perennial weeds, and make sure to pull out or cut back annual and biennial weeds before they go to seed. Make sure to pull out the entire root of perennial weeds, such as quack grass or Canada thistle, or they will return from the root remaining in the soil.

Cutting and raking. Prevent a buildup of dead vegetation (known as thatch) to help keep your prairie diverse and healthy. Removing thatch will encourage new growth and promote soil warm-up in the spring. Depending on the rate of thatch buildup, you can mow your meadow and rake off the residual vegetation before spring green-up, usually around April. Some communities may allow you to burn your meadow, but first check your local ordinances.

It's best to set up a regular rotation plan to only mow (or burn) and rake one-third to one-half of your meadow each year. This will preserve a refuge for migrating and resident birds, small mammals, and overwintering butterflies, moths, and other invertebrate pupae and eggs.

> **With the decline of the American bison and the rise of domestic cattle, the buffalo bird that followed the bison herds and the insects they stirred up became known by a new name—the brown-headed cowbird.**

GROWTH PATTERNS

Given adequate soil moisture, soil fertility, and weed control, the majority of transplants will bloom and provide cover and food sources for a variety of birds the first year they are planted. During the second and third years, each transplant will become more robust and fill its allotted 1-square-foot (30 cm) area, minimizing the need for weeding. You may need to cut back the taller and more aggressive species, such as ox-eye sunflower or New England aster; doing this in early summer will promote a bushier growth structure and help prevent them from towering over other plants, which may not get enough sun otherwise.

WILDFLOWERS ACROSS THE CONTINENT

Each pocket of the continent has its own wildflower treasures. Use native plants and grasses to attract the birds that are naturally in your neck of the woods. Seeds and fruits in a wild garden will mature continuously throughout the growing season, providing birds with a supply of food that replenishes itself with no help from you! By planting your birdseed garden densely, you'll be providing cover and leaving little room for weeds to take hold.

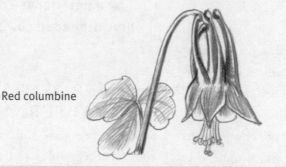

Red columbine

PACIFIC COAST/NORTHWEST

Once difficult to buy, more and more native plant species are being nursery-propagated and sold by native plant specialists who recognize their environmental value and beneficial nature.

PLANT NAME	BLOOM SEASON
Pearly everlasting (*Anaphalis margaritacea*)	Late summer
Red columbine (*Aquilegia formosa*)	Summer
Common camass (*Camassia quamass*)	Late spring
Indian paintbrush (*Castilleja miniata*)	Summer
Bleeding heart (*Dicentra formosa*)	Spring
Fireweed (*Epilobium angustifolium*)	Summer
Beach strawberry (*Fragaria chiloensis*)	Summer (fruit)
Columbia lily (*Lilium columbianum*)	Late summer
Pacific lupine (*Lupinus lepidus* var. *lobbii*)	Summer
Beardtongue (*Penstemon davidsonii*)	Early summer
Foamflower (*Tiarella trifoliata*)	Spring

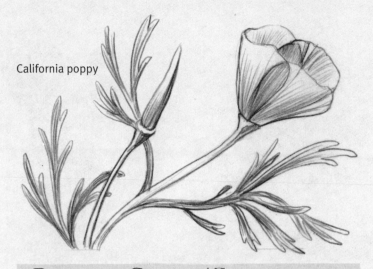

California poppy

PACIFIC COAST/CALIFORNIA

Hummingbirds are found in large numbers up and down the Pacific Coast. Red, tubular flowers do a good job of attracting hummers to your wild garden for nectar. Even though their visits are spectacular enough, hummers do double duty by assisting with pollination while making their rounds.

PLANT NAME	BLOOM SEASON
Yarrows (*Achillea* spp.)	Summer
Columbines (*Aquilegia* spp.)	Spring to summer
Sagebrush (*Artemisia californica*)	Summer to fall
Milkweeds (*Asclepias* spp.)	Summer
Calliopsis (*Coreopsis tinctoria*)	Summer to fall
Cosmos (*Cosmos* spp.)	Summer to fall
Buckwheats (*Eriogonum* spp.)	Summer to fall
Wooly sunflower (*Eriophyllum lanatum*)	Late summer
California poppy (*Eschscholzia californica*)	Summer
Wild strawberry (*Fragaria californica*)	Summer (fruit)
Sunflowers (*Helianthus* spp.)	Summer to fall
Alum root (*Heuchera micrantha*)	Spring
Monkey flowers (*Mimulus* spp.)	Summer
Sages (*Salvia* spp.)	Spring to fall

Blanket flower

MOUNTAIN WEST

Growing your own plants from seeds may be, in some cases, the only way to obtain particular plants for your natural garden. If collecting seeds from wild areas, obtain permission first, then limit what you take to no more than 10 percent of the seeds available, leaving the rest to maintain the wild population.

PLANT NAME	BLOOM SEASON
Western wheatgrass (*Agropyron smithii*)*	Multiseason (grass)
Lead plant (*Amorpha canescens*)	Summer
Sideoats grama (*Bouteloua curtipendula*)**	Multiseason (grass)
Rocky Mountain bee plant (*Cleome serrulata*)	Summer to fall
Blanket flower (*Gaillardia aristata*)	Summer
Scarlet gilia (*Ipomopsis aggregata*)	Summer to fall
Gayfeathers (*Liatris* spp.)	Summer
Colorado four o'clocks (*Mirabilis multiflora*)	Summer
Evening primroses (*Oenothera* spp.)	Summer
Penstemons (*Penstemon* spp.)	Summer
Reed canary grass (*Phalaris arundinacea*)*	Multiseason (grass)
Indian pink (*Silene laciniata*)	Summer
Green needle grass (*Stipa viridula*)**	Multiseason (grass)

* Ideal for wet meadows. ** Ideal for dry meadows.

Prickly poppy

DESERT SOUTHWEST

Desert plants have different mechanisms for survival. Herbaceous plants must act quickly—breaking dormancy, blooming, and setting seed in a matter of weeks—to assure continuing survival. The seeds can then remain dormant for 2 or more years, patiently awaiting the next rainy spring.

PLANT NAME	BLOOM SEASON
Wild hyssop (*Agastache cana*)	Summer to fall
Agaves (*Agave* spp.)	Spring
Prickly poppy (*Argemone pleiacantha*)	Spring to summer
Desert milkweed (*Asclepias subulata*)	Spring to fall
Desert marigold (*Baileya multiradiata*)	Spring to summer
Indian paintbrushes (*Castilleja* spp.)	Spring to summer
Bush dalea (*Dalea pulchra*)	Spring
Brittlebush (*Encelia farinosa*)	Late winter
Firewheel (*Gaillardia pulchella*)	Summer
Standing cypress (*Ipomopsis rubra*)	Spring
Parry's penstemon (*Penstemon parryi*)	Spring
Sages (*Salvia* spp.)	Summer
Goldeneye (*Viguiera stenoloba*)	Summer
Desert zinnia (*Zinnia acerosa*)	Spring

Purple coneflower

MIDWEST/GREAT PLAINS

The North American prairie was once dominated by deeply rooted grasses and drifts of native perennial flowers that offered variety in color and texture. Keep this natural design in mind when you plant a meadow garden, and you'll fashion a low-maintenance landscape that attracts wildlife of many kinds.

PLANT NAME	BLOOM SEASON
Big bluestem (*Andropogon gerardii*)	Multiseason (grass)
Butterfly weed (*Asclepias tuberosa*)	Summer
Smooth aster (*Aster laevis*)	Fall
Dwarf red coreopsis (*Coreopsis tinctoria*)	Summer
Purple prairie clover (*Dalea purpureum*)	Summer
Shooting stars (*Dodecatheon* spp.)	Spring
Purple coneflower (*Echinacea purpurea*)	Summer to fall
Wild geraniums (*Geranium* spp.)	Spring to summer
Prairie smoke (*Geum triflorum*)	Spring
Maximillian's sunflower (*Helianthus maximilliani*)	Late summer to fall
Prairie coneflower (*Ratibida columnifera*)	Summer
Black-eyed Susans (*Rudbeckia* spp.)	Summer to fall
Little bluestem (*Schizachyrium scoparium*)	Multiseason (grass)
Indian grass (*Sorghastrum nutans*)	Multiseason (grass)

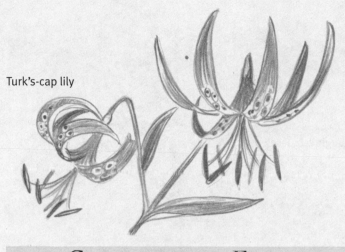

Turk's-cap lily

CONTINENTAL EAST

Fall blooms and berries add interest to the winter garden and attract migrating birds. If you counter the impulse to "neaten up" the garden, you'll be rewarded with a stream of winter visitors. Many birds will feast on seeds that remain on a plant's dried stalk long after the plant has gone dormant.

PLANT NAME	BLOOM SEASON
Anise hyssop (*Agastache foeniculum*)	Summer
Canada columbine (*Aquilegia canadensis*)	Spring to summer
Milkweeds (*Asclepias* spp.)	Summer
Aster (*Aster novae-angliae*)	Fall
Boltonia (*Boltonia asteroides*)	Summer to fall
Turtleheads (*Chelone* spp.)	Late summer
Thistle (*Cirsium discolor*)	Summer to fall
Joe-Pye weed (*Eupatorium fistulosum*)	Summer to fall
Wild strawberry (*Fragaria virginiana*)	Early summer
Turk's-cap lily (*Lilium superbum*)	Summer
Cardinal flowers (*Lobelia* spp.)	Summer to fall
Bergamot (*Monarda fistulosa*)	Summer to fall
Goldenrods (*Solidago* spp.)	Summer to fall
Ironweed (*Vernonia noveboracensis*)	Summer to fall

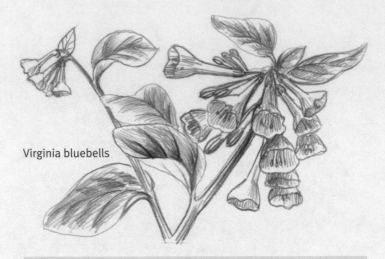

Virginia bluebells

HUMID SOUTH

A water feature is a wildlife magnet in any garden, but it can be particularly welcome during the long summers of the humid South. Even a small pond can serve as a visual focus and a cool haven for people and birds. A partially submerged rock will give visiting birds a convenient place to perch.

PLANT NAME	BLOOM SEASON
Giant hummingbird's mint (*Agastache barberi*)	Summer to fall
Swamp milkweed (*Asclepias incarnata*)	Summer to fall
Carolina aster (*Aster carolinianus*)	Fall
False indigo (*Baptisia australis*)	Spring
Wild oats (*Chasmanthium latifolium*)	Multiseason (grass)
Coreopsis (*Coreopsis lanceolata*)	Summer
Joe-Pye weed (*Eupatorium fistulosum*)	Summer to fall
Swamp sunflower (*Helianthus angustifolia*)	Summer to fall
Swamp rose mallow (*Hibiscus moscheutos*)	Summer
Blazing-stars (*Liatris* spp.)	Summer to fall
Virginia bluebells (*Mertensia pulmonarioides*)	Spring
Phlox (*Phlox carolina*)	Early summer
Goldenrods (*Solidago* spp.)	Summer to fall
Stoke's aster (*Stokesia laevis*)	Summer

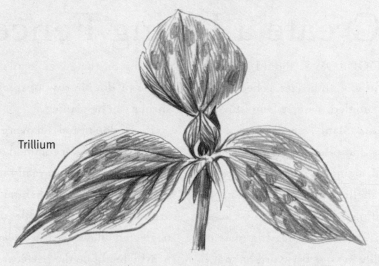

Trillium

CANADIAN NORTH

The long winters of the Canadian North mean backyard bird watchers can attract large numbers of birds to seed and suet feeders. If you stock your yard with plants that hold their food into the winter months, you may also draw in the birds that don't habitually visit feeders.

PLANT NAME	BLOOM SEASON
Angelica (*Angelica atropurpurea*)	Spring to summer
Canada columbine (*Aquilegia canadensis*)	Spring to summer
New England aster (*Aster novae-angliae*)	Fall
Bunchberry (*Cornus canadensis*)	Fall (fruit)
Joe-Pye weed (*Eupatorium fistulosum*)	Summer to fall
Boneset (*E. perfoliatum*)	Summer to fall
Queen-of-the-prairie (*Filipendula rubra*)	Summer
Jerusalem artichoke (*Helianthus tuberosus*)	Fall
Canada lily (*Lilium canadense*)	Summer
Lupine (*Lupinus perennis*)	Summer
Partridgeberry (*Mitchella repens*)	Summer (fruit)
Black-eyed Susan (*Rudbeckia fulgida*)	Summer to fall
Goldenrods (*Solidago* spp.)	Summer to fall
Trillium (*Trillium recurvatum*)	Spring

Create a Living Fence

HEDGEROWS should not be confused with hedges. A hedgerow is a tangled, assorted mixture of various plants, small trees, and vines that offer insects, birds, and small mammals an abundance of the shelter and food they need. Planting a hedgerow can be a superb way to enhance the lives of wildlife in your backyard habitat.

PLANNING MAKES PERFECT

Before you begin, study your property to decide on the best location for a hedgerow. Do you want it to define a property boundary, accent a landscape pond, provide shade, or block prevailing winds? Since the plants you choose will grow best where conditions are favorable, you'll need to assess the site for sun, shade, moisture, and wind and select suitable plants. Is the soil well drained or is it clay? Think about how tall you want the hedgerow to grow. Do you want a short hedgerow, a tall screen, or a windbreak? This decision will affect your choice of plants, too. De-

pending on the space available, a single or double row of trees and shrubs can be planted.

If you don't think an overgrown hedgerow can be accommodated in your yard, and you'd really like to create a bird-friendly habitat, look around you for a suitable site. A neglected alleyway or a vacant lot nearby might be the perfect spot if the owner is agreeable.

NATIVE, NATIVE, NATIVE

Using native plants has two huge benefits—first, the plants are bound to grow well because they are adapted to your climate, and second, they'll create a haven for the birds in your yard. The lives of plants and wildlife are interrelated.

Although exotic plants may produce a showier hedge and bear more fruit, they may not be as edible or acceptable to the wildlife in your area as native plants are. Nesting can also be affected. The nesting cycle for many species of birds corresponds to the fruit production of native plants.

Writing and Illustrating for Your Pleasure

A hedgerow takes on a life of its own, even in its first few years. You may be amazed by how busy a hedgerow can be with all of the comings and goings of birds and wildlife! If you don't keep a nature journal already, consider starting one when you plant your hedgerow. Sketch the progress of the hedgerow as it grows. Keep a count of the birds that are attracted to it and the animals that make their homes among the tangle of branches. Record what you observe by jotting notes in your journal and by making sketches of the birds that come to visit your hedgerow.

Sketching birds is a skill that you can develop over time; juggling field glasses, a sketchpad or journal, a pencil, and time is a considerable accomplishment. The following tips may help make the sketching process a bit more rewarding if you're a beginner.

■ Use binoculars or a spotting telescope to get a good look at a bird without scaring it. If you're lucky enough to have a spotting scope, you'll have both hands free to hold the sketchpad and draw.

■ Keep your sketches simple. Don't try for detail until you've made a number of action sketches. You'll learn more about the bird with each sketch.

■ Draw the moving parts first. Try to "freeze" a pose you like in your mind.

■ Don't be afraid to make dozens, even hundreds, of small sketches of the same bird. If you flub one, just make another. Don't erase.

■ Use a mechanical pencil that advances lead with a click to save time.

■ While you rest, keep watching the bird to learn more about its actions and movements. Be sure to take notes on the bird's behavior in the margins of your sketchpad. Everything you notice increases your understanding.

■ For your first sketching attempt, try big domestic birds like chickens, ducks, or geese. They'll stay reasonably still for you!

CLIMATE COUNTS, TOO

Choose native species that are adapted to your local climate. Instead of growing just one or two species of shrubs that could be susceptible to insect infestations or disease, try a variety of shrubs and evergreens to make a diverse habitat and an excellent windbreak that can provide an endless succession of leaves, flowers, seeds, buds, and colors. Your goal in planting and growing a hedgerow is to establish a wide array of shrubs and beneficial plants that provide the best food and cover for wildlife.

VARIETY AND SPACING

Strive for a combination of fruit-bearing shrubs and berry producers, vines, berry canes, and if room permits, one or two evergreens. When designing and planting a hedgerow, remember that its appearance will keep changing as the trees, shrubs, and plants grow, intertwine, and create a thickly woven habitat.

When planning, count on planting your shrubs slightly closer than suggested by the nursery. You'll create a solid wall of growth, and if a shrub dies, the gap will soon be filled by another plant as it grows and matures.

Start the hedgerow by planting heavy fruit-, berry-, and nut-bearing shrubs, such as sumac, hazelnut, barberry, viburnum, chokeberry, blueberry, and elderberry, if they're suited to your region.

MADE IN THE SHADE

Dogwood, American mountain ash, blueberry, and viburnum do well in shady conditions. In spring, the snowdrift of white dogwood blossoms are followed by brilliant fruit—a plus for birds.

Holly trees will also thrive in partial shade (and do equally well in full sun, too). The glossy dark green foliage produces a dense cover perfect for nesting. Holly berries are staples for many birds in winter, including chickadees, kingbirds, pine grosbeaks, hermit thrushes, cedar waxwings, and robins. (When planting holly, you must plant both male and female plants to get berries.)

For partly shaded, low-lying wet areas, try winterberry or inkberry. These will attract the hermit thrush, catbird, brown thrasher, and bobwhite.

THORNS CAN BE A BONUS

Thorny plants such as raspberries, blackberries, and gooseberries can be tucked in along the edge of a hedgerow to give the protection and density that brown thrashers and catbirds favor for a nesting site. Many birds, including the song sparrow, cedar waxwing, Baltimore oriole, wood thrush, and rose-breasted grosbeak, relish the berries that these thorny plants provide.

If you're looking for alternatives to brambles, try planting native roses, such as prairie or swamp rose; they provide rose hips (as well as protective thorns) for bobwhites and ruffed grouse. The thornier the plants, the better it is for wildlife, especially birds, which can slip quickly through the thorns and prickles to find a secure sanctuary from roaming cats and other predators.

Ninety-four species of birds, including the cardinal, song sparrow, wood and hermit thrushes, catbird, flicker, bobwhite, downy woodpecker, and brown thrasher, enjoy the fruit of the dogwood.

NATURAL BY NATURE

If you let nature take its course in your hedgerow, you will find that many native plants will self-sow and fill in the gaps. In some areas, you will be blessed with wildflowers that you and the birds love. However, some of the plants that move in may be invasive, so you'll need to make periodic checks to see what's growing. Birds love poison ivy, for example, but you may not want to encourage it in the hedgerow next to your child's play area. If you want to control what grows around hedgerow shrubs and trees, mulch with a thick layer of newspaper and wood chips to keep down invasive weeds.

habitats

sanctuary wildflowers diversity shelter meadow environment prairie evergreen

> **Birds apparently can sleep with one half of the brain on alert, the other half resting. This allows them to open one eye to check for predators on a regular basis.**

AN EVERGREEN FOR EVERY BIRD

Try incorporating several evergreens or conifers to help tie together your hedgerow planting; evergreens also provide color and protection in the winter.

Pines, spruces, firs, cedars, and hemlocks offer seeds and shelter to backyard birds. If space is an issue, though, try dwarf pines, such as the exotic yet noninvasive mugho pine or smaller versions of the tough, dense arborvitae clan.

FRUIT SWEETENS THE POT

If room permits, break up the uniformity of the line of shrubs with a fruit-bearing tree such as a cherry, crabapple, American mountain ash, mulberry, or serviceberry.

Your local nursery probably carries a variety of fruit trees, so visit and explore the fruit producers that grow well in your area.

Be sure not to overlook lesser-known fruit bearers, such as the serviceberry. The serviceberry is a small, shrublike tree that reaches 12 to 40 feet (3.5 to 12 m). The sweet purple fruits ripen early, and mockingbirds, cardinals, orioles, thrashers, catbirds, and ruffed grouse relish them.

LOOK A BIT LOWER

You can add perennial wildflowers, grasses, and groundcovers underneath the hedgerow to make the most of your habitat. Plant goldenrod, purple coneflower, red baneberry, and Solomon's seal, if they're suited to your region. Low-growing wintergreen tolerates a great deal of shade and reaches a height of 4 inches (10 cm)—birds that feed and nest on the ground favor this mint. A thick carpet of wild strawberry provides bright red fruit for many birds, such as the robin, wood thrush, and towhee.

VINTAGE VINES

Once the hedgerow has been in place for a year, you may want to plant vines such as Virginia creeper, grapes, American bittersweet, and trumpet creeper at intervals, encouraging growth within the hedge. Virginia creeper turns bright scarlet in the fall and produces quantities of black berries that last well into the winter; many birds eat the berries of Virginia creeper, including flickers, mockingbirds, scarlet tanagers, finches, and thrushes.

Keep in mind when adding vines that you don't want to damage your hedgerow by completely covering it with vines. Your goal is to add extra cover and food. A small hedgerow will not be able to sustain more than one vine without being overpowered.

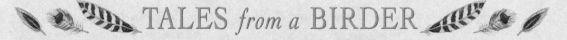

TALES *from a* BIRDER

HEDGEROWS provide great foraging and nesting opportunities for a diversity of birds, but they're also attractive to edge predators. Raccoons, opossums, and skunks consume eggs and nestlings as part of their daily diet.

Cowbirds are also fond of edge habitats and hedgerows and propagate their species by laying their eggs in other birds' nests, to the detriment of the host bird family.

In the wild, shrubby plant communities (similar to the habitat created by hedgerows) exist along the edges of forests. They grow up anywhere there's a gap in the forest created by a fallen tree. The mature forests buffer these communities, helping to protect eggs and nestlings from predators.

To create definition for your property without creating exposed edge habitat, I recommend planting hickory trees, or bur, black, or white oaks at 25- to 50-foot (7.5 to 15 m) intervals. (Such parklike savannah, with large hardwoods and a grassy understory, is a vanishing commodity.) Enhance the foraging opportunities and diversity of the landscape by planting prairie wildflowers and grasses underneath these monumental trees. The result of this planting, reminiscent of a savannah ecosystem, can attract several bird species, including red-headed woodpeckers, eastern and western kingbirds, great crested flycatchers, and northern orioles.

—*Mary Louise Boldan*

NEW LIFE FROM AN OLD HEDGE

You can revitalize an old hedge by planting a row of shrubs a few feet from the existing ones. Don't plant between the shrubs that are already there unless there are large gaps. If one of the shrubs is dead, use the skeleton of the shrub as a trellis to grow Virginia creeper or American bittersweet.

As you watch your hedgerow develop, watch for those plants that may attempt a coup d'état, and turn your diverse hedge into a monoculture. Trumpet vine, an invasive native, and Japanese honeysuckle, a viciously invasive exotic, are two to keep an eye on.

MAINTAINING IS A BREEZE

Once a hedgerow is established, maintenance is minimal. A good hedgerow is thick, bushy, and en-

Hedgerows draw even the tiniest birds. The flowering vines of the Humid South, including trumpet vine, offer sweet nectar for ruby-throated hummingbirds.

tangled with vines. If you plant one near a neighbor's property, you'll need to do some regular trimming so it doesn't fall into the adjoining yard. The mere act of clipping produces a dense, twiggy cover. Grapevines and Virginia creeper may need to be pruned annually so they don't overpower nearby shrubs.

Many experts say that regular pruning promotes strong, bushy growth. Others advocate letting plants grow naturally no matter how out of proportion they get. You'll need to decide which approach you'll take. If you can afford the space, let your hedgerow grow wild.

Be sure to avoid cutting the hedge during the nesting season. Even though you may not physically damage a nest, the dramatic change to the look of the surrounding area can cause the parent birds to desert their nest.

Hedgerows Made Simple

WHY not create a hedgerow using nature's method? Let the birds do it. Natural hedgerows grow up from wind-dispersed seeds and by the droppings of fruit- and seed-eating birds. Left alone, the hedgerow grows thick and lush, covered in time by vines and edged by the birds' favorite plants.

A Natural Hedgerow in 5 Easy Steps

1. Till the area in summer or early fall.

2. Set posts at 15-foot (4.5 m) intervals across the tilled area.

3. String a wire line a few feet above the area where you want to establish the hedgerow.

4. Fruit- and seed-eating birds will perch on the posts and wires, and drop seeds of their favorite food plants along with sufficient fertilizer. The seeds, having passed through a bird's digestive system, will be ready to germinate.

5. Let the hedgerow grow naturally, and sit back and enjoy the birds that eat and live in nature's bountiful plantings.

HEDGEROWS

PACIFIC COAST/NORTHWEST AND CALIFORNIA

Finding plants that are adapted to the sandy soils that often characterize coastal regions can be a challenge. Visiting a local wildlife preserve can yield valuable information about groundcovers, trees, shrubs, and vines that thrive in a particular area.

KEY G Groundcover   S Shrub   T Tree   V Vine

PLANT NAME	HEIGHT	SPREAD	BIRD FEATURES
Pacific Coast/Northwest			
T Western serviceberry (*Amelanchier alnifolia*)	12 feet (3.6 m)	12 feet (3.6 m)	Fruit; cover
G Bearberry (*Arctostaphylos uva-ursi*)	8 inches (20 cm)	12 feet (3.6 m)	Fruit
T Black hawthorn (*Crataegus douglasii*)	30 feet (9 m)	25 feet (7.5 m)	Fruit; forms thickets for nesting
T Pacific crabapple (*Malus fusca*)	35 feet (10.5 m)	30 feet (9 m)	Fruit
S Flowering currant (*Ribes sanguineum*)	10 feet (3 m)	6 feet (1.8 m)	Fruit; nectar
S Nutka rose (*Rosa nutkana*)	8 feet (2.4 m)	6 feet (1.8 m)	Fruit; cover
Pacific Coast/California			
S California sagebrush (*Artemisia californica*)	6 feet (1.8 m)	10 feet (3 m)	Leaves are winter grouse food; evergreen cover
S Blueblossom ceanothus (*Ceanothus thyrsiflorus*)	20 feet (6 m)	20 feet (6 m)	Fruit; evergreen cover
G Wild strawberry (*Fragaria californica*)	6 inches (15 cm)	Indefinite	Fruit
S Coffeeberry (*Rhamnus californica*)	15 feet (4.5 m)	10 feet (3 m)	Fruit; evergreen cover
S Blue elderberry (*Sambucus mexicana*)	20 feet (6 m)	20 feet (6 m)	Fruit; cover

MOUNTAIN WEST

If you plant both seed-bearing and fruit-bearing plant species, you'll attract the greatest variety of birds to your diversified hedgerow. Colorful tanagers and orioles feed mainly on fruits, while nuthatches and grosbeaks prefer seeds.

KEY　G Groundcover　S Shrub　T Tree　V Vine

PLANT NAME	HEIGHT	SPREAD	BIRD FEATURES
T Rocky Mountain maple (*Acer glabrum*)	20 feet (6 m)	15 feet (4.5 m)	Nesting; seeds
S Serviceberry (*Amelanchier* opp.)	12 feet (3.6 m)	12 feet (3.6 m)	Fruit; nesting
G Bearberry (*Arctostaphylos uva-ursi*)	8 inches (20 cm)	12 feet (3.6 m)	Fruit
T Common hackberry (*Celtis occidentalis*)	70 feet (21 m)	50 feet (15 m)	Fruit; nesting
S Rabbitbrush (*Chrysothamnus nauseosus*)	3 feet (90 cm)	3 feet (90 cm)	Seeds
V Western virgin's bower (*Clematis ligusticifolia*)	20 feet (6 m)	Indefinite	Seeds
T Rocky Mountain juniper (*Juniperus scopulorum*)	40 feet (12 m)	20 feet (6 m)	Fruit; evergreen cover
S Mountain ninebark (*Physocarpus monogynus*)	3 feet (90 cm)	3 feet (90 cm)	Fruit
T Pinyon pine (*Pinus edulis*)	50 feet (15 m)	25 feet (7.5 m)	Seeds; evergreen cover; nesting
S Western sandcherry (*Prunus besseyi*)	6 feet (1.8 m)	6 feet (1.8 m)	Fruit
S Skunkbush sumac (*Rhus trilobata*)	6 feet (1.8 m)	8 feet (2.4 m)	Fruit; cover
T Dwarf mountain ash (*Sorbus scopulina*)	12 feet (3.6 m)	5 feet (1.5 m)	Fruit

DESERT SOUTHWEST AND MIDWEST/GREAT PLAINS

Although neither the desert nor the prairie have natural hedgerows, there are native plant communities in both which are bird havens. In the desert, you'll find forestlike areas dominated by mesquite, while oak savannahs form the prairie's edge.

KEY **G** Groundcover **S** Shrub **T** Tree **V** Vine

PLANT NAME	HEIGHT	SPREAD	BIRD FEATURES
Desert Southwest			
S Catclaw acacia (*Acacia greggii*)	8 feet (2.4 m)	8 feet (2.4 m)	Fruit
G Big bluestem (*Andropogon gerardii*)	6 feet (1.8 m)	2 feet (60 cm)	Seeds; nesting
G Grama grasses (*Bouteloua* spp.)	2 feet (60 cm)	1 foot (30 cm)	Seeds
S Desert hackberry (*Celtis pallida*)	18 feet (5.4 m)	18 feet (5.4 m)	Fruit; cover
G Chollas (*Opuntia* spp.)	3 feet (90 cm)	3 feet (90 cm)	Fruit
S Mesquites (*Prosopis* spp.)	25 feet (7.5 m)	25 feet (7.5 m)	Seeds; cover; nesting
Midwest/Great Plains			
S American filbert (*Corylus americana*)	15 feet (4.5 m)	10 feet (3 m)	Nuts; nesting; cover
T Hawthorns (*Crataegus* spp.)	30 feet (9 m)	25 feet (7.5 m)	Fruit; cover
T Bur oak (*Quercus macrocarpa*)	50 feet (15 m)	30 feet (9 m)	Nuts; nesting; cover
T Black oak (*Q. velutina*)	100 feet (30 m)	80 feet (24 m)	Nuts; nesting; cover
S Brambles (*Rubus* spp.)	8 feet (2.4 m)	8 feet (2.4 m)	Fruit; cover

CONTINENTAL EAST AND CANADIAN NORTH

Trees and shrubs do not produce fruits all at the same time, nor do the fruits all last the same amount of time on trees and shrubs. To help ensure that your birds are well fed all year long, choose a variety of early- and late-flowering species.

KEY **G** Groundcover **S** Shrub **T** Tree **V** Vine

PLANT NAME	HEIGHT	SPREAD	BIRD FEATURES
Continental East			
T Sugar maple (*Acer saccharum*)	70 feet (21 m)	40 feet (12 m)	Nesting; cover
S Red-osier dogwood (*Cornus sericea*)	7 feet (2.1 m)	7 feet (2.1 m)	Fruit
T Eastern red cedar (*Juniperus virginiana*)	50 feet (15 m)	25 feet (7.5 m)	Fruit; evergreen cover
T Red mulberry (*Morus rubra*)	40 feet (12 m)	40 feet (12 m)	Fruit
S Northern bayberry (*Myrica pensylvanica*)	8 feet (2.4 m)	8 feet (2.4 m)	Fruit; cover
V Virginia creeper (*Parthenocissus quinquefolia*)	Indefinite	Indefinite	Fruit
T Chokecherry (*Prunus virginiana*)	30 feet (9 m)	25 feet (7.5 m)	Fruit; nesting
S Staghorn sumac (*Rhus typhina*)	15 feet (4.5 m)	15 feet (4.5 m)	Fruit; cover
T Mountain ash (*Sorbus americana*)	40 feet (12 m)	25 feet (7.5 m)	Fruit
Canadian North			
S Blueberries (*Vaccinium* spp.)	6 feet (1.8 m)	6 feet (1.8 m)	Fruit
S Viburnums (*Viburnum* spp.)	15 feet (4.5 m)	10 feet (3 m)	Fruit; cover

HUMID SOUTH

The many evergreen trees and shrubs of the South provide birds with protection from both occasional winter chills and oppressive summer heat. Native hollies yield plentiful fruit, a nutritious and long-lasting food source for many backyard birds.

KEY   G Groundcover   S Shrub   T Tree   V Vine

PLANT NAME	HEIGHT	SPREAD	BIRD FEATURES
T Red buckeye (*Aesculus pavia*)	20 feet (6 m)	15 feet (4.5 m)	Nectar; fruit
S American beautyberry (*Callicarpa bodinieri*)	6 feet (1.8 m)	5 feet (1.5 m)	Fruit
V Trumpet vine (*Campsis radicans*)	30 feet (9 m)	Indefinite	Nectar
T Mayhaw (*Crataegus opaca*)	30 feet (9 m)	25 feet (7.5 m)	Fruit
V Yellow jessamine (*Gelsemium sempervirens*)	20 feet (6 m)	Indefinite	Nectar; evergreen cover in warmest regions
T American holly (*Ilex opaca*)	50 feet (15 m)	40 feet (12 m)	Fruit; evergreen cover; nesting
S Yaupon holly (*I. vomitoria*)	25 feet (7.5 m)	15 feet (4.5 m)	Fruit; evergreen cover; nesting
V Trumpet honeysuckle (*Lonicera sempervirens*)	20 feet (6 m)	Indefinite	Nectar; fruit
T Southern magnolia (*Magnolia grandiflora*)	50 feet (15 m)	50 feet (15 m)	Fruit; evergreen cover; nesting
S Carolina cherry laurel (*Prunus caroliniana*)	25 feet (7.5 m)	20 feet (6 m)	Fruit; evergreen cover
T Carolina buckthorn (*Rhamnus caroliniana*)	30 feet (9 m)	20 feet (6 m)	Fruit; cover

Building a Brush Pile

BRUSH piles are ideal for attracting wildlife to your yard. They provide shelter for wintering mammals, cover for low-nesting birds, and even a spot for hibernating butterflies. And the best part—they're free and use plant material that would otherwise be put out on the curb for trash.

Don't confuse the brush pile with your compost pile, however. A brush pile is made with only branches, sticks, and twigs. A compost pile, on the other hand, consists of plant material, such as sticks and twigs, as well as lawn clippings, leaves, and some kitchen waste. Compost should not be used on a brush pile because it will compact and block off the many entrances and exits that make a brush pile the great hideout that it is.

THE PERFECT SPOT

Before you start hauling branches from the woods, consider where to put your brush pile and how much space you have. Pick a spot in the yard that is a distance from your house but is still visible so you can observe the pile's inhabitants. You probably don't want it right outside your back door because the winter mice it harbors may decide to take the short hike into your house. But you'll want a warm comfortable spot nearby that offers a view of the activities of the juncos and towhees that share the space with the little rodents.

INSTANT BRUSH PILE

To provide your birds with instant protection from predators and wind, simply lay your Christmas tree (with limbs intact) on its side near your feeders (not too close, though, or cats may hide inside and snatch your feasting birds). If you pick a spot carefully and can leave the decaying tree there permanently, you can add your new tree each year—providing a New Year's gift of habitat to your birds.

If your brush pile looks a bit too messy for you or the Christmas tree you propped up is losing its needles, grow vines for camouflage.

Try Virginia creeper, American bittersweet, morning glories, wild grapes, or moonflowers.

HOW BIG IS BIG ENOUGH?

There are no hard and fast rules to tell you how big to make a brush pile. The finished size will depend on the amount of room you have. Even a small brush pile will be home to interesting wildlife. The proportions can vary a bit too, but a good rule of thumb is to have the maximum width about twice that of the height. Be sure not to make any brush pile too dense—spaces are needed for the birds to get in, out, and through it.

TALES *from a* BIRDER

I have hedgerows and what I call "edgerows" on my 228-acre Maine farm. I've let the edgerows develop by yielding 20 feet (6 m) around the edges of my fields to whatever springs up. These edge areas have become a self-stocked pantry of viburnums, shrub dogwoods, wild red raspberries, and escaped apple seedlings from my nearby orchard.

Every few years I remove a few native trees that have self-seeded to keep it a shrub-dominant edgerow. I remove trees such as gray birch, red maple, and quaking aspen. I leave the wild apples and the best of the red oak, beech, and sugar maple trees that also appear in these edgerows for their value for wildlife, and also for my commercial maple sugaring. An edgerow of sugar maple, begun in 1975, is now mature enough to tap and is a part of my sugar bush, with a sumac understory.

A 1983 row planting of black walnut trees has become a hedgerow filled with black raspberries, self-seeded by the birds from a nearby black raspberry planting. This hedgerow of black raspberries and black walnuts has become a food cupboard for birds, small mammals, and my family.

Other hedgerows began as rows of Christmas trees. I allowed the volunteer chokecherries (*Prunus virginiana*) to remain between the trees along each row but removed brush between the rows. I share the chokecherries with the birds, then put the rest to use in my favorite jelly recipe.

—*Warren Balgooyen*

STEP-BY-STEP BRUSH PILES

Brush piles are simple to construct and require no tools. You may want a saw to make the job easier, but if you keep an eye to size as you gather brush, you won't even need that.

1 Position four logs or thick branches about 6 feet (1.8 m) long in a square. (If you want to provide a great winter hideout for rabbits, keep the corners of two of the four bottom logs at least 4 inches/10 cm apart.)

2 On top of these, place five or six thinner limbs, propping them in an upright position against each other to form an inverted cone, or teepee shape. Put the leafy ends of the branches toward the ground.

3 Place smaller branches, with the leafy ends down, against the uprights to fill the spaces. This allows roosting birds access but keeps out nighttime predators, such as raccoons and cats. Make the brush pile thickest on the side facing the prevailing winds to offer the most protection.

4 Add more branches as the pile breaks down over time. As you rebuild, crisscross the sticks to create a honeycomb effect.

Christmas in July

A cut Christmas tree makes a good shelter for birds when placed upright since most of the needles will remain on the tree for several months. As an added benefit for the birds, position the Christmas tree close to a feeder so that it can provide cover (as long as the needles remain) if a pesky cat wanders into the area. If you choose to make the tree permanent, plant vines around it to improve its appearance once the needles fall off.

To stand the tree up, you can try the following techniques:

- Tie it to a post or a deciduous tree
- Cement it in for a more permanent fixture
- Put the trunk in the ground and support it with stakes
- Anchor it in a large bucket or tub filled with sand and gravel

CREATING LIFE FROM DECAY

Let's say that along your back border an old oak stands dying. Your first inclination, being a responsible homeowner, is to have the local tree doctor cut it down. That dead tree, however, serves as an important resource for a wide variety of wildlife.

As the bark and wood decay, a host of insects and other invertebrates will feast on the decaying wood. An entirely new habitat is created on your property. Abundant insects may attract the attention of woodpeckers that chisel away at the soft wood in search of juicy beetle larvae. They may excavate some nesting cavities, too.

Screech owls, bluebirds, tree swallows, wrens, chickadees, flying squirrels, bats, and many other species of wildlife may use these cavities when woodpeckers leave them unoccupied. So, if your tree doesn't pose a threat to you or your neighbors (and you remove weakened limbs that may come down in a storm), feel free to let the tree linger to provide food and shelter for birds and their insect prey.

Even a dying tree provides habitat in a backyard. Many species of birds and animals will find food and shelter in it long after its final leaves have fallen.

How to Snag Birds

PLANTING a tree seems like the ultimate exercise in permanence. It's a pact, made with a living thing, to care for it and watch it grow, decade after decade. By contrast, you can add large, dead tree trunks and branches, which are also known as snags, to your landscape quickly and easily. Dead trees and limbs will attract cavity-nesting birds because they favor soft, rotting wood when excavating a nest site. Birds will also find a banquet of insects inside of stumps and decaying branches, making snags virtual cafeterias.

Collect snags from your woods or, with permission, from your neighbors' woods or municipality's recycling center for yard waste. Snags will offer food to woodpeckers that will search for insects in the dead wood and perches for all of your birds. Dig holes in the ground around your yard and "plant" the snags, packing the dirt around them securely. If the snags are large, you may want to mix up some cement and pour it into the hole as you set the snag. Hold the snag steady for a few minutes while the cement sets or stake it up while the cement dries to ensure that your snag won't topple over on the next windy day.

BIRDS OF THE SNAGS

Across most of the United States and Canada, you may attract nuthatches, titmice, chickadees, and various species of woodpeckers to these perches. Downy and hairy woodpeckers, white-breasted nuthatches, tufted titmice, northern flickers, and black-capped chickadees are common in many places. In the East, you may add Carolina chickadees and red-bellied woodpeckers. The pileated woodpecker may visit far into the North and near well-wooded areas in the East.

Why are snags, which seem to be merely dead wood, so attractive to birds? Aside from the potential they hold for woodpeckers to find wood-boring insects, snags lure many species of woodland birds simply because they are dead. To a bird that spends most of its time with its view obscured by twigs and leaves, a leafless, twigless snag is irresistible.

> Acorn woodpeckers store nuts in the thick bark of old trees. These granaries may contain tens of thousands of holes but do not harm the granary tree.

Almost all woodland birds, from woodpeckers, waxwings, and chickadees to tanagers, flycatchers, and orioles, like to emerge for a good look around. Waxwings and tanagers, in particular, like to vary their diet by catching the flying insects they spot from exposed snags.

In addition, a snag can function as a hunting station for open-country birds like bluebirds and kingbirds, which need good visibility to spot their insect prey in the grass or in the air. Broad-winged hawks, red-shouldered hawks, and American kestrels, which hunt small rodents, insects, reptiles, and amphibians, appreciate snags for the same reason. Woodpeckers love their clear visibility and resonating qualities, and even the shy pileated woodpecker will perch on an exposed, dead treetop for a quick look around and to announce its presence to others.

Snags also afford you the opportunity to watch birds groom themselves. In the morning and evening, birds like to relax by perching on a snag and preening, often in small, mixed flocks. Many eyes help watch for predators, and flock members can let their guard down a bit to preen and oil their feathers. A spotting scope can reward the backyard birder with sightings of species and behavior that would otherwise go unseen.

RELAX, AND APPRECIATE

Incorporating deadwood, brush piles, vine tangles, hedgerows, and even unmown meadows into your landscape may require you to relax your standards for tidiness. Even a small degree of disorder in a tidy yard offers the potential for food and cover far beyond that of a perfectly clipped lawn or a neat ball of shrubbery. Confine the "wild" area to a small corner or let it define your grounds; it's up to you. Keep a list of the birds you spot before and after you let things go a bit, and you may be pleasantly surprised at the up side of a tumbledown habitat.

5
LETTING IT GO

The Messy, Marvelous Ways of Nature

nature   dandelion diversify berries mullein nesting material goldenrod variety chicory weeds

I**T TAKES COURAGE** to let a few things go in your yard when faced with neighbors who mow, fertilize, prune, and weed like clockwork. You may feel your role as yard keeper is to neaten, eliminate, and simplify, too. Relax. Leave the weed trimmer leaning against the garage wall for a week or two longer. Let the sunflowers come up under the feeder. Watch nature take its course and begin to weave its spell on your backyard habitat. Weedy patches have a special beauty that may not brighten every beholder's eye, but the benefits of these natural backyards are numerous and alluring to birds and wildlife.

A Weedy Paradise

EVER see an abandoned lot in your neighborhood filled with crabgrass, ragweed, poison ivy, and other weeds? It may not be picturesque to you, but to birds, it's paradise. If you want to attract more birds to your backyard, then you, too, should consider growing weeds. Weeds have been described both as plants out of place and as flowers in disguise. Indeed, many of them mix in well in the garden with their interesting, if not always beautiful, flowers and seedheads.

Your job as a gardener and bird lover is to identify the weeds that will grow well in your area without becoming an overgrown tangle.

SEEDS ABOUND

Adding weeds to your backyard habitat can be wonderful for the birds *and* frustrating to you when you discover that numerous off-spring have popped up everywhere. There's no denying it—weeds produce an enormous amount of seeds.

For instance, a single plant of pigweed (*Amaranthus* spp.) or common lamb's-quarter (*Chenopodium album*), a true bird favorite, bears between 70,000 and 130,000 seeds.

Besides having a plethora of seeds, many weeds have another black mark on their record. Poison ivy (*Toxicodendron radicans*) produces an irritating rash, the pollen of the ragweed plant (*Ambrosia* spp.) is a troubling allergen, and for some reason, no one seems to like lowly crabgrass (*Digitaria* spp.). However, these plants and other weeds are some of the most important sources of food for seed-eating birds, particularly during the winter months. Most of the weeds with question-able reputations bear seed and fruit that attract birds, so backyard bird lovers willingly accept them as part of their overall gardening plan.

PROTEIN MAGNETS

A weed's usefulness is not limited just to seed or fruit production. Weeds attract insects, and insects attract wrens, chickadees, titmice, warblers, woodpeckers, and other insect-eating birds. Also, the eggs and larvae of insects overwinter in the dead leaves and flower heads of weeds, providing much-needed food for insect-eating birds over the colder months.

NECESSARY FOR NESTING

A variety of birds rely on weeds for nest-building materials. They use roots, dead leaves, plant down, and spider webs (built among the plants) to make their nests. Weeds can provide super sites for nests, too, either on the ground among the stems or in the branches of sturdier plants. This is particularly true when the plants grow in groups.

White-crowned sparrows haunt weedy fields in search of lamb's-quarter seeds.

TALES *from a* BIRDER

THE air is cooling. Yesterday, juncos visited the feeding station for the first time, looking out of place on the still verdant lawn. The dozen house sparrows that don't seem to grasp how much I dislike them were joined by an elegant, adult white-crowned sparrow, stripping the crabgrass seeds.

I wind down my gardening efforts, letting tomatoes drop from the tired vines and basil go to seed. The garden, right in front of my kitchen window, stands in glorious disorder, awash in sprawling tomatoes, springing with crabgrass, and overflowing with nasturtiums and marigolds, with proud zinnias still barely holding their heads above it all. Rustling and peeping and sorting through the tangle are the birds of summer, the birds of autumn, the birds of winter.

All summer long, the common yellowthroats, blue-gray gnatcatchers, and even a family of yellow-breasted chats used the garden as their insect larder, gleaning the bean leaves for beetles, spooking quarry out of the tomatoes, and sallying forth after flying prey from the tall pea fence that lines the back of the raised beds. The bluebirds were a constant presence on the fence and on the snags we erected as perches for them.

Now that fall is here, the shifts are changing. Chipping sparrows, and yellow-rumped, palm, and Cape May warblers—the birds of autumn—flit and pinwheel through the vines. They will not stay the winter, but while they're with us, they find the remains of my garden irresistible. Winter residents—cardinals, eastern towhees,

goldfinches, juncos, and field, song, and white-throated sparrows—have been stripping the flower heads since the first seed formed, and they'll continue to find food here until early April, when I clear the beds and dig a furrow for the sugar snap peas.

I let it all stand and slowly collapse in on itself. Put a white-crowned sparrow against this trashy backdrop and you have something distinctly lovely. Zinnias and coneflowers, blasted by frost, are sad and black like burned skeletons, but top one with a goldfinch and they're not so sad anymore. My flowerbeds may look awful all winter and well into the spring, but in them I find beauty hiding just beneath the surface, scratching on the ground, rattling the spent stem.

—*Julie Zickefoose*

SOME THINGS IN LIFE ARE FREE

One of the best things about growing weeds for birds is that they're free—many are probably already sprouting in your yard. All you have to do is let them grow unhindered. They don't need any special care, and most of them will easily make it through a drought. If you want some new plants in your landscape, all you need to do is wait. Birds have a

> **If a songbird is discovered in the process of building its nest, it may drop the nesting material, abruptly change course, and even abandon the nest.**

habit of sowing their favorite food plants just by passing through your yard, so sooner or later new ones will arrive.

The timid, ground-dwelling ovenbird builds its domed, Dutch-oven–style nest using sturdy, upright Christmas fern stalks for support.

The Top 10 Wonderful Weeds

WHICH weeds should you grow in your yard? Birds find many enticing, but the following list of their favorites will get you started. Introduced plants can sometimes become unwelcome invaders of natural plant communities. Check with your local nature center or native plant society if you are unsure if any of these plants will cause problem in your area.

Mullein is a boon for birds through many seasons. In the winter months, flickers can find food on the tall stems that reach above the fallen snow.

Chicory (*Cichorium intybus*): Only a few chicory flowers open at a time throughout the summer, so its seeds are produced over a long period of time. Once the chicory seeds are ripe, they may be visited by house finches and goldfinches.

Thistles (*Cirsium* spp.): These plants can be hard to live with because of their spines and the white down attached to each seed, but your yard will be a hot spot of bird activity if you include thistle. Goldfinches use the down to line nests and fill up on seeds. Clay-colored sparrows and indigo buntings will also eat the seeds, and hummingbirds seek nectar from the flowers.

Common pokeweed (*Phytolacca americana*): Pokeweed grows anywhere from 4 to 12 feet (1.2 to 3.6 m) tall and bears purplish black berries in fall. Doves, phoebes, thrashers, catbirds, mockingbirds, bluebirds, robins, thrushes, waxwings, and warbling vireos enjoy the luscious-looking fruit.

Knotweeds (*Polygonum* spp.): Knotweeds have small spikes of charming pink flowers that give way to tiny black seeds. Many birds eat the seeds, including pheasant, quail, doves, blackbirds, juncos, buntings, finches, cardinals, redpolls, and sparrows.

Greenbriers (*Smilax* spp.): These thorny climbing vines produce bluish black berries eaten by grouse, pileated woodpeckers, flickers, crows, thrashers, catbirds, mockingbirds, bluebirds, robins, thrushes, waxwings, and cardinals.

Climbing nightshade (*Solanum dulcamara*): This climbing plant produces red berries summer to winter. Catbirds, mockingbirds, thrashers, thrushes, cardinals, and towhees find the berries irresistible.

Goldenrods (*Solidago* spp.): Once the golden yellow flowers of goldenrods go to seed, those seeds remain a food source for birds through winter. Grouse, orange-crowned warblers, juncos, indigo buntings, goldfinches, and tree sparrows are among the birds that feast upon goldenrod.

Dandelion (*Taraxacum officinale*): These yellow-flowered plants flourish across the continent and are some of the earliest to bear seeds, making them indispensable to birds. Grouse, quail, house finches, pine siskins, chipping sparrows, and indigo, painted, and lazuli buntings dine with goldfinches at the dandelion diner.

Common mullein (*Verbascum thapsus*): Flower stems of mullein grow 2 to 6 feet (0.6 to 1.8 m) tall, packed with small, light yellow flowers. In winter, erect stems remain above the snow, keeping the seeds accessible for sparrows, goldfinches, and others, while insect eaters like flickers find insect larvae overwintering on the seedstalks.

Grasses: Wheat, oats, milo, canary, and the various millets are types of grasses. Some of the best for growing in your yard are switch grasses (*Panicum* spp.), little bluestem (*Schizachyrium scoparium*), and fountain grass (*Pennisetum setaceum*). Quail, doves, bobolinks, indigo buntings, cardinals, towhees, and many sparrows include grass seeds in their diets.

A Little Shabby

PUT those pruners away and rest the rake this fall, and you will be rewarded for your lack of labor in extra time and energy this autumn and, with any luck, the sounds of young birds next spring. If you are one of those neatnik gardeners who can't wait to trim back ragged perennials and rake up each leaf from under every shrub, think about changing your ways.

Many gardeners hesitate to leave debris in the landscape in the fall for fear it will harbor unwanted pests. Others believe that they need to "put their garden to bed" in the fall. Some just want to get a jump on spring cleanup by taking care of it in fall.

There is no biological reason to put your garden to bed, only a psychological one. Gardeners living in cold and snowy climates know that winter can be dreary enough. If you chop all the perennials to the ground and dig up the annuals,

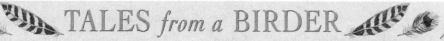

TALES *from a* BIRDER

MY curiosity was piqued one beautiful April day while watching a busy black-capped chickadee in my Fort Collins, Colorado, backyard. It zoomed from point A to point B to point C with as much regularity as one might expect from a frenetic chickadee during nest building. The bird emerged from a neighbor's yard, pulled up in a snap to land momentarily on the top branches of a still dormant, dwarf mock orange, scanned the surroundings for any cats, and then disappeared into the stalks of my butterfly garden. In a few seconds, it went straight back to point A, where it again disappeared.

Its task was too quick for me to see with the naked eye, so I pulled out my binoculars for a better look. The little bird repeated the steps, and when it got to point C, I discovered it rummaging in the debris on the ground of the butterfly garden for whatever would fit into its tiny beak. It paused just long enough for me to clearly see a beak stuffed with the strings of daylily leaves and leaf litter.

That day I learned the value of leaving your landscape on the shabby side, autumn through spring.

—*Miles Blumhardt*

your landscape can be pretty monotonous. Leaving perennial and annual stalks standing to poke through winter snow gives a pleasing winter appeal to these plants. Refraining from dead-heading in fall also leaves a valuable natural food supply for birds migrating south and for those birds ready to fatten up for the winter.

> **Bullock's orioles like to nest close to the nests of more aggressive birds, such as the western kingbird and scissor-tailed flycatcher, presumably benefiting from their spirited defense of their own nests.**

MAKING WEEDS WORK FOR YOU

When you include weeds and wildflowers in your landscape, group the plants together. Even when not looking for a place to nest, birds are more attracted to weeds when several plants of the same type are growing in the same area. Grouping the plants also gives birds some shelter during inclement weather, which is especially important in the winter.

Allow your dead plants to stand throughout winter to ensure that seeds, berries, and insects will be available during the cold months. The most important weeds for winter food are those with stiff, weatherproof stems that hold their seeds above the snow.

Deadheading is fine. If you snip off the blossoms of spring- and summer-blooming perennials after the first flush of color, you will usually get a second, albeit smaller, show of blooms in the fall. This way, you'll enjoy two blooming periods, and the birds will have food when the seeds dry in the fall.

Also, when you deadhead the first time, allow the snipped seedheads to lie on the ground to dry out, which will provide more food for the birds and result in an occasional seed that beats the odds and grows into a flower.

With invasive plants, such as evening primrose, you may not want to try this, in case these aggressive self-sowers overrun your garden and backyard.

nature

dandelion diversify berries mullein nesting material goldenrod variety chicory weeds

LEAVE THE LEAVES

Keep autumn cleanup to a minimum. Instead of raking leaves and taking them to the curb for the trash truck, make them into homemade mulch by mowing over them to chop up the leaves. Scattering a layer of shredded leaves around your flowers and underneath your shrubs will provide an insulating winter mulch that will enhance your soil and help to alleviate the problem of plants heaving out of the ground in areas with fluctuating winter temperatures.

GLORIOUS GRASS

Leaving your string trimmer in the garage or shed has two major benefits—it cuts back on the chores you have to do *and* provides nesting material for birds. If the untidy look gets you in trouble with your spouse, roommates, or neighbors, strike a compromise—at least refrain from trimming the last couple of mowings of the year. Birds such as the warbling vireo and yellow-rumped warbler may just thank you for the dried grass by building a nest in your yard.

Warbling vireos weave their hanging-basket nests from grasses and plant fibers. The nests are often difficult to spot in shade trees.

Going Wild from Sea to Sea

EVERY gardener can have a delightfully wild garden that encourages birds to settle in it. Use the plants native to your area, leave some edges untidy, heap brush in piles instead of carting it off, and let a little corner of your yard go wild!

FALLING FOR FALL

In a Pacific Northwest garden, brown-eyed Susan is bright and blowsy in the fall. This prairie native is a plant of many virtues having made the transition from the central United States to moist Oregon gardens with no complaints. Although this member of the black-eyed Susan clan can grow up to 6 feet (1.8 m) tall, the multi-branched stems sport small flowers, only 1½ inches (4 cm) in diameter. The gaiety of these plants, with their hundreds of little, dark-centered, yellow daisy flowers dancing in the breeze, is irresistible.

NURTURE NATURE (AND YOU!)

BIRD watchers just might be the salvation of nature. Many bird watchers like having flowers and birds share their garden. From that basic starting point, bird watchers like you can be inspired to adopt a genuine and all-encompassing reverence for life, which is referred to as *ahimsa* in Buddhist and Hindu doctrine. Ahimsa is a spiritual tenet that stresses the importance of not harming any living being. Because of your love of birds and flowers, you can gradually teach yourself to love other kinds of animals, other kinds of vegetation, then even insects, and finally—the supreme test for some—spiders and snakes. You must go that far to create a backyard not just attractive to but also nurturing of nature. Then, one backyard at a time, the effect of bird watchers, gardeners, and other naturalists will build a collective conscious striving for the same goal—true natural preservation that will benefit all living things.

nature

dandelion diversify berries mullein nesting material goldenrod variety chicory weeds

The dark-eyed junco feasts on the brown-eyed Susan, but a few seeds are left to ensure next year's bounty.

Dark-eyed juncos head right for this plant as they move back to lower elevations for the winter. They leave only a few seeds, insuring there will be a seedling or two in the spring for you to give to friends. When new growth emerges in spring, cut back the dead stems.

BRINGING BIRDS IN

If you live near the California coast, let your leaves gather in order to bring sparrows and California towhees to scratch among them for insects. Allow the cosmos and sunflower to go to seed. Resist the temptation to prune salvia — the flowers provide a welcome food source for hummingbirds in fall.

Fall is an ideal time to plant native perennials in this ecoregion. Try Pacific dogwood for a flowering tree; its red autumn fruit will attract woodpeckers, cedar waxwings, and purple finches. Toyon, also called California holly, offers bright red or yellow berries throughout the fall and winter that attract northern mockingbirds, western bluebirds, and wrentits. For color, add a few perennials such as California lilac and California buckwheat.

LONG GROWING SEASONS

In many parts of the desert Southwest, September and October are still quite warm. After the long, hot season, trees, shrubs, and perennials are dense with growth — providing perfect shelter and roosting habitat for birds. And, yes, some birds are still raising their young. Prolific nesters such as mourning doves may be working on their fourth or fifth broods by this time in fall.

Letting Your Garden Go

Q I like the idea of not cleaning up the garden in the fall, letting the birds use the seedheads and cover it provides. Are there any flowers that should be cut back for their own good?

A The hard, spiky stalks of spent perennials left to overwinter will actually help protect the small, basal rosettes of living leaves from herbivores in early spring. These perennials will get a better start if you leave the dead stalks until the weather warms up and new growth is well underway. Woody perennials such as roses should be cut back about the time the forsythia blooms, in early spring, before new leaf growth starts. If your roses have had trouble with black spot fungus, you may wish to cut them back in fall, disposing of all leaves and leaf litter by burning (if allowed in your area). The fungus will live in the soil around the plant and re-infect it in the spring if you do not clean up around the plant.

Q I love the look of ornamental grasses, especially fountain grass. I had thought that it wouldn't spread, but it seems to be seeding itself around my garden. Is this any cause for concern?

A Ornamental grasses, especially cultivars of eulalia grass (*Miscanthus sinensis*), are extremely popular in foundation plantings. In some areas, however, they can become troublesome and invasive weeds, taking over pastures and clearings. Keep a close eye on your ornamental plantings and consider removing them and replacing with native grasses that won't become a threat to your local habitat.

denrod variety chicory weeds

Unlike some other parts of the continent, fall is the ideal time to plant in the low deserts. The cooler weather of winter encourages root establishment and gives plants a fighting chance to withstand the next year's heat.

Why not consider some plants that will provide cover for towhees, sparrows, verdins, and bushtits, while producing flowers that will feed hummingbirds? If you've got room for a sprawler, the tubular red flowers of chuparosa (*Justicia californica*) will stage an impressive display until cold weather arrives.

> **Northern birds such as the evening grosbeak, the snowy owl, and the pine siskin are called irruptive species. They may invade southern climes one winter in ten, or three in a row, without a discernible pattern.**

Native to southeastern California and southern Arizona, chuparosa, a 5-foot (1.5 m)-tall deciduous shrub, is a desert stalwart that hummingbirds love.

TALES *from a* BIRDER

PAINTED buntings have given me my greatest reason for nurturing a shabby garden throughout fall and winter. One year my husband, Steve, and I had allowed weeds to grow between rows in the vegetable garden near our sunflower-seed feeders. Over the years, the sunflower seeds have lured such migrants as goldfinches, purple finches, indigo buntings, and rose-breasted grosbeaks. However, no painted bunting had ever stopped at the feeders.

One afternoon I glanced out the back window to see three parrot green birds with yellow undersides pulling down weed stalks with their heavy bills. These female painted buntings were ample reward for not clearing the garden. Then the male—with his blue head, red underside, and yellow-and-green back—arrived and began prancing around, pulling off the choice weed heads. The picture was complete. Their favorite? Chickweed! The painted buntings enjoyed it so much that I'm considering planting an entire bed of chickweed.

—*Jeanne Lebow*

You might also want to try flame acanthus (*Anisacanthus quadrifidus* var. *wrightii*), a drought-tolerant Texas native that grows from 3 to 4 feet (0.9 to 1.2 m) high and often blooms well into the autumn.

MIXING MOODS

Throughout the Midwest and in the East, a mix of prairie and woodland perennials, arranged using the organized-chaos approach, will welcome many a bird. You don't need to adhere to the dictates of the color wheel or consider texture and line when planting for the birds because nearly anything goes.

While annual flowers produce copious amounts of seeds, perennials such as daisies also provide seeds for birds. You may find that some perennials offer fruit instead of seed; no matter, the birds will come in droves when offered a flower, seed, and fruit feast.

The magenta flowers of rough blazing star can be delightful next to the yellow ox-eye sunflower, and the orange butterfly weed will do just fine next to the pale purple coneflower. Goldfinches and indigo buntings don't mind as they flit from flower to flower through the summer and autumn gathering seeds. If you don't cut the garden

When fruit and vegetables are past their prime for picking, don't toss them on the compost pile. These rotting, splitting treats will attract hungry birds day after day.

down in the fall, the standing residual grasses and flowerstalks collect snow during winter. Under this newly fallen snow, deer mice and meadow voles hide. Occasionally these rodents surface, providing a nutritious winter meal for great horned and screech owls.

TALES *from a* BIRDER

THE buzzwords for the decade seem to be "simplify, simplify"; and contrary to what you might think, it's not a positive message. People want the inside of their houses to be perfectly free of spiders or insects of any kind. People tend to want their yards to boast little variety: They prefer a lawn with all the grass of one species with no others mixed in. Out in the yard, two or three species of trees stand isolated, preferably trees that flower but do not grow any sort of messy fruit.

Nature is completely opposite—"How many angels can I get to dance on the head of a pin?" Nature crams as much diversity as it can into a tiny space—studies have even been done on the numbers of creatures that live inside an acorn.

Humankind's and nature's ways are fundamentally at odds. We continue to increase our numbers and our use of power tools and chemicals. We are gradually turning, not only our houses and gardens, but also our towns and cities, and finally the countryside, the forests, the deserts, the watersheds, and even the oceans themselves into a pattern of "simplicity."

In my favorite daydream, I win the lottery, and with my millions pick the Nature Conservancy as my favorite charity, and I help them buy huge tracts of land to keep pristine forever. But the reality is that I'm such a cheapskate I don't even buy lottery tickets, so the only tract of land I can preserve, even for my lifetime, is the acre of land my house is on just outside the city limits. Even this is no small thing. I have recently read how many million square miles of backyards there are in this country. Think what a difference it would make if even a sizable portion of these backyards were managed according to nature's rhythm rather than people's; if only the owners tried for maximum diversity because of their love of living things rather than maximum order and limitation because of human exclusivity.

—*Norman Lavers*

WHERE WINTER IS WARMER

If you want winter interest in humid southern climates, leave standing tall goldenrod, dog fennel, boneset, and giant coneflower stalks. Don't cut down the dried flowers of oak-leaved hydrangea until new stalks pop up in spring— butterflies and other insects will enjoy them into the cooler months. And these insects provide food for birds, both resident and migrating.

Red-osier dogwood is a lovely native that forms clumps via spreading underground roots. In late summer, its fruits are welcomed by a variety of birds, and in winter, its blood red stems enliven the landscape with color. Such specimen plantings look best when they're clumped, and red-osier dogwood takes care of that on its own, lending a natural, thicketlike aspect to your wildlife plantings.

BRRR AND THE BIRDS

It can be chilly year-round in the North, but there are plenty of plants to keep the birds coming around. Eastern red cedar and winterberry will attract mockingbirds, robins, bluebirds, and cedar waxwings. Add an American cranberry bush, too, and you might be surprised and delighted to find a wild turkey or ruffed grouse wandering into your backyard habitat.

The aromatic northern bayberry can count on having yellow-rumped warblers, red-bellied woodpeckers, and tree swallows (on their fall migration route) among its visitors. If you have eastern hemlocks on your property, you'll probably find golden and ruby-crowned kinglets searching their needles for scale to eat, while eastern white pines often attract black-capped chickadees and red-breasted nuthatches.

Pines are native to many parts of the country, so before you go to a nursery for an Austrian black pine or a mugho pine, consider the native species. Virginia pine, a short-needled species, is superbly adapted to much of the East and lower Midwest, and it may be a better, hardier, and more natural-looking choice all around. When planting for wildlife, always remember to look around you to see what occurs naturally.

Weeds—The Good Outweighs the Bad

AFTER all this information about living in harmony with weeds, there are some cases where cleanliness and neatness is the better route. If you've had trouble with rusts, wilts, black spots, and other fungal diseases, especially in your beans, tomatoes, and roses, it's best to remove and burn those plants at season's end. (Whatever you do, though, don't just toss them on the compost heap because the spores will survive the winter to infect next year's plants.) If burning is prohibited in your area, put the diseased plants in the trash.

No matter the down side, weeds will enhance your backyard habitat and entice birds to it. Once you realize the benefits of weeds, you'll find yourself fascinated by the weedy world at your feet. When you take time to learn about them, you'll discover how easy it is to incorporate weeds (the appropriate ones!) into your landscape (if they haven't found their way there already!). When you learn to love everything wild—weeds included—you'll create a yard that pleases both you and wildlife. And that's when the future of nature becomes a little more secure.

6

SAVING
GRACES

Solutions for Times When Trouble Swoops In

THE COLORFUL CARDINALS and gold-finches that make their homes in your backyard live moment to moment in a quiet struggle for life. A whispered alarm call sounds, and all freeze, as the streamlined form of a sharp-shinned hawk carries one of the clan away — now a random bit of protein to fuel the hawk's frantic fire. Natural predation such as this may horrify some observers and engage others. Perhaps more troubling are the misfortunes befalling backyard wildlife that are caused, directly or indirectly, by humans. When your windows intercept the natural flight lines of birds or when a house cat roams unattended, you realize that caring for your backyard habitat means caring for its inhabitants as well.

Predators on the Prowl

THE natural world revolves around prey and predators, and the birds in your yard are no different. Birds eat and are eaten. However, when you create a bird haven in your backyard by providing food, shelter, water, and nesting sites, you could be luring your wild visitors toward danger.

It's natural for predators to stalk and pounce or swoop and snatch prey. Despite your sense of loss when the sharp-shinned hawk snatches the songbird, you can still appreciate the finely tuned manner in which the hawk has evolved to feed itself.

In your bird-friendly backyard, you must remember that everything you do affects your mini-ecosystem: House cats can roam free and fill up their stomachs at the base of your feeder; disease can run rampant through your feeding station; and even the tadpoles you import can become predators.

TALES *from a* BIRDER

ABOUT a year into enjoying our first water garden, all 200 gallons of it, I decided to introduce a few bullfrog tadpoles into my little ecosystem. They changed into froglets in their second summer. One grew very fast, especially when I started tossing mealworms to him. I named him Fergus, and he became tame enough to hold and talk to.

Fergus liked to sit right under the pink blossoms of my 'Firecrest' water lily. He looked grand there. I soon found that this had less to do with froggy aesthetics than his sinister hunting strategy. One July morning, I found 10 tiny tail feathers from a ruby-throated hummingbird floating on the surface of the pond. The shafts were bent, so I could tell they'd been pulled out with some force. It suddenly hit me that Fergus was the culprit, and his round, fat sides doubtless hid a recent hummingbird meal. Buzzing low to check out the pink water lily, the hummer had been easy prey for Fergus's lightning-fast strike. Butterflies met the same fate.

A short while later, I was shocked to find Fergus with the tail of a chipping sparrow protruding from his jaws. Furious, I grabbed him by the hind legs and tried to work the sparrow out. It was too late, though, and in one mighty gulp Fergus finished swallowing the bird. If he could kill hummingbirds and chipping sparrows in his first summer of froghood, what a deadly force he'd be when he reached full size! My little water garden was the only water around on our dry, Ohio ridge top. Birds were irresistibly drawn to this resource. Fergus was a spider with a pond-size web. He had to go.

Still fuming, I plopped Fergus in a pickle jar, the same one he'd arrived in as a tadpole, and walked him, sloshing, across a wide alfalfa field to the neighbor's farm pond. I figured his chances of catching birds would be greatly diminished by many more yards of shoreline. The next evening, I drove slowly by Fergus's new home, taking in the beauty of the scene. A great blue heron stood on the shore, looking out over the smooth water.

Most gardeners may attach little significance to a few tail feathers or a drowned bird floating on their ponds; fewer still happen to catch a bullfrog red-handed, stuffing a bird down its gullet. But all water gardeners should watch for such signs of frog predation and think twice before introducing this voracious predator into their miniature Edens.

—*Julie Zickefoose*

FEROCIOUS FROGS

There are a lot of water gardens in America, and many of them have a resident bullfrog or two. Bullfrogs eat birds and butterflies, however, and they can eat a lot of them.

Bullfrogs must eat, too, and butterflies and small birds are often the preferred prey for these aquatic predators.

Many water gardeners buy tadpoles and frogs because they eat algae and insects, respectively, but the risks to the wildlife who frequent a pond with a frog are great. If birds regularly visit your water garden, you may want to forego the frogs and add more fish instead.

SAVAGE NATURE

Accipiters, such as sharp-shinned hawks, Cooper's hawks, and northern goshawks, are woodland hawks with long tails and short, rounded wings that give them quick wing beats followed by a glide. They are fast, agile, and perfectly designed for their niche, and they also eat birds. Attracted to the flocks that frequent bird feeders, accipiters feast on migrating warblers and dine on the delightful woodpeckers in your woods and hedgerows. They are a perfect example of the savage beauty of nature. As a bird lover, it may be difficult to appreciate an animal that systematically devours your songbirds. But accipiters are natural predators and fill an essential need in a well-balanced ecosystem—the need to control populations.

Blue jays and other large songbirds will often harass a sharp-shinned hawk when it perches. Jays target immature hawks like this one, rarely bothering adults.

DIVING FOR COVER

A raptor specialist describes accipiters as the James Bonds of the hawk world. "They always get their man," he says. He may have confused James Bond with the Canadian Mounties, but his point is valid. A buteo—like a red-tailed hawk—is larger, with a wide tail and broad wings that allow it to soar high; in diving to take a rabbit, it will veer off if the rabbit reaches cover. However, a sharp-shinned hawk, Cooper's hawk, or goshawk whose prey makes cover will dive in right after it, ripping out leaves and twigs in a ferocious effort to uncover its victim.

Death and raptors are two things sure to be found together. A peaceful scene at a backyard birding station will be completely disrupted as a sharp-shin swoops in to grab one of the slower or less-watchful juncos or sparrows pecking at mixed seed. In autumn, when the leaves are turning and the air has a snap to it, you may hear the hushed *seet* calls of sparrows and warblers as they dive for cover. When a sharpshin perches, jays and flickers may stay nearby to harass it. The tormenters sometimes press their luck too far, though: The sharpshin can dispatch them with ease. Jays voice a special raucous *raack* as they flirt with death, coming ever closer, pinwheeling around a perched sharpshin. Flickers, too, perhaps confident in their size and toughness, love to torment the little hawks, nervously *churring* and giving *woika* calls.

MORE PREY, MORE PREDATORS

Lots of birds have profited by the growing popularity of bird feeding. Cardinals, titmice, red-bellied woodpeckers, and house finches are a few that have ex-panded their ranges in response to ample food at feeding stations. Evening grosbeaks now range as far south as the Gulf Coast in search of sunflower seeds. With these peaceful, colorful hordes come their predators. Should we be surprised that hawks have fig-ured out where to get an easy meal? Is it any wonder that more and more birds are spending the winter farther north, aided by bird feeders, feeding stations, and homeowners supplying them with gourmet treats?

TALES *from a* BIRDER

I remember my first sharp-shinned hawk. I was cross-country skiing in a Massachusetts woodland, gliding along on a newly broken trail through old orchard and white-pine stands. The sun cast sky blue shadows on the sparkling snow. I heard the rushing of feathers as they sliced the air, and felt the bird's presence. A startled *yawp* from a blue jay, and suddenly there was a double bird at eye level in front of me, the top half slate and rust, and the bottom, the brightest cobalt. A sharp-shinned hawk bore the screaming jay away, even though it was nearly as big as the hawk itself was. The jay, still flapping, met his end somewhere deep in the pines. I was left breath-less, leaning on my ski poles, mind racing, figuring out that I had just seen my first sharp-shinned hawk.

They still do that to me, those sharpies—make me drop my pencil or wooden spoon to race to the window to see what they are up to. Fierce of eye and prickly in temperament, they settle in a snag for a moment, assess prospects around the feeder, and either strike or take off. The moment passes as swiftly as it starts.

—*Julie Zickefoose*

The Dangers Posed by Cats

CATS, like accipiters, eat birds. While there are some cats that show little interest in killing backyard birds and others that derive more entertainment from chasing squirrels than birds, it remains a grim fact that many cats kill backyard birds on instinct.

Cats are extremely popular pets and many are allowed to roam freely through all the yards in the neighborhood. Many bird lovers like cats, too. Certainly anyone who can revel in the predatory nature of a hawk can appreciate the same nature in a cat. The sleek, athletic bodies and round, intelligent faces of felines make them hard not to love and respect.

Should we be concerned about this booming love affair with cats? You bet! Studies show that both feral and house cats have an enormous impact on bird populations.

The warm and cuddly feline on your lap may become a predator once it steps into your backyard. Songbirds such as this young robin may quickly fall victim to a cat's predatory instincts.

solutions

danger alarm call flurry of feathers disease prowling alert predator prey

What Can Be Done?

Whether the problem is feral cats or house cats killing or chasing away birds from backyard feeders, there are ways that cat owners themselves can lessen the impact of their pets on bird and small mammal populations, those hardest hit by hunting cats.

Though many cat lovers insist that cats must be allowed to roam freely for their own good, they may be putting their feline friends in peril. Pam Johnson, writing in *Cats* magazine, recommends keeping your cat inside to prolong its life. On the average, free-roaming cats live only 3 to 5 years, while indoors

> A 4-year study estimated that 1.2 million pet cats in Wisconsin kill 400 million animals each year, including at least 7.8 million birds.

they live 17 years or more because they are not exposed to the cars, dogs, or diseases that kill 1.5 million cats each year. Free-roaming cats may also develop wanderlust and may simply disappear, leaving behind grieving family members.

Some cat owners may be sympathetic to the predation problem and want to take action but can't quite take the step to keep their cats in-

Many cat lovers have taught their cats to enjoy exploring on a leash, thus giving the cats a taste of the outdoors without a taste of your birds.

doors permanently. Many cat lovers have trained their cats to walk on a leash, while others have built a pen or run, or even screened in their porch to give their cats access to the outside without access to the birds. Some cat owners have successfully kept their cats on leash-runs.

CAT CURFEWS

If you feel you must let your cat run free, attach one or more bells to its collar. Unfortunately, the tinkling bell probably won't alert birds to the approaching predator, but it will warn mammals. Even declawed cats are quite adept at knocking birds down from the air with only their paws.

Perhaps the best compromise is to control the time of day and season that you let your cat out. Birds are most active during early morning and early evening. Protect the more vulnerable baby birds by keeping your cat indoors as much as possible during the breeding season from May to August. If you feel it's absolutely necessary for your cat to roam the neighborhood, winter may be the best time because the snow and lack of foliage make it easier for birds to spot their stalkers.

Discouraging a neighbor's cat from killing birds in your yard may

An Indoor Cat "Habitat"

MAKE your home more comfortable for your cat and it won't need, or want, to go outside. Think like a cat when you create your cat-friendly indoor habitat—provide access to windows, toys, and pots of catnip to help meet physical needs, and give plenty of love and attention for emotional needs.

- Provide a good scratching post.
- Add a potted indoor tree near a sunny window.
- Play with your cat frequently with toys.

- Leave surprises for your cat, perhaps a toy in a paper bag.
- Grow indoor grass for your cat to nibble on; grass-growing "kits" are available at pet stores.

- Grow catnip and offer it to your cat as a treat.
- Provide a large litter box and clean it often.
- Shower your cat with loads of love and attention daily.

be one of the most difficult problems faced by suburban, backyard-habitat stewards. First, try the obvious things. Make sure your feeder is located far from any shrubs or other cover where a cat may lurk. Avoid ground feeding; stick to hanging tubes or hopper feeders. You might try spraying the cat with water from a hose whenever it appears. (Nifty motion-activated automatic sprayers are now available in catalogs.) Or, as a last resort, tell the owners that you may live-trap the animal and take it to a pound if it continues to roam free.

STEMMING THE TIDE

Every cat owner and cat lover can do something to keep the cat problem in check by helping to control the burgeoning cat population. Cat owners should have each cat neutered or spayed within 6 months of obtaining it. Like rats and rabbits, cats have an amazing ability to be prolific breeders.

The Humane Society of the United States calculated that one female and her offspring are capable of producing 420,000 cats in a span of just 7 years.

A Reflection on Window Kills

WHAT kills roughly 97 million birds each year in the United States? Windows. Glass is a ruthless killer. Potential victims are fit or unfit, common or rare, big or small. It matters little if a bird is male or female, young or old, breeder or migrant. Large windows reflect nature outside, and many birds may perceive a window as a natural flight corridor. South-facing windows are the biggest threat because glass panes tend to be larger.

WHY BIRDS HIT WINDOWS

Some researchers have speculated that birds may collide with windows because of inadequate depth perception, impaired vision due to smoke, blinding glare, mist, alcohol (birds can get drunk on fermented berries), or diverted attention. Distracted individuals chasing one another, prey escaping danger, predators pursuing prey, and birds becoming disoriented by adverse weather or lighting conditions are prime candidates for window collisions. Raptors cause panic in fleeing birds. Loud noises, passing cars, or blue jay arrivals at the feeder may startle a bird and cause it to fly into a window. Studies show that wherever birds and windows coexist, collisions occur—no matter what the conditions. The avian eye appears incapable of detecting clear or reflective glass.

IDENTIFYING DANGER

Observers tally more window strikes in favorable weather, and collisions occur far more often during morning hours. This makes sense when one remembers that birds forage for food more frequently in the mornings and during nice weather. There are fewer strikes in the summer, perhaps because fewer people feed birds in summertime, and the birds aren't drawn close to our windows.

Birds strike windows of single homes almost exclusively during daylight hours. Of those birds striking windows, roughly half die. Some are killed instantly, and some are knocked unconscious to die later from their injuries or from scavengers. Some are able to recover to fly off weakly, and the lucky ones are just startled but unaffected. Even the smallest flying birds can generate enough momentum to sustain serious injury.

The most common injuries reported are broken bills, internal injuries, and brain hemorrhages. Sometimes paralysis sets in. Contrary to popular belief, few birds die from a broken neck.

A GROWING PROBLEM

Were birds flying into windows always such a serious problem? Picture windows were a relatively uncommon thing until the end of World War II, and there was little reason to be concerned about their threat to birds, Daniel Klem Jr.

Birds and Windows

Q **A bird hit my window, and I can still see its imprint. How did that happen?**

A When a bird hits a window with any speed, powder and oils that occur naturally in its plumage are deposited on the glass. Powder down is a special kind of feather that degrades into slightly oily particles, helping the bird shed moisture and dirt from its feathers. The deposit left in a collision may be only a smudge, or a breath-takingly beautiful impression of the bird, with every feather in sharp detail. Species that have more powder down in their plumage, such as hawks and doves, are renowned for such detailed impressions.

Q **I have a hawk in my yard that keeps ambushing my feeder, and the panicked birds often hit my window. Could it be doing that on purpose?**

A Individual hawks, often sharp-shinned or Cooper's hawks, are capable of exploiting a large window to their advantage. The typical scenario: A hawk rushes at a feeder. The startled flock scatters, and one bird hits the window, is stunned, and falls. The hawk picks up this easy prey, and the pattern is set. You might try moving your feeders either farther from the window, or right up next to it, so that the birds have a chance to scatter, or, con-versely, not build up enough speed to hurt themselves by hitting the window.

Q **I rarely find dead birds out-side my windows. Could birds be hitting my window without my knowing it?**

A Possibly. Sometimes birds aren't killed immediately and fly a short distance away after striking a window, only to die later. A wandering cat may pick up any dead birds before you notice them. Generally, you can recognize a collision by noting the smudges, or feathers stuck to the glass. You can usually hear a loud thud if you're inside when the bird hits.

points out in his doctoral studies. In the postwar period, a building boom stimulated the rapid expansion of the sheet-glass industry, and large glass windows were incorporated into the designs of both new and re-modeled structures. Today it is not uncommon to find modern build-ings that are entirely surfaced with glass, says Klem.

Birds are more vulnerable to large (6 square feet/1.8 m or more), clear, or reflective windows at ground level and at heights above 9 feet (2.7 m). It doesn't matter whether the windows face north or south during migratory periods. Glass corridors, stairways, or rooms that create the illusion of a clear passageway are especially bad. Even glass telephone booths and the windows of stationary vehicles have claimed victims.

WHICH BIRDS ARE AFFECTED

Windows cause the death of a great variety of birds. American robins, northern cardinals, dark-eyed juncos, purple finches, and waxwings are some of the most frequent victims. Ground-dwelling birds like thrushes and sparrows also seem vulnerable. Water birds, soaring hawks, and species occu-pying unpopulated or sparsely pop-ulated desert, grassland, and forest areas are obviously less likely to encounter windows.

In a 1990 Project FeederWatch survey, 66 species were reported to have died by crashing into windows in the homes of participating bird watchers. The top 9 species, begin-ning with those with the highest mortality rates, were

- Pine siskins
- American goldfinches
- Dark-eyed juncos
- Northern cardinals
- Mourning doves
- House finches
- Purple finches
- Evening grosbeaks
- Black-capped chickadees

The members of this list are not surprising since they are common visitors to bird feeders in eastern North America. Three of the raptor species—sharp-shinned hawks, Cooper's hawks, and American kestrels—were among the remaining 57 species.

When a bird strikes a window, you may see slight smudges of powder and oil from a bird's plumage, but a violent collision could leave a full impression of the bird with every feature clearly identifiable.

WHAT WORKS, WHAT DOESN'T

How can you minimize bird collisions around your home? Interestingly, studies show that homes with the greatest frequency of window kills had many feeders and were located in rural settings. If this sounds like your little corner of the world, don't worry! You don't have to close down your backyard feeding operation; just use a little common sense.

Put white cloth drapes or sheer curtains on your windows during daylight hours to show birds there is no clear passage through the living room window. You might also try placing objects on the window, such as decals or vinyl window-clings. Cloth strips hung vertically about 4 inches (10 cm) apart are ideal. One cottage owner solved her problem by hanging vertical strips of silver Mylar on the outside of the window. In warmer weather, you

WINDOW KILLS at a glance

IF birds collide with the windows in your home, try these ideas to prevent or lessen the chance of an occurrence:

- Close curtains during the day.
- Hang Mylar strips outside the window.
- Break up the expanse of window with decals.
- Move feeders a few feet away from large windows.

could also tie a couple of silver party balloons near the problem window; even the slightest movement will put the balloons in motion to help a bird detect a barrier. Or, place black plastic netting (used primarily for protecting gardens) on frames mounted about a foot (30 cm) from the window to keep birds away.

If you have a lot of bird strikes at a particular window, close the drapes during the day and break up the reflection by hanging something in front of the window to warn the birds and keep them away.

PLACEMENT IS PARAMOUNT

If you place a feeder and other, similar bird attractants in front of a window, you definitely increase the hazard of window collisions. However, if you place feeders within just 1 foot (30 cm) of your window (or right on the window), birds won't be able to gain enough momentum to hurt themselves. If you have a serious collision problem, locating all of your bird attractants as far away from your windows as you possibly can may be your best solution.

Old Wives' Tales

BIRD watchers have tried everything to keep their windows from being death traps. You've probably heard half a dozen old wives' tales about birds successfully shunning windows because of this gizmo or that gadget. But the truth is that many of these sure-fire tricks don't really work.

Unsuccessful Diversions

- Blinking lights
- Falcon silhouettes
- Hanging plants
- Large eye patterns
- Owl decoys
- Wind chimes

There are falcon silhouettes and owl decoys commercially available that may appear to work—but not because the birds are frightened away by the specter of a potential predator. Birds very quickly acclimate to an inanimate object, no matter how scary it might look to us. Rather, these products may be keeping birds away because their presence breaks up the expanse of the window, no longer making the window look like a clear passageway to a bird in flight.

Since many window strikes are caused by panic flights, observe the normal escape patterns of the birds, then position your feeders, water features, and plantings to lead birds away from your windows and not into them.

A Tip on Windows

Many windows reflect the sky and the surrounding habitat, which may lure birds to their deaths. If you're building a new home or replacing windows, you may be able to install new windows at angles to reflect the ground instead of the surrounding habitat or sky to decrease window kills. (Of course, it's important to first check your local zoning and building requirements and the specifics of the manufacturer's warranty before installing windows at an angle.)

Certainly, in the greater scheme of things, designing and constructing fewer buildings with mirror sides would be a long-term advantage to bird populations.

Rat-a-Tat

You may not experience the horrifying sound of a bird hitting a window of your home, but you may hear a gentle tap, tap, tap every now and again. Upon closer inspection, you'll probably find a bird pecking repeatedly at your window. Birds tap at windows because they think they may be seeing another bird, possibly a rival; in essence, they are unable to recognize their own reflections.

Cardinals can be especially persistent reflection fighters, but any species, including bluebirds, buntings, and woodpeckers, may suddenly spot an imagined rival and take up the fight. Try to discourage the bird as soon as possible after the behavior starts. Apply clear plastic cling wrap over the window, and any adjoining windows, in the zone that the bird is fighting. Hanging an inflatable balloon next to the offending window may help frighten the bird away. In rare instances, a bird simply moves to another window, going around to every window in the house with single-minded obsession.

Serving Up Disease

FOR all the beauty and joy we associate with bird feeding, the pastime has an ugly side. Bird feeding has the potential to increase the occurrence of certain diseases among birds, and you need to take care not to help spread disease beyond what would occur naturally. In other words, your bird feeding should not make the situation worse. Discussing the subject of disease at bird feeders is difficult because very little research has been done on backyard birds. Most disease research with birds has focused primarily on game birds, poultry, and zoo stock. Nevertheless, some basic information about bird diseases applies equally well to bird feeders as to poultry pens.

DISEASE — THE SILENT DANGER

Six diseases may occur in bird species that typically use feeders. They each have their own symptoms and may be spread through

GARDENING UNDER FEEDERS

KEEPING the ground tidy under heavily used feeders may help keep diseases at bay but that doesn't have to mean another list of chores for you to do. If you design a garden around and under your feeder, you can sit back and enjoy both birds and plants at a single glance without lifting a finger.

First, add a 2- to 3-foot (60 to 90 cm)-diameter circle of shredded mulch or bark chips under the feeder to capture dropped seeds and empty hulls. This mulch can be raked up and removed periodically as it becomes soiled.

Second, think plants! Find out which plants are suited to the site. Consider adding groundcovers and low-growing plants outside of the mulched circle to keep the farther reaches tidy, too. And, most of all, be sure the plants you'd like to add to your feeder garden bear fruit or berries to welcome ground-feeding birds. Wild strawberry, low-growing blueberry, and evergreen bearberry are terrific choices!

TALES *from a* BIRDER

I miss the birds. Only 10 days ago I counted 85 red-polls on my hillside home's upper deck. I had barely put out new seed when they swarmed my feeders and wood railings.

What a raucous bunch they were! Chirping loudly, wings fluttering, these sparrow-sized birds with red-splotched heads and black bibs voraciously pecked at seeds and occasionally each other, apparently in territorial disputes over prime feeding spots.

Now as I look out my window on this February afternoon, no birds sit at my feeders. And when I open the door to the back deck, I hear no song. The birds are gone. I've sent them away because the redpoll disease, salmonellosis, has returned to Anchorage, Alaska.

I didn't want to stop feeding. I wanted to believe that the redpolls in my neighborhood would somehow avoid the salmonellosis plague. Then I began seeing sick redpolls. One bird was so sluggish I easily caught it. I took the redpoll to the Anchorage Bird Treatment and Learning Center, but all they could do was euthanize it. I found another redpoll shivering on the ground. I picked it up, and the bird just sat there, too weak to even flutter its wings. It died within an hour.

What to do? If I cleaned my feeders but didn't re-supply them, the birds might instead be drawn to the debris on the ground below. Or they might simply move to another, dirtier feeder.

I felt bad about the birds—and selfish. When I began feeding birds a few years ago, it seemed like a wonderful, harmless thing to do, a gift to both the birds and me. Now I was faced with a dilemma. I called a local ornithologist for advice. Shutting down feeders is not the same as removing a reliable food supply in the dead of winter, she assured me. The birds will adapt; they'll find other food. So I cleaned and disinfected my feeders and kept them empty. Then I called a neighboring couple who also feed birds to warn them about the epidemic.

Now I sit at my desk, looking out the window at empty feeders. And I wonder about this ritual of feeding birds, whether it's a good thing. I have no answers for the larger questions, but I believe I've done what's right, what's best for the birds, in these circumstances. Still, I greatly miss their bright energy, their songs, and the delight their visits bring.

—*Bill Sherwonit*

different means. If you start to notice diseased birds enjoying your feeder fare, stop your feeding program for a few weeks, and clean and disinfect the feeders. These are the most common diseases you'll see in backyard birds:

Salmonellosis (sal-muh-nel-LOW-sis) is a group of bacteria; different strains of the salmonella bacteria affect different species. (Typhoid fever is the most infamous of the salmonellosis diseases that afflict human beings, but birds do not transmit it to humans.) The most commonly detected disease at bird feeders, salmonellosis spreads among birds through active bacteria passed in bird droppings. The disease can be lethal by itself, but it also often leads to secondary problems that ultimately cause death.

Avian pox is quite common. It's a virus that causes wartlike growths around a bird's face, on the bend of its wing, and on its legs, feet, and toes. Birds can get the virus by direct contact with infected birds or by picking it up from contaminated feeders. Severely infected birds may not be able to perch, fly, or open their eyes wide enough to find food. This leaves them vulnerable to hypothermia, predation, and starvation. Grackles and blackbirds are frequent victims of avian pox.

Aspergillosis (as-per-jill-OH-sis) is a disease caused by a widely distributed, naturally occurring fungus, aspergillus. When birds inhale its spores, the fungus spreads throughout their lungs and air sacs, and they develop the disease. Weakened birds easily develop bronchitis or pneumonia—two diseases that are nearly always fatal.

Trichomoniasis (trick-oh-mo-NYE-uh-sis) is caused by protozoans that are pathogenic parasites and is characterized by sores in a bird's throat. The sick bird tries to eat but finds it cannot swallow, so it drops the now-contaminated food back on the feeder where other birds inevitably eat it. Infected birds usually starve to death. (Blue jays are often afflicted with gapeworms, which cause similar symptoms.)

Coccidiosis (cock-sid-ee-OH-sis) is also caused by protozoans. Coccidia parasites live in birds'

danger alarm call flurry of feathers disease prowling alert predator prey

intestines and are passed in droppings. Dehydration follows, and the weakened birds succumb to starvation or predators. (Coccidiosis has not been proven to spread at feeders.)

House finch disease, also called conjunctivitis, causes red, swollen, crusty eyes in affected birds. The bacterium, *Mycoplasma gallisepticum*, appears to have spread to goldfinches as well. Sick birds sit quietly at feeders or baths, too weak to eat or protect themselves, and many die from exposure, starvation, or predation.

To report sick birds and learn more about diseases, call the National Wildlife Health Center. (See "Resources and Supplies" on page 232.)

HEADING OFF DISEASE

Just because you feed birds does not automatically mean you're spreading bird diseases, but just because you don't find dead birds doesn't mean you have no disease problem at your feeder.

Here's how to minimize the chances of spreading disease at your feeding station:

Be alert for the first signs of ill birds at your feeders. A sick bird will usually puff up its feathers to help retain heat. It may huddle low with half-closed eyes and be lethargic.

1 Provide enough feeder space so that birds do not have to crowd together to feed. Select the larger feeders and use more than one feeder. Multiple feeders will also allow you to separate your food types to keep larger birds from bullying the smaller ones. Birds shouldn't have to touch each other to eat at your feeders.

2 Don't use feeders that have sharp points or edges. Home-made feeders fashioned of scrap materials can be especially hazardous. Chicken wire, popular for fencing out cats and squirrels, and welded wire, popular for suet feeders, can have many exposed sharp ends. They can nick, cut, and scratch birds' feet and toes. The sores that result then allow viruses and bacteria to enter.

3 Regularly clean and disinfect your feeders. Just endlessly re-filling feeders is an easy but care-less habit. Each time before you refill, you should remove the debris with a stiff-bristled brush or a hard spray from a hose. Bacteria and fungi can thrive in the debris that cake up in corners and crevices. At

FIGHTING DISEASE
at a glance

THESE five steps will help you fight disease at your feeders:

- Provide plenty of feeders.
- Remove feeders with sharp edges.
- Clean feeders regularly.
- Keep the feed clean and dry.
- Clean up under feeder.

least once a month your feeder should be completely immersed in a warm solution of 1 part liquid chlorine bleach added to 9 parts of water. Let it soak for 2 to 3 min-utes, then rinse. Allow all parts of the feeder to dry thoroughly before reassembling and hanging it. If sick or dead birds show up at your feeder, disinfect weekly.

4 Keep your feed clean. You'll achieve nothing by putting contaminated feed into a clean feeder. Use containers with lids

that seal tightly to store food away from water and rodents. Aspergillus grows on damp seed, so discard any seed with a musty odor or visible signs of fungal growth. Mice and squirrels can carry germs internally and on their feet and fur. If they get into seed, they can contaminate the entire batch with their droppings or just by burrowing around in it. If you must discard a batch of seed, be sure to disinfect the container and the scoop the same way you would a feeder.

5 Clean up the spilled feed, bird droppings, and the other debris that accumulate beneath your feeders. Aspergillus and salmonella thrive in such waste material. A shovel and small broom will work well to scoop up the mess, but a workshop-type vacuum sweeper will work even better. Clean the ground under the feeder at the same time that you clean and disinfect your feeder. When you are finished with everything, dip the broom and shovel or vacuum parts

before discarding the chlorine solution, and of course be sure to thoroughly wash your hands with hot, soapy water when you're all done.

Unfortunately, you can follow all these precautions and still have sick birds if your bird-feeding neighbors do not participate in this "bird-feeding hygiene." Do not mistakenly assume disease only involves an individual site; birds do move among feeders, so disease involves an entire feeding community.

IT'S UP TO YOU

If you feed wild birds, you are obligated to practice ethical stewardship. Don't wait for someone else to pressure you into more thoughtful bird feeding. You'll find, like many others who've been convinced to clean up their bird-feeding program, that you enjoy feeding the birds more when you know you're doing it right. Do the right thing on your own, and set the example for your neighbors to follow. Then evangelize!

7
BOXES
FOR BIRDS

Addressing the Housing Shortage

housing

EVEN THE MOST DIVERSE backyard habitat, with various kinds of trees, shrubs, flowers, and water features, may lack one valuable commodity—nesting cavities. By adding a variety of birdhouses, you can encourage several species not only to dine at your flowers and feeders but also to raise their young outside your window. There's stiff competition for suitable nest sites in most areas. You can actually boost populations of species that have limited nesting sites by providing well-maintained birdhouses that are safe from predators.

Who Nests in Cavities?

APPROXIMATELY 85 North American species nest exclusively in cavities. A smaller segment of this set will nest in backyard habitats, and an even smaller number will use artificial nest boxes and birdhouses. Bluebirds, swallows, wrens, and woodland songbirds, such as chickadees and titmice, will take up residence in a well-placed, well-protected birdhouse. Flickers, great crested flycatchers, purple martins, wood ducks, hooded mergansers, American kestrels, screech owls, and barn owls need specially designed boxes.

Not every backyard will attract all of these cavity nesters. If your backyard habitat is heavily planted with trees, shrubs, and hedges, or is adjacent to woodland, you may want to add nest boxes designed to host wrens, chickadees, titmice, and nuthatches. If you have large expanses of open, grassy habitat nearby, such as pastures, hay fields, agricultural land, public parks, or even golf courses, you have a very good chance of attracting the likes of bluebirds, tree swallows, or violet-green swallows.

THE HANDY WOODPECKER

Many North American cavity nesters depend on woodpeckers to make their homes, especially when they don't have houses provided for them by bird enthusiasts. These avian carpenters chisel fresh homes for nesting in spring and for roosting in fall, and when they move on, other birds move in. Downy woodpeckers are found all across North America, and they make a neat 1½-inch (4 cm)-diameter entry hole. A hole of this size lets small birds like wrens, chickadees, titmice, nuthatches, and bluebirds in, while excluding bigger birds like the European starling, that many birders don't consider a desirable tenant. It's no accident that the 1½-inch (4 cm) diameter is a "magic" hole size for bird-nest boxes—the downy woodpecker set the standard!

The bigger woodpeckers, such as flickers, make a 2-inch (5 cm)-diameter hole that's just right for great crested flycatchers. The king of woodpeckers, the crow-sized pileated woodpecker, makes a generous excavation that a kestrel or even a wood duck can fit into!

The great crested flycatcher takes advantage of a deserted flicker cavity to raise its young in relative safety and comfort. It will often trail a snakeskin out of the hole, perhaps to deter other occupants.

housing

nest cavities protection competition open fields woodland roosting insulation

BUILDING THE PERFECT BOX

WHETHER you're making your own nesting boxes or purchasing them, remember that the dimensions of the box, both inside and out, the size of the entry hole, and the placement of the box will determine who your tenants will be. Use this handy chart to help you attract the birds you want flitting around your backyard.

KEY

⌂ Length and width of box in inches (cm)
▮ Height of box in inches (cm)
◖ Entrance-hole diameter in inches (cm)
▯ Box placement height in feet (m)
❈ Habitats for box placement

CHICKADEE
⌂ 4 × 4 (10 × 10)
▮ 9–12 (23–30)
◖ 1⅛–1½ (2.8–4)
▯ 5–15 (1.5–4.5)
❈ Open woods and edges

A 1⅛-inch (2.8 cm) hole excludes all other birds except house sparrows.

LUCY'S WARBLER, PROTHONOTARY WARBLER
⌂ 4 × 4 (10 × 10)
▮ 12 (30)
◖ 1¼ (3.1)
▯ 5–12 (1.5–3.6)
❈ Wooded swamps

Mount box on a metal pole above open water.

TITMICE, WHITE-BREASTED NUTHATCH
⌂ 4 × 4 (10 × 10)
▮ 12 (30)
◖ 1½ (4)
▯ 5–12 (1.5–3.6)
❈ Wooded areas and edge habitat

HOUSE WREN
⌂ 4 × 4 (10 × 10)
▮ 9–12 (23–30)
◖ 1–1½ (2.5–4)
▯ 5–10 (1.5–3)
❈ Old fields and thickets

Carolina wrens need 1½-inch (4 cm) hole, and Bewick's wrens 1¼-inch (3.1 cm) hole.

EASTERN BLUEBIRD
⌂ 4 × 4 (10 × 10)
▮ 12 (30)
◖ 1½ (4)
▯ 5–6 (1.5–1.8)
❈ Open land with scattered trees

WESTERN BLUEBIRD
⌂ 5 × 5 (13 × 13)
▮ 12 (30)
◖ 1½–1⁹⁄₁₆ (4)
▯ 5–6 (1.5–1.8)
❈ Open land with scattered trees

MOUNTAIN BLUEBIRD
⌂ 5 × 5 (13 × 13)
▮ 12 (30)
◖ 1⁹⁄₁₆ (4)
▯ 5–6 (1.5–1.8)
❈ Open meadows above 5000 feet (1500 m)

TREE SWALLOW
⌂ 5 × 5 (13 × 13)
▮ 10–12 (25–30)
◖ 1½ (4)
▯ 5–10 (1.5–3)
❈ Open land near water

Place exit ladder on inside of front of box.

VIOLET-GREEN SWALLOW
⌂ 5 × 5 (13 × 13)
▮ 10–12 (25–30)
◖ 1½ (4)
▯ 5–10 (1.5–3)
❈ Pastures, fields, parks

PURPLE MARTIN
- 6 × 6 (15 × 15)
- 6 (15)
- 2⅛ (5.3)
- 15–25 (4.5–7.5)
- Open country near water

Position entrance hole 1 inch (2.8 cm) above the floor.

GREAT CRESTED FLYCATCHER
- 6 × 6 (15 × 15)
- 12 (30)
- 1¾–2 (4.5–5)
- 6–20 (1.8–6)
- Open woods and edges

Use a 1⁹/₁₆-inch (4 cm) hole if starlings are a problem.

ASH-THROATED FLYCATCHER
- 6 × 6 (15 × 15)
- 12 (30)
- 1¾–2 (4.5–5)
- 6–20 (1.8–6)
- Open, semi-arid country

NORTHERN FLICKER
- 7 × 7 (18 × 18)
- 16–24 (40–60)
- 2½ (6.5)
- 10–20 (3–6)
- Farmland and open country

WOOD DUCK
- 12 × 12 (30 × 30)
- 24 (60)
- 3 × 4 (7.5 × 10)
- 5–20 (1.5–6)
- Wooded swamps

Hole is a horizontally oriented oval.

HOODED MERGANSER
- 12 × 12 (30 × 30)
- 24 (60)
- 3 × 4 (7.5 × 10)
- 5–30 (1.5 9)
- Wooded swamps

SCREECH-OWLS
- 8 × 8 (20 × 20)
- 18 (45)
- 3 (8)
- 8–30 (2.4–9)
- Farmland, orchards, woods

BARN OWL
- 12 × 36 (30 × 90)
- 16 (40)
- 6 × 7 (15 × 18)
- 15–30 (4.5–9)
- Open farmland and marshes

Hole should be 4 inches (10 cm) above floor.

AMERICAN KESTREL
- 9 × 9 (23 × 23)
- 16–30 (40–45)
- 3 (8)
- 12–30 (3.6–9)
- Farmland

FOR ALL NEST BOXES: The height listed above refers to the inside back panel. Always place baffles below nest boxes. Sizes above are the minimum for each species. Handmade next boxes should have walls that are ¾ inch (2 cm) or more thick to provide adequate insulation against cold and heat.

FOR WREN BOXES: Larger, oblong holes make it easier to get twigs into box.

FOR SWALLOW BOXES: Carve grooves or place hardware cloth on inside front of box.

FOR PURPLE MARTINS: Size listed here is for one compartment in a multi-unit martin house.

FOR WOODPECKER BOXES: Pack cavity full with wood chips and sawdust.

Keeping It Safe

BIRDS usually have a choice of where to nest, but artificial housing is a powerful attractant, especially where natural cavities are scarce. As a landlord, you owe it to your tenants to make sure their digs are well located, clean, and, most importantly, safe. While natural cavities are by their nature well hidden, nest boxes are fairly conspicuous, and predators are quick to key in to this fact. Probably the worst predator of nest boxes is the raccoon, closely followed by climbing snakes such as black rat and bull snakes. House cats, opossums, squirrels, chipmunks, and mice can all wreak havoc in nest boxes, eating eggs, young, and even adult birds. All of these predators can be stopped cold by properly mounting your box.

MOUNTING THE BOX

Though it's easy to nail a nest box on a tree or fence post, don't succumb to the temptation! Tree- or post-mounted boxes are the most vulnerable to climbing predators. An 8-foot (2.4 m) length of galvanized pipe with a ¾-inch (2 cm) inside diameter will give you the most latitude in siting and

A NATURALLY GOOD NEST BOX

LOOK at what nature provides to see what's best for cavity-nesting birds. The neat homes chiseled out by woodpeckers illustrate the characteristics of a good nesting cavity. Follow the three rules for great boxes, and you'll be rewarded with brood after brood of nesting birds.

Nest boxes should be protected from predators. Woodpecker cavities are inconspicuous, unlike many manmade boxes. Their concealed nature helps protect them from marauding raccoons, cats, and opossums. You should use baffles when building birdhouses to protect birds from climbing predators.

Nest boxes should be well insulated. A typical woodpecker cavity in a tree is made 5 inches (13 cm) or greater in thickness, giving the cavity thick walls that

mounting the box. (Galvanized pipe is available at hardware stores.) Sink the pipe 1 or more feet (30 cm) in the ground, and mount the box by screwing pipe flanges into its back.

Raccoons are among the most avid predators of bird-nest boxes.

BAFFLING PREDATORS

A baffle is a guard made of plastic or metal that is mounted below the box to keep animals from climbing up to raid it. As bird feeding gains popularity, more baffles are becoming available commercially, but most are meant to discourage squirrels and aren't up to the task of deterring raccoons and snakes. And many of the baffles being sold simply don't work at all, so choose carefully when buying one. Of all baffle designs, the stovepipe, or tubular, baffle is the most effective. It uses motion to deter invaders, wobbling when a predator tries to climb.

keep cold out and heat in. This helps keep eggs and young birds from becoming chilled in early spring and overheated on the hottest summer days. Handmade nest boxes should have walls that are ³⁄₄ inch (2 cm) or more thick to provide adequate insulation against cold and heat.

Nest boxes should be weatherproof. Natural cavities are often on the underside of a limb, situated near the branch collar where the limb joins the trunk, or on the lee side of a tree where they are protected from rain. Nest boxes are best when made of wood that naturally sheds water, such as cedar or redwood, or when treated on the outside with waterproof stain or paint. Renew the stain or paint as needed. (Note: Don't use pressure-treated wood because the chemicals used to make it water resistant may leach from it and harm birds.)

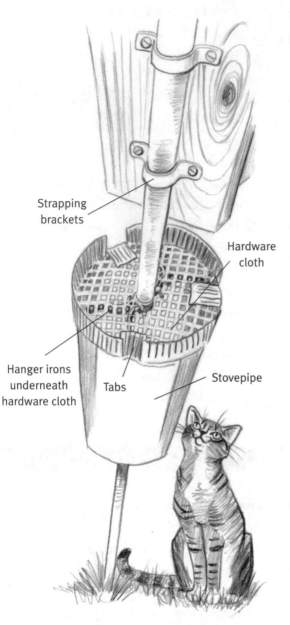

Strapping
brackets

Hardware
cloth

Hanger irons
underneath
hardware cloth

Tabs

Stovepipe

Make housing safe for tenants by
installing baffles on nest-box poles
to frustrate would-be predators. The
baffle wobbles on the pole, preventing
a predator from reaching the box.

To make a tubular baffle, you'll
need a 6-inch (15 cm) circle of
½-inch (1.25 cm)-mesh hardware
cloth, a 6 × 24-inch (15 × 60 cm)-
galvanized stovepipe, a galvanized
pipe with a ¾-inch (2 cm) inside
diameter for the box mounting
pole, a hanger iron in two 7-inch
(18 cm) strips, machine screws
with nuts, duct tape, and strapping
brackets and weatherproof screws
to mount the nest box to the pole.

Place the hardware cloth over
the end of the stovepipe, bending
the edges down so that it will fit
snugly into the pipe, about 1 inch
(2.5 cm) down from the top. Be
sure to close any gaps between the
hardware cloth and the stovepipe
to thwart snakes.

Use tin snips to cut three tabs in
the top of the stovepipe. Bend the
tabs over the hardware cloth. Cut a
small hole in the middle of the cloth
so the assembly can slip over the
pole. Set the baffle aside.

Using machine screws and nuts,
bolt the two strips of hanger iron
securely on either side of the
mounting pole about 3 inches (8
cm) below where you'll place the
nest box; bend the hanger irons to
support the hardware cloth. Wrap

duct tape around the pole to hold the hanger irons in place. Slip the baffle over the hanger irons (it should wobble a little so that it discourages climbing predators). Mount the nest box on the pole, using the strapping brackets and weatherproof screws.

SITING THE BOX

If at all possible, put some of your birdhouses where you can see them easily from a window or a porch swing, and, install several boxes around your property to encourage different birds to move in. For bluebirds and swallows, put the boxes as far from shrubs and trees as possible. Woodland songbirds, such as chickadees and titmice, prefer their boxes close to the cover of the woods. When you put boxes near trees, be sure that no branches hang over the box, allowing a predator to leap onto the box from above.

For most songbirds, mounting the box at eye level is fine. You'll be able to peek in easily.

Put your boxes up at any time of year. In the fall and winter, some birds may use them for roosting.

Fall-mounted boxes will be in place for birds prospecting for nest sites in late winter and early spring.

BOX MONITORING

Yes, it is okay to check on the nesting birds! If you put up a box and never open it, you'll miss out on a lot of interesting observations. The birds may even benefit if you check their nest regularly. The old wives' tale about birds deserting their nests if you touch them is a myth. Birds are so strongly bonded to their eggs and young that they will put up with a surprising amount of helpful intervention.

There are certain times when you should keep your distance, though. Stay clear of the box while eggs are being laid and incubated when adult birds are more likely to desert the nest. Make your checks in late morning or early afternoon. Most eggs are laid in early morning, and it's best not to disturb the female then. Curtail box checks when the nestlings are about 12 days old. You'll be able to tell because they'll be well feathered and bright eyed. Checking the box after that may result in premature fledging

housing

nest cavities protection competition open fields woodland roosting insulation

MONITORING BIRDHOUSES
at a glance

FOLLOW these guidelines when monitoring birdhouses to disturb your tenants as little as possible:

■ Check boxes in late morning or early afternoon only.

■ Limit peeking to just a few seconds of time.

■ Halt checks when nestlings are about 12 days old.

■ Replace soiled or wet nests with fresh nests of dry grass.

(frightening the nestlings into leaving the box before they're ready to fly). Keep your peeks brief; a few seconds is all you'll need to note the nest contents.

Don't monitor boxes unless you've equipped them with a predator baffle. An unprotected box is more vulnerable to attack when you check it regularly because predators will follow human-scent trails out of curiosity. If you intend to monitor boxes regularly, it's also important to purchase or build bird boxes that open easily, with a front or side panel that swings open and is simple to re-fasten. Avoid top-opening boxes; they're hard to check and clean.

You may want to carry a light-weight plastic bag full of fresh, dried grasses with you when you check boxes. If you discover a nest that is wet, dirty, or overrun with parasites, remove the nest and re-place the nestlings in a fresh nest of your own making. Wind the grass tightly and form a cup with your thumbs, packing it down firmly before replacing the young birds.

ONE FOR THE BOOKS

Plan to check your box once or twice weekly while it's in use. As you watch the activity around the nest box, keep a written record to give you a good idea of what's going on inside. Record your observa-tions on type and amount of nesting material, number of eggs, number of hatchlings, and age of the young birds at fledging (the moment of leaving the nest). Take note of any food items you see the parents bringing to the young. It's worth recording anything that piques your interest. Keep a separate page for each box if you're lucky enough to have residents in more than one, and be sure to date each entry.

The great crested flycatcher often trails a snakeskin out of the entrance to its nesting cavity. This is thought to deter predators and competitors that might otherwise enter.

WINTERIZING YOUR BOXES

As autumn arrives and the weather starts to sharpen, it's a good idea to make sure that your boxes are ready for winter. Apply a new coat of stain or sealant on a mild, sunny day. (If you do this without taking the box down, wear latex gloves to avoid sealing your hands at the same time.) Use flexible, weather-strip putty to plug the ventilation holes at the top or sides of the box to make it more snug against winter winds. (Make a note on next year's calendar to remove this in the spring.) You can add pine straw, dried grasses, or wood shavings to the box for extra winter comfort and insulation. You may be lucky enough to see bluebirds, wrens, titmice, chickadees, nuthatches, or woodpeckers entering the box around dusk, or find the droppings, feathers, or regurgitated seeds that indicate you've got a tenant roosting in your winter-ready nest box.

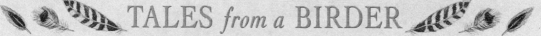

TALES *from a* BIRDER

WE clean out our nest boxes each fall and replace the old, messy nests with fresh, clean, dried grasses that we form into a loose cup and place in the bottom of the box. Next, we use the flexible putty strips that are made for window insulation to help block off the large ventilation holes at the top of the nest boxes. These two winterizing steps help to convert our nest boxes into cozy winter-roosting sites.

—*Julie Zickefoose*

housing

COMPETITORS IN THE NEST BOX

Unfortunately, not all of the birds that will nest in boxes *should* nest in boxes. Two birds are particularly troublesome: the European starling and the house sparrow. House sparrows can easily fit into a 1½-inch (4 cm) hole, and they are destructive pests, killing incubating bluebirds and swallows on the nest, and throwing out eggs and young birds as they usurp the nest box. Starlings are less bothersome because they cannot enter boxes with holes smaller than 1¾ inches (4.5 cm), but they can still cause plenty of trouble. They mainly plague woodpecker and martin houses, leaving the smaller birds alone to nest unmolested.

Both starlings and house sparrows should be evicted the moment they begin to build a nest in your

House sparrow

House wren

A few of your backyard visitors may not be polite guests. House sparrows, house wrens, and European starlings may invade nest boxes and force out less aggressive species.

box. But look before you leap and be sure you are throwing out an unwanted tenant and not a bluebird or swallow! One quick way to tell whether you have desirable tenants or not is by identifying the nesting materials—starlings and house sparrows favor coarse straw and trash for their nests. If that's what you see, monitor the box to confirm you have starlings or house sparrows, then remove the nest.

House wrens are stiff competitors for nest sites. Their tight nests are composed of small, interlaced twigs, lined with grasses and feathers. Unlike the starling and house sparrow, house wrens are native birds protected by law. If house wrens take over your nest box, you must leave them undisturbed and put up another box as far out in the open as possible for other tenants.

European starling

Nesting Birds

Q **I thought a pair of bluebirds was going to move into my nest box, but they disappeared! What happened?**

A You may still have tenants; they're just being sneaky. After the initial flurry of courtship, bluebirds often make themselves scarce, with the female building the nest surreptitiously. During the egg-laying period, you may hardly see the birds; the female lays a single egg around dawn, then leaves until the next sunrise. Even during incubation, which takes 12 to 14 days, you won't see much activity. Not until the young have hatched will you see birds visiting the nest with any frequency.

Q **I opened my nest box just to a peek at the young birds, but they jumped out and landed on the ground! What did I do wrong?**

A After nestlings are well feathered, they are vulnerable to premature fledging should the box be opened. They can't fly yet, but their parents' alarm calls urge them to flee. You should stop checking the nest after the young are 12 days old. Should it happen again, replace the young birds in the box and temporarily plug the hole with a cloth (for perhaps 10 minutes) until the birds have settled down.

Q **I checked a nest box that had eggs in it just the day before, and there was nothing. What might have happened?**

A If your box doesn't have a baffle, a snake may have slipped in and eaten the eggs, without disturbing the nest. Another possible culprit is a house wren; however, you'll usually find bits of eggshell on the ground when a wren is to blame. Should you find an unbaffled box with the nesting material pulled out of the hole, and remains of eggs or birds on the ground, assume a raccoon or house cat paid your nest box a visit.

Tiny Tenants: Bugged in the Box

JUST like birds, insects are only too happy to find a warm, dry place to raise their young. Insects in birdhouses, though, are bothersome to the tenants. Wasps and bees often hang their papery nests from the ceiling of boxes and can easily prevent birds from entering or using the box. Remove their nests with a long, stout stick. And never use pesticides in or around a nesting box because birds are highly sensitive to such toxins.

Ants can also be a problem for cavity nesters. Should ants swarm into the nest, treat the pole with a thick coating of petroleum jelly, solid vegetable shortening, or axle grease, just under the box where the birds won't come in contact with it but where it will stop ants from reaching the box.

Blowflies parasitize all box-nesting species by laying their eggs in the nest lining. Their maggotlike larvae live in the nesting material, emerging at night to suck the blood of vulnerable young birds, then retreating back into the nesting material during the day. Though they are not usually fatal to the young, heavy infestations can slow their development or hasten their death in adverse weather conditions.

If you notice wasps buzzing around a nest box, they've probably moved in and forced out bird guests. Remove the papery wasp nest from the ceiling of the box with a long stick at dusk when wasps are likely to be less active.

Mites and lice also feed on the blood, skin, and feathers of young birds, and heavy infestations can make a nest look as if it's covered by moving gray felt.

Taking Action

If you notice large numbers of blowflies, mites, or lice in your boxes, it's time for cleaning. Follow these steps to get the job done quickly and efficiently:

■ Remove the young to a temporary container, such as an ice-cream tub or small bucket.

■ Remove the infested nest.

■ Sweep the box clean.

■ Fashion a new nest from clean, dry grasses, formed into a cup and packed firmly in the bottom of the box.

■ Replace the young carefully.

Good Nest Keeping

Some controversy surrounds whether or not a landlord should clean out the nest box between broods. Birds often raise two or more sets of young in a season in the same box. Some studies have shown that birds are more likely to nest in a box that contains the remnants of an old nest. By the time a brood of bluebirds, chickadees, titmice, or swallows have fledged from a nest, however, it is usually smashed flat and heavily soiled, and may be teeming with parasites. Filthy or parasite-ridden nests are no asset to birds and should be removed to clear the slate for the next brood. Be sure to do a thorough cleaning of the nest box, too, including the roof, front, and opening, in order to give the next inhabitants a fresh start.

8

HABITATS
THROUGH THE
SEASONS

Continent-Wide Observations

migration snow monsoon humidity desert mountains prairie frost ecoregion

WHO BETTER TO SHARE information about bird gardening than those who are successful at it? These eight gardeners have turned their backyards into havens for birds in very diverse ecoregions. This ecoregions map reflects the natural boundaries of birds. Climate and habitat play the biggest role in determining what species live in a given region. Wherever you live and garden and no matter which birds frequent your backyard, you'll find the experience of sharing your plot of earth with birds rewarding and joyous.

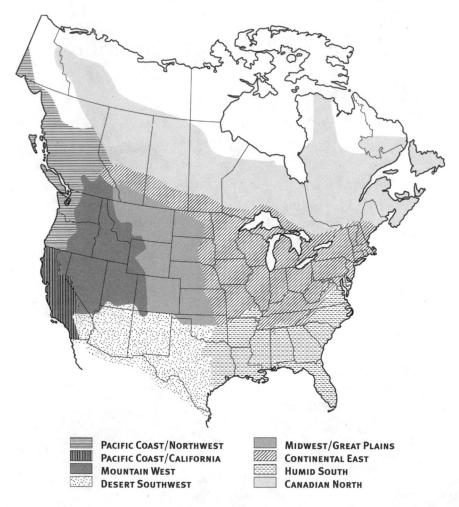

PACIFIC COAST/NORTHWEST
PACIFIC COAST/CALIFORNIA
MOUNTAIN WEST
DESERT SOUTHWEST

MIDWEST/GREAT PLAINS
CONTINENTAL EAST
HUMID SOUTH
CANADIAN NORTH

PACIFIC COAST/NORTHWEST

More Than Rain

Though there is plenty of rain in the Northwest much of the time, there are glorious days in the garden, too. Linda Beutler tells you how to work with the seasonal changes and how to give your backyard birds what they need.

SPOTLIGHT ON A BIRD GARDENER

LINDA BEUTLER

Linda Beutler is a native Oregonian and lifelong birder. She hails from a family of gardeners and is herself a garden writer and instructor.

It's easy to make jokes about the weather in the Pacific Northwest, such as: "How do you know when it's summer in Oregon?" Answer: "Easy. The rain warms up." We do have wonderful summers; they just start later and linger longer than most people might expect.

WINTER DAYS

The coldest months in the Northwest are January, February, and March. Extended cold is unusual, though, and seemingly endless strings of gray, rainy days are the norm. Gardening for winter interest has become a hot topic. Winter-blooming plants are what gardeners are adding to their landscapes these days—plants such as daphnes and witch hazels; fruit-bearing, deciduous shrubs, such as barberries, beautyberry, and native roses; and conifers with gold or silver foliage, such as hemlocks, deodar cedars, and hinoki cypress. Crabapples and other small trees that hang onto their fruit are popular because they give the gardener something to look at when flowers of spring seem a long way off.

BIRDS OF WINTER

The benefits of all of this "birdscaping" are many. Fruit-bearing shrubs and trees bring winter food into the garden, and conifers make great cover for the small birds. Common birds in urban winter gardens include scrub and Steller's jays, black-capped chickadees, Oregon juncos, numerous kinds of sparrows and finches, downy woodpeckers and northern flickers, and spotted towhees.

Varied thrushes, known locally as Alaskan robins, fly in when American robins fly south. Anna's hummingbirds will stay in an area if there is a ready food source, like an artificial feeder, but this puts the burden on the bird watcher to see that the nectar is kept fresh and that the feeder doesn't freeze. Otherwise, Anna's hummingbirds will migrate south into California and west to milder coastal areas once natural food sources have stopped blooming and artificial nectar feeders have been removed.

SEGUE TO SPRING

There's no getting around the fact that spring is wet in the Northwest. As temperatures rise, native rhododendrons, currants, and roses draw birds from their winter haunts. Native roses such as *Rosa*

woodsii, R. gymnocarpa, and *R. nutkana* provide favored cover all year long. Flocks of bushtits, loosely mixed with both kinglet species (ruby-crowned and golden-crowned), twitter through the garden in waves, feeding on the aphids and larvae they find on hybrid roses and other ornamentals. Evening grosbeaks pass through the area in April and May to follow tree-seed production, and goldfinches become bright yellow again before leaving urban feeders for rural nesting areas. Both red- and white-flowering currants will lure Anna's hummingbirds back into your garden in March.

Birds are your natural pest-control officers. In the Northwest, bushtits and kinglets devour the larvae and aphids that often devour your roses.

SUMMER SIMMERS

A sure sign of summer in the Pacific Northwest are the violet-green swallows that soar high over open green spaces. Gardeners prize these violet-green and tree swallows as mosquito eaters *extraordinaire*. Joining them near wetlands are red-winged blackbirds that will stop for sunflower seeds at urban feeders before switching over to an insect-based diet at nesting time.

Summer is a time of plenty if you garden for birds in this eco-region. To make your experience more successful, look to the following ideas for guidance.

Use Water Wisely. Gardeners should provide water sources for birds from July through September. The abundance of water during the winter makes rationing rare come summer, but many gardeners try to keep the need for irrigation at a minimum when adding plants to their landscape. By removing lawns of turf grass and mixing in more native plants to garden beds and borders, you'll reduce your watering duties.

Temperatures do occasionally top 100°F (38°C); and there's no doubt that if there's an extended period of heat, your native plants will whine excessively! It is not uncommon to be without measurable rain for 30 to 40 days running in the Northwest, with highs above 80°F (27°C) the whole time. The most successful plants in your backyard will be those that can tolerate warm, dry summer weather.

Invite Hummers. Salvias (ornamental sages) and hardy fuchsias are at the peak of bloom in summer. You're sure to see resident and migrant hummingbirds visiting them often. Hummingbirds are also drawn to agapanthus, fragrant lamb's-ears (*Stachys albotomentosum*), and our native snowberry (*Symphoricarpos albus* var. *laevigatus*). The snowberry has tiny, white, bell-shaped flowers that must bear lots of nectar, for both Anna's and rufous hummingbirds are wild for these seemingly inconsequential flowers.

Hummers also frequent the many different forms of the summer-blooming bulb, crocosmia. A bright red cultivar, known as 'Lucifer', is sure to cause squeaky squabbles among your hummers, and they will dive-bomb you fearlessly if you approach their plants. *Crocosmia ma-sonorum*, which is orange, has been widely naturalized along the populated areas of the Oregon and Washington coast, giving hummingbirds there a long season of nectar.

Fill Your Feeders. Western tanagers are welcome summer visitors to suburban and rural seed feeders. Several of the warblers, including Townsend's and Wilson's, will visit suet feeders during their warm-weather stay. (Aside from eating from a feeder, a Townsend's warbler will even dig in your lawn for grubs unless it is run off by a territorial northern flicker.)

FADE TO FALL

The tanagers and warblers are the first birds to disappear from autumn feeders, but the sparrows take over, feeding aggressively as the days shorten. Really fine weather often continues well into October, when the prairie native brown-eyed Susan (*Rudbeckia triloba*) is brightening the garden, along with late-blooming salvias, such as *Salvia guaranitica*, which has vivid blue florets that hummingbirds love.

Cedar waxwings will arrive to start stealing berries from hollies and hips from roses. Both waxwings and the remaining robins eat the brilliantly colored berries of mountain ash, and fruit-loving house finches will make quick work of unpicked apples.

NATURAL BALANCE

Garden fads come and go, with hot plants and new garden plans flowing in and out of fashion like the tide. In the horticulturally active Pacific Northwest, this is particularly true. The trend to create gardens that reflect our dramatic environment will also invite birds in to assist in maintaining an organic balance.

Both public and private gardens continue to grow increasingly aware of this natural partnership. Local governments and conservation organizations are now acknowledging gardens designed to entice wildlife, bestowing awards and organizing tours of gardens where habitat creation thrives hand in hand with the ornamental function of gardening.

PACIFIC COAST/CALIFORNIA

Always in Season

Along the Northern California coastline, Amy Stewart has created a bird haven in her backyard. Her California-specific gardening ideas will inspire you to bask in the glory of colorful gardens and enchanting birds.

SPOTLIGHT ON A BIRD GARDENER
AMY STEWART

A writer and gardener living in Eureka, California, Amy Stewart is the author of *From the Ground Up: The Story of a First Garden.*

From great egrets standing majestically in a coastal marsh to spotted owls roosting in an old-growth redwood forest to mockingbirds building a nest in a backyard citrus tree, California's bird population is as diverse as the geography of the state itself. From my window, I see Anna's hummingbirds visiting late-blooming salvia, double-crested cormorants perching in a eucalyptus tree across the street, and a yellow-rumped warbler paying a visit to my neighbor's feeder. The good news for California gardeners is that no matter where you live, your garden can play host to a variety of year-round and migratory birds.

CALIFORNIA WINTER

Resist the temptation to tidy up your yard too much during the winter. Each December, I prune the roses, remove dead tree limbs, and trim back the salvia to encourage new growth, but otherwise, I leave things alone. I put all my cuttings into a rather untidy pile in the far corner of my garden.

I put my Christmas wreaths and swags on the pile after the holidays, and I let fallen leaves litter the ground. As the oranges ripen on my tree in January, I cut a few in half and place them in the tangle of twigs and branches.

This brush pile becomes the winter living room for the birds. Song sparrows forage there for insects and seeds, wrens come to seek its shelter, and a bright yellow western tanager appears sometimes to perch on an orange rind to enjoy eating the fruit. The birds that spend their winter in California are always on the lookout for an undisturbed place to nest, for insects and seeds to eat, or for shelter during storms.

BERRIES, ETC.

You'll find that berry-producing trees and shrubs are the real treasures in a winter garden. The toyon, also known as the Christmas berry or the California holly, is a California native that produces bright red clusters of berries from November through January.

Junipers offer berries as well as winter shelter for the birds. The low-growing shore juniper is popular along the coast, and the tall California juniper grows well in desert areas. Check with your local nursery or local extension office for advice on varieties that will grow well in your area.

A WET SPRING

Coastal gardeners often experience wind and rain throughout the early weeks of spring, with only a few, warm, balmy days to hint at the calmer weather to come. In the mountains, snow will continue throughout March, making shelter and well-stocked feeding stations more important than ever. But once the warm spring weather arrives, I look forward to the spectacle of bird-friendly trees coming into bloom in my neighborhood.

Pacific dogwood, which is a California native, and flowering dogwood make excellent focal points for the spring garden. Both will burst into spectacular bloom in April or May, with a second flowering possible in September. And as if that wasn't enough, the leaves turn a glowing red, yellow, or pink in fall. After the leaves drop, clusters of scarlet fruit provide a feast for the birds during fall and winter months.

Flowering plum and cherry trees also offer spectacular spring blossoms and fruit for the birds later. I like the native holly-leaved cherry and the hardy wild goose plum for their reliability and lovely pinkish white flowers.

NESTING MOCKINGBIRDS

I look forward to spring each year because a pair of mockingbirds faithfully builds a nest in my lemon tree. Both birds share the task of building a nest of dead twigs and grass about 10 feet (3 m) above the ground. It's a joy to watch them forage for food among the berry-producing shrubs and vines. They stop frequently to chatter at one another, or they hop onto the roof of the garden shed, where they protest loudly any time a gull dares to fly over their territory.

Mockingbirds are drawn to backyards that feature a multitude of fruiting plants and dense shrubbery.

BY THE BUNCH

Spring is a good time to plant flowers that will produce seed in summer and fall for finches, towhees, juncos, and sparrows. The trumpet-shaped blossoms of the columbines attract hummingbirds. Forget-me-nots can be invasive but they offer bright, early spring flowers and plenty of seeds later, and calendulas and marigolds attract beneficial insects to the vegetable garden.

For a gentle transition from spring into summer, interplant bachelor's buttons along with spring bulbs; the color combinations are delightful. The highlight of my flower garden, however, is a patch planted with meadow wildflowers, such as California poppy, yarrow, purple coneflower, and pincushion flower. Many of these flowers attract butterflies, too!

FOR HUMMERS

I've devoted a wide perennial border along my house to hummingbird plants, and summer is their time in the sun. I've planted penstemon and pineapple sage, Canadian columbine (*Aquilegia canadensis*), and lupine to attract the Anna's and rufous hummingbirds. (Desert gardeners may want to consider drought-tolerant natives, such as California fuchsia and monkey flower.) Aloes and red-hot poker plants thrive in both desert and seaside areas and attract hummingbirds with their bright orange blooms.

In a cottage garden, flowering plants, such as the butterfly bush, bee balm, penstemon, and foxglove, will attract hummingbirds and butterflies in droves. I've even drawn both to the vegetable garden with scarlet runner beans, which sport bright red flowers and edible pods.

FALL PLANTING

October is the best month to plant in California since the rains are just starting and the weather is still warm enough to encourage young growth in new plants. A good layer of leaf mulch in the garden helps keep roots warm in winter. It's also fun to watch the sparrows forage for insects under the decaying leaves.

One of my favorite vines comes into its prime in the fall—Virginia creeper. It will scramble over the ground, climb up a trellis, and provide erosion control when planted as groundcover on slopes. Virginia creeper leaves turn a dramatic orange-red in fall, and its berries are attractive to flickers, titmice, and robins, among others. Here in coastal California, I look to the long-blooming Mexican sunflower, the Virginia creeper vine, and the migratory monarch butterflies to provide fall color in my garden.

NATIVE HEDGEROWS

A hedgerow planted with the fall in mind can be the highlight of your year-round California garden. Many birds will find food and shelter in a hedgerow tangle, and you'll enjoy the seasonal changes that your plantings will offer. Stick with native plants to attract the most birds. Try grouping any of these plants together to create a bird-friendly hedgerow: wild buckwheat, California sagebrush (*Artemisia californica*), 'Blueblossom' ceanothus (*Ceanothus thyrsiflorus*), coffeeberry (*Rhamnus californica*), coyote willow (*Salix exigua*), elderberry, lupine, poppy, wild strawberry, and yarrow.

MOUNTAIN WEST

Rewarding Challenges

The weather and altitude make it tough for bird gardeners in the Mountain West. But Miles Blumhardt has found that choosing the right plants and providing the little extras for birds will make the experience truly rewarding.

SPOTLIGHT ON A BIRD GARDENER

MILES BLUMHARDT

Miles Blumhardt is a landscape designer, avid birder, and home-and-garden writer at the *Fort Collins Coloradoan* newspaper. His yard is a certified backyard wildlife habitat.

It's inconceivable to me how one can be a gardener and not garden for the birds. Oh, sure, the birds might have stolen a few cherries you had planned for that pie, and yes, there was that early morning revelry when you really wanted to sleep in. But birds are the bonus for being a truly good gardener. They're the movement, color, and sound in a landscape. And like perennials, the bird species that frequent my yard change with the season, keeping the landscape alive even in winter.

ROCKY TIMES

Gardening in the Rocky Mountain region of the United States is challenging. But if you roll with the punches of temperature fluctuations, clay and rocky soil, ferocious winds, and untimely early fall and late-spring frosts, you'll be blessed with a bounty of birds and blossoms.

Gardening for pleasure and attracting birds go hand in hand. To make your landscape attractive to birds, you'll need to provide cover, food, places to raise young, and water. Trees and shrubs that provide four-season interest to you are also the best selections for birds.

SPRING PROMISE

Spring is a season of anticipation. You're anxiously watching for migrating birds and for signs of new *ecoregion*

migration snow monsoon humidity desert mountains prairie frost

growth from perennials, shrubs, and trees. Spring, like no other season in the Rockies, is a season of uncertainty, though. Warm days that have coaxed leaves to emerge can suddenly turn nasty. Cold winds and heavy snows will combine to wreak havoc on young plants and migration-weary birds alike.

It's important to provide shelter for birds during spring. Conifers, or evergreens, can offer shelter from the biting winds. Dense conifers, such as Colorado blue spruce and Rocky Mountain juniper, provide some of the best protection, especially when planted together on the north or west side of a property to protect birds from the prevailing wind.

PRACTICAL PLANTS

There are few plants in this region that actually produce spring fruit, but many ornamental plants bear fruit in the late summer and fall that often lingers on the branches until early spring. Bird gardeners should include as many of these plants as possible—both for their aesthetic value and their fruit-bearing qualities. Landscape-worthy trees, such as mountain ash, hawthorn, and crabapple, may grow well in your region, and equally pleasing shrubs, such as pyracantha, European and American highbush cranberry, cotoneaster, coralberry, and mahonia, will provide fodder for the birds.

FEEDER FRENZY

Seed-eating birds feed heaviest at feeders during the spring and early summer. This extra gobbling is probably due to the energy they expend migrating, setting up and defending territories, courting, nesting, and rearing young.

Just when the spring migrants arrive, the natural food supply is at its lowest. If you've done your part by landscaping for the birds and filling feeders well into the summer, though, these birds will be attracted to your yard for the goodies you have to offer.

SUMMER BLISS

As the spring warms into summer, the importance of providing places for birds to nest and to raise their young only heightens.

These sites include both large and small deciduous trees, conifers, thickets, and nest boxes.

Some of my favorite trees for nesting include common hackberry, green ash, apple, cherry, cockspur hawthorn, crabapple, Rocky Mountain juniper, and Colorado blue spruce. All of these trees are valued for their ornamental qualities, and all of them produce food as well as offering nesting sites.

THICK THICKETS

Many of the birds in the Mountain West ecoregion use thickets for nesting, shelter, and food. Every bird gardener should give summer-blooming chokecherry and American plum a try. Both trees are beautiful and attract birds.

Other berry-producing shrubs that bear fruit during summer and form ideal thickets include golden currant, red twig dogwood, juneberry, elderberry, and buckthorn. With the right plantings, you can expect a variety of birds to nest in your yard, including mourning doves, blue jays, house finches, chickadees, downy and hairy woodpeckers, robins, and house wrens.

Let a thicket of berry canes and fruit trees grow up along your property's edge, then grab a lawn chair and enjoy the parade of birds, including the common yellowthroat.

FALL LOITERERS

Every fall, American and lesser goldfinches seem to know when my purple coneflowers have gone to seed. They stop for a day or week or more to gather strength for migration by eating the seeds of perennials, such as coneflowers, asters, and blanket flowers, and of annuals, such as zinnias, Mexican sunflower, cosmos, and marigolds.

As autumn progresses and the migrants head southward, dark-eyed juncos and pine siskins begin their own migration, descending from the mountains to spend the winter around my foothills home. Each fall, I return to feeding the birds, placing several tube feeders filled with black oil sunflower, a thistle feeder or two, and a suet feeder around my backyard.

WINTER VIEWS

Winter is warmed by the sight and sounds of juncos, pine siskins, black-capped and even a few mountain chickadees, house finches, blue jays, American magpies, common flickers, and robins.

These birds are also occasionally joined by evening grosbeaks, cedar waxwings, spotted towhees, red-breasted and white-breasted nuthatches. During extremely cold stretches, red crossbills, common redpolls, sharp-shinned hawks, and a single Townsend's solitaire have visited my yard.

OFFER UP WATER

Water is important for birds year-round, but it might be the most important in winter. I leave my water feature, which includes two small ponds and a 23-foot streambed, running as long as I can during winter. When the snow gets too deep, I disconnect the hose that feeds water from the lower pond to the upper pond, and I allow the pump to bubble. The bubbling keeps the water open for the birds, even in the most frigid winter-weather temperatures.

You could also place a small floating heater in your water feature, be it a pond, a birdbath, or a fountain. Open water is the single, best bird magnet you can have in your backyard, especially during the desperately cold days of winter.

UP ON HIGH

Despite its rigorous climate, gardening in the Rockies can be very rewarding. Incorporate the trees, shrubs, vines, perennials, and annuals that thrive here in the mountains in clusters in your yard, add feeders filled with various seeds for supplemental food, provide water, and don't be too diligent a gardener, and you'll find yourself enjoying your landscape as much as the birds do.

DESERT SOUTHWEST

Desert Diversity

Lynn Hassler Kaufman revels in her Desert Southwest garden, enticing resident and migrant birds to her backyard. Her bird-friendly plantings have even attracted some exciting Mexican hummingbird visitors.

SPOTLIGHT ON A BIRD GARDENER

LYNN HASSLER KAUFMAN

Lynn Hassler Kaufman has been bird watching, gardening, and studying plants for more than 25 years. She is on the staff of the Tucson Botanical Gardens and is the author of *Birds of the American Southwest*.

The Desert Southwest is a region very rich in bird life because it encompasses a number of different elevations and habitats. The climates in these zones are vastly different, so it is nearly impossible to make generalizations about gardening in this part of the world. Each elevation supports a distinct set of plants and a different group of birds, and gardening practices vary. The Southwest also has many subtropical species of birds that spill across the border from Mexico, increasing the chances for unexpected avian visitors to the backyard bird garden.

REGIONAL REALITY

While the Desert Southwest supports an incredible array of interesting plants, most gardeners in this region have to face challenging site conditions. Gardening successfully means facing up to the regional realities. Whether your backyard is at a high or low elevation or whether most of your rain falls in summer or winter, choosing suitable plants, especially native ones, should be your number one priority.

Soil types vary throughout the region, from the rocky soil in the foothills and mountain slopes to the almost pure sand in the arroyos. The presence of caliche, a layer of calcium carbonate found at the surface of the soil or slightly below it, is a problem in some parts of the region. Caliche forms a cementlike soil layer that is nearly impenetrable, so plant roots have nowhere to grow and drainage can be a problem.

The desert at the lowest elevations is hot and dry for a good portion of the year. One thing is certain—in arid regions like the Southwest, gardeners need to use water-efficient perennials, shrubs, and trees in their landscape.

Spring Glory

Spring blooms warm and beautiful in the desert lowlands. In years of good winter rains, the desert can be ablaze with color. Annual wildflowers abound, supplying copious amounts of seed for goldfinches, sparrows, quail, and doves. The daisylike flowers of brittlebush (*Encelia farinosa*) literally cover some south-facing hillsides and produce abundant seed for birds and small mammals.

Ocotillo provides a great perch for passing birds and forms clusters of red-orange flowers at the end of long, whiplike stems. Hooded orioles often build their woven nests on the underside of the fronds of the date palm, a tree found in many southwestern gardens. At higher elevations, black-and-lemon-yellow–colored Scott's orioles reappear for the nesting season. They sip nectar from flowering agaves and often build their elaborate nests in native yucca plants.

White-winged doves return for another year of nesting, and the air is filled with the sound of their rich, cooing voices. Mourning doves are already into their second or third brood of the year, nesting in acacia, mesquite, or palo verde trees, or in large shrubs like hop bush.

Summer Heat

Plants and birds try to cope with the merciless sun and heat in the desert. Broad-leaved plants are subject to sunburn, and many garden plants stop flowering completely as they attempt to withstand the temperature extremes. Birds struggle to find much-needed water sources and the shaded spots that are out of the direct rays of the sun.

| Quick Reference | **BIRD-FRIENDLY PLANTS** |

DESERT SOUTHWEST

BIRDS flock to a multitude of plants in the Desert Southwest ecoregion for food, shelter, or roosting and nesting opportunities.

HOST PLANTS	BIRDS THEY SUPPORT
Agaves (*Agave* spp.)	Scott's orioles
Mimosas (*Albizia* spp.)	Mourning doves
Bird of paradise (*Caesalpinia gilliesii*)	Orioles
Saguaro (*Carnegiea gigantea*)	Summer tanagers, gila woodpeckers, and gilded flickers
Hop bush (*Dodonaea vicosa*)	Mourning doves
Ocotillo (*Fouquieria splendens*)	Hummingbirds, verdins, and Bullock's orioles
Blanket flowers (*Gaillardia* spp.)	Lesser goldfinches
Chuparosa (*Justicia californica*)	Anna's, black-chinned, and Costa's hummingbirds
Texas rangers (*Leucophyllum frutescens*)	House finches and Gambel's quail
Cholla (*Opuntia* spp.)	Cactus wrens
Palo verde (*Parkinsonia florida*)	Cactus wrens and mourning doves
Parry's penstemon, rock penstemon (*Penstemon parryi, P. baccharifolius*)	Anna's, black-chinned, and Costa's hummingbirds, and house finches
Date palm tree (*Phoenix dactylifera*)	Hooded orioles
Mesquites (*Prosopis* spp.)	Mourning doves, cardinals, and pyrrhuloxias
Texas sage (*Salvia coccinea*)	Hummingbirds and lesser goldfinches
Autumn sage (*S. greggii*)	Anna's, black-chinned, and Costa's hummingbirds
Texas betony (*Stachys coccinea*)	Anna's, black-chinned, and Costa's hummingbirds
Cape honeysuckle (*Tecoma capensis*)	Verdins and hummingbirds
Yellow bells (*T. stans*)	Black-chinned and Costa's hummingbirds
Yuccas (*Yucca* spp.)	Scott's orioles

But, the news is not all dismal. A few plants thrive in the intense heat: The red bird of paradise's dazzling red-orange flowers are unequalled for showy summer color, and orioles often flock to them. Yellow bells is in its glory in May and June, and rock penstemon's scarlet tubular flowers are reliable summer bloomers for hummingbirds. Red salvia blooms attract nearby hummingbirds, and its seeds offer a feast for lesser goldfinches.

SPLENDID SAGUARO

One of the plant highlights in parts of the Sonoran Desert is the blooming of the saguaro cactus. This plant provides food, moisture, shelter, and nesting sites for many desert birds. The waxy, white flowers are followed by red, pulpy fruits that are fed upon by scores of birds, providing them with much-needed moisture. Summer tanagers may venture forth from slightly cooler streamside habitats to feed on saguaro fruits in adjacent desert areas. Gila woodpeckers and gilded flickers attend to their nests in holes excavated in the saguaro.

BRING ON THE RAIN!

The summer monsoons in the Sonoran and Chihuahuan Deserts arrive in July and August. Towering thunderheads form over the mountains as tropical air masses bring much-welcomed moisture. This is a major growing season for many shrubs and trees. Plants lose their withered look, start to green up, and many perennials and summer wildflowers resume blooming.

In response to the increased humidity, Texas rangers (*Leucophyllum frutescens*) produce a profusion of lavender-pink flowers, which are eaten by house finches and Gambel's quail. Firewheels or blanket flowers (*Gaillardia* spp.) bloom continually at this time of year; their globular seedheads are very popular with flocks of lesser goldfinches. Weeds also take advantage of the increased moisture to sprout.

HUMMERS ON THE MOVE

A late summer highlight in the Southwest is hummingbird migration. One August day, seven species of hummingbirds visited my Tucson yard. Hummingbirds that breed farther north, such as rufous, broad-tailed, and calliope, have begun their southward journey, following the blooms of wildflowers.

Species that breed locally, as well as their offspring, are still in the area, adding to the numbers. Because mountain ranges are not contiguous in this part of the world, but rather broken up into what we call sky islands, many birds, including hummingbirds and other higher-elevation species, must move through the desert lowlands as they head south. You never know what species might drop by to feed on garden plants.

RELISHING FALL

White-crowned sparrows arrive in October to spend the winter in the desert lowlands where they rummage for grass and weed seeds. Cardinals and pyrrhuloxias feed on the fallen seeds of mesquite trees. Cape honeysuckle begins its cooler weather flowering period. In milder areas, it sports red-orange tubular flowers that are relished by verdins and hummingbirds, from fall well into winter.

UNPREDICTABLE WINTERS

There's not much for the gardener to do during the cold and rainy southwestern winters, so many of us do a bit of bird watching. Despite the cold temperatures, Anna's hummingbirds will begin to nest in winter, sometimes as early as January in some of the lower desert areas.

The berries of pyracantha that ripen in the winter attract mockingbirds, curve-billed thrashers, cardinals, pyrrhuloxias, and white-crowned sparrows. If there's a shortage of food in the higher elevations, we may occasionally see American robins, hermit thrushes, and cedar waxwings outside of their normal winter ranges gorging on pyracantha berries.

A VISUAL FEAST

With the varied habitats in the region and the many birds that migrate through the area, there's a chance you could see almost any type of bird in the Desert Southwest. It's the possibility of the unexpected that makes bird gardening so special in this region.

MIDWEST/GREAT PLAINS

Prairie Roots

When settlers came to the Great Plains, they transformed the wild prairies into farmland. Now, Jennifer L. Baker spends her time returning the land to its prairie beginnings using native plants in her noteworthy garden designs.

SPOTLIGHT ON A BIRD GARDENER

JENNIFER L. BAKER

Jennifer L. Baker is an ecological consultant and landscape designer for Prairie Nursery, and the vice president for Lawson Ridge Native Landscaping in Westfield, Wisconsin. Jennifer balances her consulting work with competitive trail and endurance riding.

My passion for birds was sparked in childhood while I was growing up on a small farm in the heart of a Midwest farming community. My self-acclaimed heroic rescues of young robins and starlings that had fallen from nests developed into a full-blown crusade through the years to learn as much as I could about birds and their field marks, signature calls, and re-spective habitats. My career as an ecological consultant and landscape designer offers me the opportunity to re-create and restore native prairie grasslands and savannahs, both vital for bird habitats in the Midwest.

PRAIRIE SPRING

Fresh southern winds breathe new growth into the scattered oak canopy and prairie ground layer. Each spring, my husband, Keith, and I ride our frisky Arabian horses through the prairie and savannah landscape that we are in the process of restoring. These longer, warmer days promote a new flush of leaf growth from bur and white oak branches. Their lime green leaf buds attract a diversity of insects, which are quickly devoured by

ecoregion

migration snow monsoon humidity desert mountains prairie frost

the migrating yellow-rumped and chestnut-sided warblers. On the sandy, dry soils characteristic of our area, the Pennsylvania sedge blooms early, its yellow seedheads interspersed by blue-eyed grass, lupine, and bird's foot violet. The endangered Karner blue butterflies emerge and deposit small masses of eggs on the fuzzy lupine leaves. We catch a rare glimpse of the delicate white blossoms of a pasque flower that managed to escape the hungry mouths of the prolific white-tailed deer herds that browse through the understory.

SIGHTS AND SOUNDS

Although they're rarely seen, Savannah sparrows are definitely heard as a buzzy accompaniment to the clear songs uttered by the more conspicuous eastern meadowlarks. Vesper sparrows are also easily identified by the white triangles framing their tails as they disappear into clumps of little bluestem. A bobolink demands the attention of our horses as it takes flight from its perch on top of last year's compass plant. Prairie smoke, adorned with wispy, red flowers, blankets the ground with creeping fernlike foliage. Jacob's ladder with bell-shaped, blue flowers brightens up the shade cast by a red cedar.

SUMMER HEAT

When the prairie and savannah go from fresh and breezy to hot hazy, and humid, water is a precious commodity in our backyard. The birdbath was getting so busy on blistering hot days that we added a small rain garden, which intercepts the runoff from our rooftop, runs through gutters and downspouts, and provides pooled water at ground level for the birds. Bluebirds and their fledglings take turns drinking, bathing and, until they're through, defending this precious water from other thirsty avian onlookers.

Tree swallows visit during the day and whippoorwills come at dusk. We've even had whippoorwills nearly land in our laps as we have watched the sunset from our back porch; they are often so busy jockeying for the best calling position that they're oblivious to their surroundings.

ecoregion *prairie frost mountains desert humidity snow monsoon migration*

RADIANT FLOWERS

Pale purple coneflowers (*Echinacea angustifolia*) and the butterfly weed bloom in early summer, but once the yellow and other purple coneflowers (*E. purpurea*) bloom, I know that the summer months are starting to pass. The bluestem grasses grow rapidly under the heat of the sun and fill in between the flowers, providing support and additional cover. Blazing stars, their sturdy straight stalks a perfect song perch for dickcissels, come alive late in the season and their clusters of diminutive, deep pink flowers begin to open gradually from the top of the stalk downward. Ox-eye sunflowers are everywhere, their sunny yellow blooms providing an amazing backdrop to the iridescent blue shine of indigo buntings.

HAWK WATCH

Red-tailed hawks are a common sight during the summer, and they will descend from their stately oak perches to hunt for the unsuspecting rodents that are scooting through the dry prairie below. On rare occasions, we may see harriers hover over the prairie wildflowers and grasses, seeking meadow voles that have wandered from their thatch-covered trail systems.

Raptors, such as this northern harrier, search meadows for food, playing key roles as predators in the prairie ecosystem. They typically fly low over fields, then hover and drop down to catch voles, mice, and other rodents.

A WELCOME FALL

Fall is the highlight of my year as the heat starts to wane, the humidity lifts, and the deer flies and mosquitoes call a cease-fire. Keith and I spend as much time as possible out-of-doors, adding plants to small gardens around the house, sowing seed into old crop fields, taking out nonnative weeds that have crept in, and watching birds as they search for and harvest food.

MIGRANTS ON THE MOVE

Anticipating a meal of nectar, ruby-throated hummingbirds zoom in to inspect the cardinal flower and great blue lobelia that we're adding to the edge of the rain garden. Blackbird and sparrow families mass together and descend upon the prairie to gorge themselves on late-hatching insects and seeds to fuel their engines for long, southerly flights. Yellow-rumped and chestnut-sided warblers are back for a few quick meals of insects en route to their wintering grounds. White-throated sparrows shuffle through the oak-leaf litter like mechanical toys, their thin, clear song an echo of their confident spring yodels.

RAINBOW OF COLOR

Asters are one of the finales to the wildflower show, and they decorate the landscape with blooms of sky blue, white, clear pink, and deep purple. Sporting bright lemon flowers, goldenrods pull attention away from neighboring coneflowers that have started their dormancy cycle under the blanket of cool, fall evenings. Goldfinches, disguised in their fall and winter colors as they flit through the yellow blooms, search for ripening seeds on more mature flower heads.

FIRST FROST

The unwelcome first frost provides a dose of reality to those of us who think fall can keep winter at bay. Frost, however, transforms the blue-green leafy clumps of little bluestem to coppery penny red; a stunning contrast to the white, fuzzy fringe of the delicate seedheads. Wild turkeys peck through the thin ice layer that has formed over our rain garden for a much-needed drink. Some of their hard-earned summer fat is burned off as they launch into the oak canopy, escaping the pursuit of a hungry coyote pair. Snow is not far off and will be a welcome change to the freezing rain that coats the naked, craggy, bur-oak limbs.

SNOW SCENES

The now-dead stalks of anise hyssop, coneflowers, and Indian grass still harbor a wealth of ripe seeds, which will keep juncos, chickadees, and nuthatches full of protein during frigid winter days.

Indian grass punctuates the solid white of the snow blanket with flaxen leaves and arching seed-heads. Turkeys and deer abound, scratching through the fresh snow in search of acorns. Blue jays are next on the scene, taking advantage of the disturbed sites to cache the acorns that remain.

The crevices created by the rocks of the old, stone-barn foundation act as a vise grip for jays to crack tough acorn shells. White- and red-breasted nuthatches push seeds into cracks running along the bark of oak trees to create leverage for the seed as they pry it open with hammerhead blows. On occasion, we find a sunflower growing out of this vertical environment, evidence of a lost or forgotten seed.

For barred owls, winter marks the beginning of a new breeding cycle. Even on frigid nights, we hear them calling from the oaks that fringe the edge of our prairie.

As winter marches on, the simple palette of white, blue-gray, and black wears out its welcome. When the bright sun peers out from behind a thick bank of clouds for a few hours, it brings with it the anticipation of warm breezes, vibrant color, and the buzz of new life.

EVERY MOMENT A TREASURE

This great continent is ours only to borrow. As bird gardeners we relish the birds and the life they bring to the landscape. If we choose our plants carefully and provide the food, shelter, and water the birds need to survive, we contribute to the fascinating complexity that is the natural world.

CONTINENTAL EAST

Season for Everything

Ed Kanze shares what he's learned from turning his garden into a bird's paradise. Living in a part of the continent where the weather changes markedly means each season has its distinct delights and pleasures.

SPOTLIGHT ON A BIRD GARDENER
EDWARD KANZE

Ed Kanze is a writer, naturalist, and photographer who lives in New York. He is the author of *Wild Life: The Remarkable Lives of Ordinary Animals.* He recently finished a book about a 9-month, 25,000-mile journey of discovery that he and his wife, Debbie, made through Australia.

Watching birds in the Continental East has taught me that hope isn't all it's cracked up to be. You can be passive and long for the birds that fill the pages of field guides to appear before you, or you can get to work to bring the birds in. Make your 100 acres, ½ acre, ¼ acre, or 6 × 8-foot plot an irresistible rest stop, eatery, and watering hole, and you won't be sorry.

WISHFUL WINTERS

Winter is a great time for watching birds and dreaming and planning. You never know what birds will turn up in forests, in fields, and at shores at this time of year, so brave the cold, and head outside as often as you can.

This is the season when juncos arrive in great number, and flocks of pine siskins and common redpolls appear out of nowhere to snatch up thistle and sunflower seeds. Brilliantly colored evening grosbeaks turn up, too, and if you're really lucky (or diligent), you may get a look at a feathered predator from the Far North that has ventured southward in search of better hunting—a northern shrike, perhaps, or a rough-legged hawk or snowy owl.

ountains prairie frost ecoregion

More Than Seed

Like many bird lovers, I began feeding and attracting winter birds by putting up a number of feeders. But I noticed that no matter how much seed and suet I put out, there were always neighboring yards whose birds outnumbered mine. Then I saw the light. I realized that birds need much more than seed, and they weren't finding what they wanted in my yard.

So I began to plant. I transplanted wild trees and shrubs that were important to birds in my part of the country. I let some of the grass grow long, much to the delight of the sparrows (including a dainty field sparrow with a flesh-colored bill that stayed all winter long). I learned my lesson: Increase the appeal of a yard with natural foods and more birds will come to visit feeders.

Winter Birds

My favorite bird to see in the winter is the evening grosbeak. Some years I don't see grosbeaks at all, and in other years they arrive in squadrons.

With its enormous, pale greenish bill and flamboyant plumage, the evening grosbeak reminds me of a

Bird Shrubs and Trees

GARDENERS in the East have many plants to choose from when setting the table for the birds. These shrubs and trees make great additions to your yard, providing food, shelter, and nesting spots.

Maples
  (*Acer* spp.)
Gray dogwood
  (*Cornus racemosa*)
Red-osier dogwood
  (*C. stolonifera*)
Ashes
  (*Fraxinus* spp.)

American holly
  (*Ilex opaca*)
Black tupelo
  (*Nyssa sylvatica*)
Pines
  (*Pinus* spp.)
Mapleleaf viburnum
  (*Viburnum acerifolium*)

Arrow-wood
  (*V. dentatum*)
Blackhaw viburnum
  (*V. prunifolium*)
American cranberry
  (*V. trilobum*)

parrot. It comes to feeders for the sunflower seeds, but bird gardeners in my part of the world also attract it by encouraging tree and shrub growth in the vicinity of the feeding station. Maples and viburnums are grosbeak favorites.

I'm also partial to nuthatches, especially the red-breasted. While white-breasted nuthatches flourish in the deciduous forests, the red-breasted, which looks like a sawed-off, more colorful version of its cousin, inhabits northern evergreen forests and shifts its range southward for the winter. You can increase your chances of attracting the red-breasted by planting evergreens such as pines and spruces. These trees also provide birds with shelter from wind and cold.

SPRING ANEW

When the snow melts and the streams are clear of ice, it's time to plant and dig. Spring is my favorite time of year to be out planting and pruning because the weather is neither too cold nor too hot, and the presence of migrants give my every glance into a tree or bush the possibility of surprise.

Transplant woody plants in early spring or wait until late fall, when the plants are dormant and the ground isn't frozen. Even in humid regions in the East, considerable care is necessary to keep unearthed plants from drying out. I like to replant the same day I dig, and I always work in the cooler, least sunny parts of the day.

The red-breasted nuthatch is a delight in the winter months in the East. It seeks out conifers for seed and cover but may visit sunflower and suet feeders.

SPRING SPECIES

Though we've seen more than a dozen different species of warblers, tree swallows, and eastern bluebirds, Baltimore orioles are among the favorite birds that come to our yard in the spring. Orioles tend to seek out big deciduous trees in which to feed and weave their socklike nests. You can't grow a big tree overnight, but you can protect those you already have. This will improve your chances of having black-and-orange orioles around to sing you awake in the morning.

Eastern bluebirds, tree swallows, and house wrens will nest in birdhouses built for them. Early spring is a good time to get them up and ready. By the time the weather has grown consistently warmer, it may be too late.

Spring gives way to summer, sending off all but the nesting migrants and introducing other chores for you to do in the garden. Too hot to mow on a summer day? Don't! A ragged yard is a "welcome" sign for birds. Yards that regain some of their wildness, boasting brushy, overgrown areas, will abound in avian visitors. The song sparrow and house wren are two of my favorite birds that love the ragged look. Both will sing and sing and sing some more, and between outbursts they'll help manage your garden's insects.

BABY BIRDS ABOUND

The best part of bird gardening in summer is being able to watch the offspring of the birds you've attracted make their first, awkward visits to birdbaths, flowers, fruits, and feeders. It's guaranteed that you will take a paternal or maternal interest in them. I particularly enjoy watching young American robins pull their first worms out of the sod and speckled, juvenile eastern bluebirds struggle to balance on utility wires. Mastering the high wire is difficult, even for birds that will spend about half their lives perched on them.

Make your yard "birdy" and summer may well bring you a nest full of eastern phoebes. Get used to having these birds around, and you will find yourself pitying the people that don't have their company to enjoy. Phoebes, being flycatchers, spend a lot of time catching insects, so they're not only fun to watch, but they also provide practical aid in keeping down biting bugs.

You will often spot a phoebe near bridges, along streams and creeks, and around outbuildings where it can find insects. You can distinguish the eastern phoebe from other flycatchers by the phoebe's habit of wagging its tail downward while sitting on a tree or shrub branch.

Flycatchers such as this eastern phoebe will keep you entertained with their airborne antics and keep a handle on your insect populations.

FALL FRENZY

I associate the fall with colored leaves, cool weather, and the cries of blue jays. After a summer in which most of the birds have grown silent, it's a relief to have autumn arrive and have the blue jays start their vocalizing. They cry, *jay*, *jay*, their shrill trademark, and make other sounds, too, such as the call that sounds like the turning of a rusty gear or pulley.

Fall brings renewed activity and restlessness to other birds in the garden too. Migrants, such as hummingbirds, will feed hungrily and then vanish. Overhead, hawks drift toward the south, making smaller birds nervous. Songbirds pass through, stopping in the yard to pad on just a little more fat, before they flit off and disappear over the horizon.

RENEWAL

No matter what the season, there is always something to do and something to watch in your eastern garden. As the seasons change, so do many of the birds; so if you plant what the birds like, you'll like what you see.

Seasons of Joy

Jeanne Lebow's garden at her home in Mississippi is a favorite hangout for the neighborhood birds. She always appreciates the colorful changing of the guard as birds migrate in and out of her Humid South ecoregion.

> ### SPOTLIGHT ON A BIRD GARDENER
> ## JEANNE LEBOW
>
> Jeanne Lebow is a writer, photographer, naturalist, and former literature professor. She and her husband, Steve, enjoy gardening for birds and growing Louisiana irises around the pond in their front yard.

I was a college student in Virginia when I first became a bird watcher. On winter days, I would walk down to the swampy edges of a nearby lake to watch the most thrilling birds I had ever seen—the pileated woodpeckers. Such a handsome display of black-with-white wing linings and the large, brilliant red crests! I am just as thrilled now when these mighty woodpeckers stop by our yard on the Mississippi Gulf Coast.

A NEW VIEW

Winter is an exciting season because the hardwoods have dropped their leaves, and I can see the birds more easily. When white-throated sparrows arrive in our yard, I know winter won't be far behind. When I lived in Virginia, the dark-eyed juncos were my "winter signal" birds. Both of these birds seem cheerful on the coldest days, as they go about their chores, foraging on the ground for seeds and insects. Three types of finches also join us in our Gulf Coast backyard for winter—American goldfinches, purple finches, and house finches.

WINTER BERRIES

Trees that are particularly important to wintering birds in the Humid South, both for their berries and for their sheltering qualities, include hollies, waxmyrtle, and eastern red cedar.

A dozen hollies are native to the Southeast. In addition to pleasing wintering robins, holly berries are eaten by 48 other species of birds, including the flicker, mockingbird, gray catbird, brown thrasher, cedar waxwing, and eastern bluebird. American holly, yaupon holly, dahoon holly, possumhaw, and winterberry do well in our region.

If you want to enjoy flowers from December through February in the South, consider growing the evergreen, nonnative camellias that do so well here. Not only are the blossoms lovely in your garden but they also attract many small insects that birds can eat.

SLICE OF HEAVEN

Wintering hummingbirds are an exciting, new backyard birding possibility here in the Humid South. My husband, Steve, and I have been lucky to have a banded rufous hummingbird stay with us for five or six winters. When this Queen of the Yard arrives, she runs off all the ruby-throats,

helping launch them on their southward migration. She sticks around to enjoy the red carpet treatment that we now include in our daily feeding routine.

We maintain one or two nectar feeders for our rufous royalty, but she also visits all the red flowers and ginger lilies in the yard until the first hard frost. She gets her protein from the many gnats and other insects that stick close to our compost pile. A tough little bird, she even went through the fierce winds of Hurricane Georges with us in early October 1998. She escaped George's fury with nary a ruffled feather.

In addition to the rufous, you may find an Allen's, Anna's, black-chinned, calliope, or broad-tailed hummingbird in your yard if you maintain your nectar feeders. Reports of wintering hummingbirds extend from coastal Louisiana to Arkansas, Alabama, Georgia, and even to North Carolina.

AN EARLY SPRING

Spring arrives early with the blooms of yellow jessamine and red maple. The most widespread of

ecoregion

migration snow monsoon humidity desert mountains prairie frost

the North American maples, the red maple is nicknamed the swamp maple because it flourishes in swamps and river flood plains. However, it is tolerant enough of various types of soils to be considered a street tree, and people plant it in many places for its shade and beautiful fall color.

About a month after the tree flowers, you'll find winged seeds dangling from the branches. Grosbeaks, purple finches, pine siskins, and cardinals will eat those ripe seeds come summertime.

WORTH THE WAIT

Spring is the season when you and the birds begin benefiting from what you have planted in past winters. Red buckeyes, bottlebrush buckeyes, native azaleas, and cross vines all flower when the ruby-throated hummingbirds arrive on the Gulf Coast and begin migrating throughout the South.

The South's native red buckeye is a real showstopper in spring when it unveils its hand-shaped leaves and opens its clusters of fire-engine red flowers.

Red buckeyes are the most important small trees to have for those who want to attract ruby-throated hummingbirds to their yards. People on the Gulf Coast supply hummers with a needed boost of nectar in March and April as the birds return from Central America. Then, as the hummers continue to make their way north, the red blooms open along their flyway, with some ruby-throats stopping for the summer and others heading onward until the range is filled.

The bloom of the red buckeye fuels the northward migration of ruby-throated hummingbirds.

Trees such as the red maple, the black willow, the tulip poplar, and the red mulberry together provide food for at least 60 species of birds. In our yard, cedar waxwings stick around long enough to tear at the black willow catkins and at the sweet, cupped, tulip poplar blossoms before heading north.

SULTRY SUMMER

Most birds are on the nest and rearing their babies in the hot summer months. Few birds are uglier than the young, gray cardinals in our backyard. Yet, we enjoy watching these ugly ducklings becoming swans, as their head feathers perk up and their flight feathers gradually turn red.

We never tire of watching young cardinals learn to land on small limbs and on the seed feeders. Sometimes they'll sit at the feeder for a few moments and then fly off, not quite knowing what to do. Often they will beg on the ground or on a limb, their wings fluttering until dad or mom brings them a seed or caterpillar.

It's a special treat to watch the red-headed and red-bellied woodpeckers raising their young. The busy parents grab sunflower seeds and either fly back to the nest or stash them in the pine tree they use as a pantry. We wouldn't get as many close-ups of the adult red-headed woodpeckers as we do if they did not use feeders in summer. Sometimes we get a bonus peek at juveniles when they learn to land on perches and platforms.

SUMMER'S TABLE

Insects and berries are essential summer food for birds. By providing a backyard habitat of trees, shrubs, flowers, and grasses, birds will find plenty of insects.

Berries are easy to offer, too. Birds love the fruit of the wild black cherry tree and the common elderberry. The elderberry is a small tree that reaches 10 to 16 feet (30 to 50 m) tall. The purplish black berries can be so heavy that the tree will bend to the ground with the weight. No matter how small your backyard, make room for the common elderberry tree — 120 species of birds eat the fruit, including bluebirds, rose-breasted grosbeaks, and catbirds.

FRUITFUL FALL

Fall is the season of acorns, sweetgum balls, purple beauty-berries, pine and magnolia cones, and, of course, colorful falling leaves. The great horned owls begin their courting calls on the coast, and the barred owls start their *who, who cooks for you?* calls in the southeastern river swamps.

THE MIGHTY OAK

Every bird-friendly yard needs at least one oak to provide roosting and nesting spots, acorns, and insects. Here on the Gulf Coast, the evergreen live oak is the queen. Her long, outstretched branches are covered with resurrection fern and Spanish moss.

The water oak is a lovely tree as well. Although the water oak may not live as long or be as strong and as graceful as the live oak, it is a good shade tree for backyard gardens and can produce as many as 28,000 acorns a year—enough for blue jays, squirrels, thrashers, and just about anybody else who turns up. Think what it could do for your backyard!

A PLETHORA OF PINES

Just as no bird-friendly yard is complete without an oak tree, no bird-friendly yard—no matter how small—is complete without at least one conifer. Pines are among the most friendly trees for birds. Chickadees, evening and pine grosbeaks, nuthatches, jays, pine siskins, meadowlarks, red-cockaded and red-bellied woodpeckers, brown creepers, brown thrashers, and pine warblers all eat pine seeds.

Large pines provide roosting sites for migrating robins and nesting sites for mourning doves, purple finches, and magnolia warblers. Cavity nesters, such as the pileated, red-bellied, red-headed, and red-cockaded woodpeckers, rely on pines in the South.

DAILY SCENES

There is always something exciting happening in the bird gardens of the Humid South, and the list of plants to choose from is lengthy and inspiring. Include as many of those plants as you can to see what birds you can draw into your world.

Trees for All Seasons

The shorter growing season in the North can be a challenge for many gardeners, but Warren Balgooyen suggests that you should simply enhance what nature offers by adding the hardy plants that birds will love.

SPOTLIGHT ON A BIRD GARDENER

WARREN BALGOOYEN

Warren Balgooyen is a naturalist and field botanist. From his home in Maine, he runs a successful landscaping service and grows native plants on his small farm in order to create wildlife habitat.

Do you want to make your yard a bird-friendly paradise? Have you just moved into a new home? Are you anxious to get out there with a chainsaw or a string trimmer? Hold it! Before you unleash a bulldozer, take the time to explore and discover the varied features of your land. I always tell people who are new to a property or to an area to wait and watch through four seasons before undertaking a landscaping project. My advice is to explore, then enhance. Know, then nurture. Discover, then develop.

RESPECT FIRST, CHANGE SECOND

A part of the fun of being a landowner is sharing your land with cohabitants—the plants and wildlife, which, like you, find your piece of the planet the right place to be. As a caretaker, you should strive to create bird habitat, beautify the land, and establish places that are rich in life.

First, familiarize yourself with the local flora. Good, bird-friendly botanicals may already grace parts of your property. Identify which plants you have and which new plants you could add to your yard as companions. If you choose new plants carefully, your plants will grow and thrive, and they will attract birds of all kinds.

CAUTION FIRST

I heard of a man who moved north in January. He looked out his window and saw two "dead fir trees," bare of needles. He could hardly wait for the moving van to leave so he could grab his chainsaw. As he cut the trees down, a neighbor ran out to ask him why he was removing his larch trees. The poor homeowner. He didn't know larch trees are deciduous conifers. Siskins, crossbills, and ruffed grouse visit bare branches of larches in winter to feed on the seed-rich cones.

Gone was the joy of watching them. Gone was the pleasure of seeing new, bright green needles in spring. Gone was their display of gold. It would take 40 years to bring them back.

If you don't know a sunflower from a forget-me-not, you may want to consider bringing in an expert to do a botanical inventory or asking a knowledgeable neighbor before you embark on your bird gardening journey.

BIRCH BLESSINGS

A lone gray birch tree stood out back in my field. I planned to cut it down because it was difficult to mow around. Then one winter day I looked out on a white landscape to see dozens of goldfinches in it, feeding on seeds in the pendant catkins. There seemed to be a bird on every twig—an awesome sight. I never cut down that tree, nor can I fell that scene from my memory.

Starkly beautiful gray birches serve a catkin feast to goldfinches on cold winter days in the North.

Quick Reference — SHRUBS AND TREES

CANADIAN NORTH

HERE are a few of my favorite shrubs and trees that are proven winners for hardiness and for bird food in this northern ecoregion. If you have the room, group these plants together in mass plantings to attract the most birds throughout the winter.

KEY   S Shrub   T Tree

PLANT NAME	PRODUCES	ATTRACTS
T Serviceberry, juneberry, shadbush (*Amelanchier* spp.)	June fruit	Variety of birds
T Pagoda dogwood (*Cornus alternifolia*)	Blue berries in the summer	Variety of fruit-eating birds
S Red-osier dogwood (*Cornus stolonifera*)	Late summer berries	Variety of fruit-eating birds
S Winterberry (*Ilex verticillata*)	Fall through early winter fruit	40 or more bird species
T Flowering crabapples (*Malus* spp.)	Fall and winter fruit	Variety of birds
T American mountain ash (*Sorbus americana*)	Summer fruit	Robins, catbirds, and yellow-bellied sapsuckers
S Snowberry (*Symphoricarpos albus* var. *laevigatus*)	Fall through early winter fruit	Many species, particularly evening and pine grosbeaks
S Highbush blueberry (*Vaccinium corymbosum*)	Summer fruit	Variety of fruit-eating birds
S Nannyberry (*Viburnum lentago*)	White flowers become sweet, blue-black fruits	Robins, flickers, and waxwings
S American cranberry bush (*Viburnum trilobum*)	Translucent red berry clusters	Ruffed grouse, wild turkey, brown thrasher, cedar waxwing, and eastern bluebird
S Weigela (*Weigela florida*)	Summer flowers	Hummingbirds

PLAN, THEN PLANT

These four planning suggestions work well in the far northeastern corner of our country (and probably across the continent as well).

1 **Work with what you've got.** You may want to favor some plants and eliminate others. Thin, prune, and work around what's already in place. You may have topographic features that can be put to good advantage. Wet areas, rough areas, and hedgerows can be bird magnets. Birds like the unkempt, untidy areas of a landscape.

2 **Add water.** Birds, like us, need water as a priority for survival. A simple birdbath is helpful. If you have the room, consider a water garden or even a farm pond.

3 **Provide shelter.** This is important in the North if you want to attract the winter birds. A dense evergreen tree near your bird feeder adds to its avian appeal.

4 **Avoid invasive species.** There are many exotic shrubs and trees that make good bird habitats and food sources but that otherwise damage a natural forest ecosystem. Here in Maine, we are losing understory natives to Japanese barberry, Tatarian honeysuckle, and Oriental bittersweet. Along our riverbanks and roadsides, Japanese knotweed is taking over, and in our wetlands, purple loosestrife is on the move. Do your research before you plant to avoid unleashing nonnatives in your region.

HELP AND HOPE

There is a lot of gardening advice out there when you decide to establish a more bird-friendly landscape. In addition to the pleasure of improving your landscape for beauty, there is the added benefit of offering a helping hand to those migrating birds that are in decline due to loss of habitat. If each of you does your part for the birds, you'll see an increase in the number of species you can attract, and you'll feel great knowing you played a part in creating a bird-friendly backyard.

Contributors

JULIE ZICKEFOOSE

Julie Zickefoose is a widely published natural history writer and artist. Educated at Harvard University in biology and art, she worked for 6 years as a field biologist for the Nature Conservancy before turning to a freelance career.

She has lectured across the country, and exhibited her watercolors of birds at universities, museums, galleries, and juried shows. Illustration credits include *The New Yorker*, *Smithsonian Magazine*, *Country Journal*, *Spider*, *Cricket*, *Ladybug*, and *Bird Watcher's Digest*. She has executed 15 cover paintings and dozens of articles for *BWD*. Other illustration clients include the U.S. Fish and Wildlife Service, the National Wildlife Federation, Boy Scouts of America, Yale University Press, the American Ornithologists' Union, the Academy of Natural Sciences, the Smithsonian Migratory Bird Center, and Cornell's Laboratory of Ornithology.

With her husband Bill Thompson III, editor of *Bird Watcher's Digest*, and their two children, Phoebe and Liam, Julie lives on an 80-acre nature sanctuary in the Appalachian foothills of southeast Ohio. A 42-foot-tall bird-watching tower atop their home helps them enjoy and catalog the wildlife of the sanctuary, which includes 175 bird species and 73 butterflies to date. Their five-piece band, the Swinging Orangutangs, has an eclectic repertoire and a large following.

BILL THOMPSON III

Bill Thompson III is the editor of *Bird Watcher's Digest*, the popular bimonthly magazine that has been published by his family since 1978. An avid bird watcher from the age of 8, Bill knew that birds would someday become the focus of his career, in addition to being his main hobby. He holds a bachelor of philosophy degree from Western College at Miami University of Ohio.

Bill was a senior account executive at the advertising firm of Ogilvy & Mather in New York City prior to joining *Bird Watcher's Digest*. In January 1995 he became the magazine's editor. He also edits *Backyard Bird News*, a bimonthly newsletter, and has written several volumes in BWD Press's bestselling Backyard Booklet series, which he edits. He has also created several Web sites, including birdwatchersdigest.com, birdbuzz.com, and the site opticsfinder.com. He is the author of *Bird Watching for Dummies*.

In pursuit of birds, Bill has trekked to many of the great birding hot spots around the world, including sites in Europe, the Middle East, and Central America. He has led birding field trips all over North America. But some of his favorite bird watching is done near home in the boondocks outside of Whipple, Ohio.

Acknowledgments

IT'S a continuous thrill to have Bill Thompson III, editor of *Bird Watcher's Digest*, as one's husband. Quite outside of the love and companionship factors, he lobs art and writing projects my way so thick and fast sometimes that I have to wear a hat. I am particularly grateful to have intercepted this one and to have had the opportunity to work with the editors at Rodale. Thank you, Will.

The wonderful columnists, writers, and contributors to *BWD* have planted the stake for this book; I've just wound a few vines around it. For their contributions, I am very grateful. I've also enjoyed collaborating with Fern Bradley, Karen Bolesta, and Nancy Biltcliff of Rodale.

Phoebe and Liam, my thanks for your patience and forbearance with your distracted mother. Modern technology makes it possible for us all to be together in our Appalachian hideaway a half hour from town, playing with blocks, drawing butterflies, and plugging away at a book. Firing manuscripts across cyberspace is particularly satisfying when you can look out the window and meet the liquid gaze of a doe and her fawns (and jump up to shoo them away from your newly planted birch saplings!). —*J. Z.*

Information Sources

SOME of the information in this book originally appeared in the pages of *Bird Watcher's Digest* and *Backyard Bird News*. Chapter 8 contains original essays by the authors listed.

1: THE BEST PLANTS FOR BIRDS

Adams, George. *Birdscaping Your Garden.* Emmaus, PA: Rodale, 1994.

Baker, Jennifer L. "Gardening with Exotics." *Bird Watcher's Digest*, March/April 2000.

Isaacson, Richard T., comp. *Andersen Horticultural Library's Source of Plants and Seeds.* Minneapolis: University of Minnesota, 1996.

Kanze, Edward. "Gardening for Hummers." *Bird Watcher's Digest*, May/June 1999.

Kaufmann, Lynn H. "Catalog Dreams." *Bird Watcher's Digest*, January/February 2000.

Piper, Kathy. "Berries for Birds." *Bird Watcher's Digest*, March/April 1998.

——. "Enjoying Junipers." *Bird Watcher's Digest*, November/December 1999.

——. "Vines for Birds." *Bird Watcher's Digest*, May/June 1998.

Swengel, Ann. "Planting for Birds and Butterflies." *Bird Watcher's Digest*, May/June 1995.

2: THE NEW LAGOON

Bird, David. "Bathing Birds." *Bird Watcher's Digest*, July/August 1996.

Day, Susan. "Water in Winter." *Bird Watcher's Digest*, November/December 1999.

Stephens, Sandra. "Cool, Cool Water." *Bird Watcher's Digest*, July/August 1996.

3: SETTING THE TABLE

Dornan, Laura. "Feeder Cleaning Made Easy." *Bird Watcher's Digest*, March/April 2000.

Youth, Howard. "Summer Feeding, A-Z." *Bird Watcher's Digest*, May/June 1998.

Zickefoose, Julie. "Feeders Provide Lessons of Bird Life." *Backyard Bird News*, Spring 1998.

———. "Fledglings at the Feeder." *Backyard Bird News*, Summer 1998.

4: MAKING A HAVEN

Ayick, Paul. "Creating Hospitable Habitat." *Bird Watcher's Digest*, January/February 1993.

Baker, Jennifer. "Wonderful Meadows." *Bird Watcher's Digest*, July/August 1999.

Boldan, Mary L. "Creating a Living Fence." *Bird Watcher's Digest*, July/August 2000.

Donnelly, David. "How to Make a Brush Pile." *Bird Watcher's Digest*, September/October 1998.

Piper, Kathy. "Holiday Treat." *Bird Watcher's Digest*, November/December 1998.

Watkins, O. W. "Make a Log Feeder." *Bird Watcher's Digest*, January/February 1998.

Webster, Harvey. "A Wild Backyard." *Bird Watcher's Digest*, March/April 1995.

5: LETTING IT GO

Blumhardt, Miles. "My Shabby, Wonderful Garden." *Bird Watcher's Digest*, September/October 1999.

Lavers, Norman. "Backyard Ahimsa." *Bird Watcher's Digest*, July/August 2000.

Piper, Kathy. "A Weedy Paradise." *Bird Watcher's Digest*, March/April 1996.

Zickefoose, Julie. "Letting It Go." *Bird Watcher's Digest*, Early Winter 1998.

6: SAVING GRACES

Bird, Dr. David. "The Dangers Posed by Cats." *Bird Watcher's Digest*, May/June 1997.

———. "A Reflection on Window Kills." *Bird Watcher's Digest*, July/August 2000.

Cook, Kevin. "Feeding Birds Responsibly." *Bird Watcher's Digest*, January/February 1997.

———. "Keeping Feeder Birds Healthy." *Bird Watcher's Digest*, January/February 1993.

Sherwonit, Bill. "Missing Redpolls." *Bird Watcher's Digest*, November/December 1998.

Zickefoose, Julie. "Paradise Lost." *Bird Watcher's Digest*, July/August 1997.

———. "In Praise of Sharpshins." *Bird Watcher's Digest*, January/February 1997.

7: BOXES FOR BIRDS

Original material by Julie Zickefoose

8: HOME HABITAT THROUGH THE SEASONS

Baker, Jennifer L. "Midwest/ Great Plains: Prairie Roots."

Balgooyen, Warren, "Canadian North: Trees for All Seasons."

Beutler, Linda. "Pacific Coast/ Northwest: More Than Rain."

Blumhardt, Miles. "Mountain West: Rewarding Challenges."

Kanze, Edward. "Continental East: A Season for Everything."

Kaufmann, Lynn Hassler. "Desert Southwest: Desert Diversity."

Lebow, Jeanne. "Humid South: Seasons of Joy."

Stewart, Amy. "Pacific Coast/ California: Always in Season."

Resources and Supplies

BIRDING PUBLICATIONS AND INFORMATION

Bird Watcher's Digest
P.O. Box 110
Marietta, OH 45750
Phone: (800) 879-2473
Fax: (740) 373-8443
Web site:
   www.birdwatchersdigest.com
Bimonthly magazine devoted to birds and bird watching. Subscriptions are $18.95 for one year (six issues).

Backyard Bird News
P.O. Box 110
Marietta, OH 45750
Phone: (800) 879-2473
Fax: (740) 373-8443
Web site:
   www.birdwatchersdigest.com
Bimonthly newsletter for backyard bird enthusiasts. Tips on feeding, housing, and gardening for birds. Subscriptions are $15 for one year (six issues).

www.birdwatchersdigest.com
P.O. Box 110
Marietta, OH 45750
Phone: (800) 879-2473
Fax: (740) 373-8443
Complete online resource for bird watchers.

ORGANIZATIONS

Avid bird watchers might enjoy learning more from any of these organizations striving to promote bird counts, environmental awareness, and habitat conservation.

The American Birding Association (ABA)
P.O. Box 6599
Colorado Springs, CO 80934
Phone: (800) 850-2473 or
   (719) 578-9703
Fax: (719) 578-1480
Web site: www.americanbirding.org
Contributes to bird conservation and aids birders in gaining knowledge and skills

The Cornell Laboratory of Ornithology
159 Sapsucker Woods Road
Ithaca, NY 14850
Phone: (800) 843-BIRD (2473)
Fax: (607) 254-2415
Web site:
   www.birds.cornell.edu/PFW
Project FeederWatch; the Great Backyard Bird Count; lists of birds common to different areas

The Hummer/Bird Study Group
P.O. Box 250
Clay, AL 35048-0250
Phone: (205) 681-2888
Fax: (205) 681-1339
Web site: hummingbirdsplus.org

The Hummingbird Society
P.O. Box 394
Newark, DE 19715
Phone: (302) 369-3699 or
   (800) 529-3699
Fax: (302) 369-1816
Web site: www.hummingbird.org

National Bird-Feeding Society
P.O. Box 23
Northbrook, IL 60065-0023
Phone: (847) 272-0135
Fax: (773) 404-0923
Web site: www.birdfeeding.org

The National Wildlife Federation (NWF)
Backyard Wildlife Habitat Program
8925 Leesburg Pike
Vienna, VA 22184
Phone: (703) 790-4000 or
   (800) 822-9919
Web site: www.nwf.org
Information on preserving wildlife, from specifics on making backyard wildlife habitats, to getting involved in saving the wetlands

National Wildlife Health Center
6006 Schroeder Road
Madison, WI 53711
Phone: (608) 270-2400
Fax: (608) 270-2415
Web site:
   www.nwhc.usgs/nwhchome.hmt

The Nature Conservancy
4245 N. Fairfax Drive
Suite 100
Arlington, VA 22203
Phone: (800) 628-6860
Fax: (703) 841-1283
Web site: www.thc.org

The North American Bluebird Society (NABS)
P.O. Box 74
Darlington, WI 53530
Phone: (608) 329-6403
Web site: www.nabluebirdsociety.org
Advice on how to contribute to bluebird recovery

Purple Martin Conservation Association
Edinboro University of Pennsylvania
Edinboro, PA 16444
Phone: (814) 734-4420
Fax: (814) 734-5803
Web site: www.purplemartin.org
Advice for purple martin landlords

U.S. Department of Agriculture (USDA)
14th & Independence Avenue SW
Washington, DC 20250
Phone: (202) 720-2791
Fax: (202) 720-2166
Web site: www.fsa.usda.gov/edso
    (for state agencies) and
    www.usda.gov/news/garden/htm
    (for gardening info)

BIRD FEED AND SUPPLIES

Wild bird shops, feed mills, and garden centers are great sources of bird feed and feeders, but the following sources may provide additional seed mixes and products.

Arundale Products
P.O. Box 4637
St. Louis, MO 63108
Phone: (800) 352-9164
Web site:
    www.skycafe.com/main.html
Squirrel-proof bird feeders

Bill Chandler Farms
R.R. 2
Noble, IL 62868
Phone: (800) 752-2473
Birdseed in bulk

Duncraft, Inc.
102 Fisherville Road
Concord, NH 03303
Phone: (603) 224-0200;
    (800) 593-5656 (order line);
    (800) 763-7878 (help line)
Web site: www.duncraft.com
Birdbaths, feeders, houses, and seed

Nature's Way
P.O. Box 7268
Hamilton, OH 45013-7268
Phone: (800) 318-2611
Fax: (513) 737-5421
Web site:
    www.herp.com/nature/nature.html
Mealworms in bulk

Perky Pet Brand Feeders
2201 South Wabash Street
Denver, CO 80231
Phone: (800) 782-3514 or
    (303) 751-9000
Fax: (303) 368-9616
Web site: www.perky-pet.com
Hummingbird and other feeders

Wild Bird Centers of America, Inc.
7370 MacArthur Boulevard
Glen Echo, MD 20812
Phone: (800) 945-3247
Fax: (301) 320-6154
Web site: www.wildbirdcenter.com
Broad range of bird products

Wild Birds Unlimited
11711 North College Avenue
Suite 146
Carmel, IN 46032
Phone: (888) 302-2473
Fax: (317) 571-7110
Web site: www.wbu.com
Tips for feeding and housing birds

PLANTS

The Andersen Horticultural Library's Source List of Plants and Seeds is a good source for finding specific plants and mail-order sources.

American Meadows Inc.
4750 Shelburne Road
Shelburne, VT 05482
Phone: (877) 309-7333 (toll free)
Fax: (802) 985-9268
Web site:
    www.americanmeadows.com
Wildflower seeds, including a butterfly and hummingbird mix

Andersen Horticultural Library
Minnesota Landscape Arboretum
3675 Arboretum Drive
P.O. Box 39
Chanhassen, MN 55317-0039
Phone: (612) 443-2440
Web site: http://plantinfo.umn.edu.

Bear Creek Nursery
P.O. Box 411
Northport, WA 99157
Phone: (360) 733-1171
Rare and classic plants, featuring the best varieties for a long season of interest and ease of care

Comstock Seed
917 Highway 88
Gardenerville, NV 89410
Phone: (775) 746-3681
Fax: (775) 746-1701
Web site: www.comstockseed.com
Seeds of drought-tolerant native grasses and plants of the Great Basin

Edible Landscaping
P.O. Box 77
Afton, VA 22920
Phone: (804) 361-9134 (help line)
    (800) 524-4156 (order line)
Fax: (804) 361-1916
Web site: www.eat-it.com
Variety of beautiful and delicious plants

Fieldstone Gardens, Inc.
620 Quaker Lane
Vassalboro, ME 04989-9713
Phone: (207) 923-3836
Fax: (207) 923-3836
Web site:
    www.fieldstonegardens.com
Perennials, grasses, and vines for cold-climate gardeners (catalog $2.50)

Forestfarm
9990 Tetherow Road
Williams, OR 97544-9599
Phone: (541) 846-7269
Fax: (541) 846-6963
Web site: www.forestfarm.com
Plants for birds, butterflies, and other wildlife

Logee's Greenhouses
141 North Street
Danielson, CT 06239-1939
Phone: (888) 330-8038 or
    (860) 774-8038
Fax: (888) 774-9932
Web site: www.logees.com
Rare, hard-to-find tropicals and subtropicals (Catalog $4.95, refundable on first order)

Niche Gardens
1111 Dawson Road
Chapel Hill, NC 27516
Phone: (919) 967-0078
Fax: (919) 967-4026
Web site: www.nichegdn.com
Perennials, trees, shrubs, shade plants, including drought-tolerant varieties (catalog $3.00)

One Green World
28696 South Cramer Road
Molalla, OR 97038
Phone: (503) 651-3005 or
    (877) 353-4028 (toll-free)
Fax: (800) 418-9983
Web site: www.onegreenworld.com
Unique fruiting plants and unusual ornamentals

Plants of the Southwest
Agua Fria Road
Route 6, Box 11A
Santa Fe, NM 87501
Phone: (800) 788-7333 or
    (505) 438-8888
Web site:
    www.plantsofthesouthwest.com
Specializing in drought-tolerant native plants and seeds

Prairie Moon Nursery
Route 3, Box 163
Winona, MN 55987-9515
Phone: (507) 452-1362
Fax: (507) 454-5238
Web site:
    www.prairiemoonnursery.com
Large selection of native seeds and plants for wetland, prairie, savanna, and woodland; catalog lists butterfly and hummingbird favorites

Prairie Nursery
P.O. Box 306
Westfield, WI 53964
Phone: (800) 476-9453
Fax: (608) 296-2741
Web site: www.prairienursery.com
Range or prairie mixes for differing growing conditions; native flower and grass seeds and plants

Sandy Mush Herb Nursery
316 Surrett Cove Road
Leicester, NC 28748-5517
Phone: (828) 683-2014
Rare herbs, flowering perennials, fragrant foliage plants, and flowering plants for garden cutting, and drying; bee balms, buddleias, coral bells, fuchsias, hostas, lobelias, and salvias

Shady Oaks Nursery
1101 South State Street
Waseca, MN 56093
Phone: (800) 504-8006
Fax: (888) 735-4531
Web site: www.shadyoaks.com
*Specializing in hard-to-find plants that
thrive in shade; great hosta selection*

Sunlight Gardens
174 Golden Lane
Andersonville, TN 37705
Phone: (800) 272-7396 or
    (423) 494-8237
Web site: www.sunlightgardens.com
*Nursery-propagated wildflowers of the
Northeast and Southeast*

Tripple Brook Farm
37 Middle Road
Southhampton, MA 01073
Phone: (413) 527-4626
Fax: (413) 527-9853
Web site: www.triplebrookfarm.com
Catalog of wildflowers, fruits, and shrubs

Underwood Shade Nursery
P.O. Box 1386H
North Attleboro, MA 02763-0386
Phone: (508) 222-2164
Perennials, ferns, and grasses.

Wayside Gardens
1 Garden Lane
Hodges, SC 29695
Phone and fax: (800) 845-1124
Web site: www.waysidegardens.com
*Variety from groundcovers and perennials
for the sun and shade, to trees, vines, and
shrubs*

We-Du Nurseries
2055 Polly Spout Road
Marion, NC 28752
Phone: (828) 738-8300
Fax: (828) 738-8131
Web site: www.we-du.com

Wildlife Nurseries
P.O. Box 2724
Oshkosh, WI 54903
Phone: (414) 231-3780
*Annuals, native grasses, perennials for
wildlife, and water garden plants*

Wildseed Farms
425 Wildflower Hills
P.O. Box 3000
Fredericksburg, TX 78624-3000
Phone: (800) 848-0078 or
    (830) 990-8080
Fax: (830) 990-8090
Web site: www.wildseedfarms.com
*Varieties of wildflowers, regional
wildflower mixes, and herbs*

Woodlanders, Inc.
1128 Colleton Avenue
Aiken, SC 29801
Phone: (803) 648-7522
*Native ferns, perennials, shrubs, trees,
and vines*

Yucca Do Nursery
Route 3, P.O. Box 104
Hempstead, TX 77445
Phone: (979) 826-4580
Web site: www.yuccado.com
*Tough plants that thrive in hot, humid
climates*

WATER GARDEN PLANTS AND SUPPLIES

Avian Aquatics
Georgetown-Lewes Highway (Rt. 9)
Harbeson, DE 19951
Phone (800) 788-6478
Web site: www.avianaquatics.com
*Recirculating birdbaths, fountains, pools,
ponds, and creeks molded from fiberglass*

Lilypons Water Gardens
6800 Lilypons Road
P.O. Box 10
Buckeystown, MD 21717-0010
Phone: (800) 999-5459
Fax: (800) 879-5459
Web site: www.lilypons.com
*Spectacular water-lily selection and other
plants for backyard ponds*

Van Ness Water Gardens
2460 North Euclid Avenue
Upland, CA 91784-1199
Phone: (800) 205-2425 or
    (909) 982-2425
Fax: (909) 949-7217
Web sites: www.vnwg.com
*Wide variety including water lilies, bog
plants, fish, and snails*

William Tricker, Inc.
7125 Tanglewood Drive
Independence, OH 44131
Phone: (800) 524-3492
Fax: (216) 524-6688
Web site: www.tricker.com
*Perennial water garden specialist;
plants, books, and water-garden-care
products (catalog $2.00)*

Index

Ecoregions Map

Plant communities and their associated birds have natural geographical limits, and these limits have been recognized and mapped into a series of areas known as ecoregions. Robert G. Bailey, heading a team of ecologists and geographers, has developed the ecoregions mapping concept. Using climate, topography, and vegetation, Mr. Bailey mapped natural boundaries across the continent. This ecoregion system helps the backyard bird watcher better understand seasonal movements and behavior in birds and select plants that will attract birds to the home landscape.

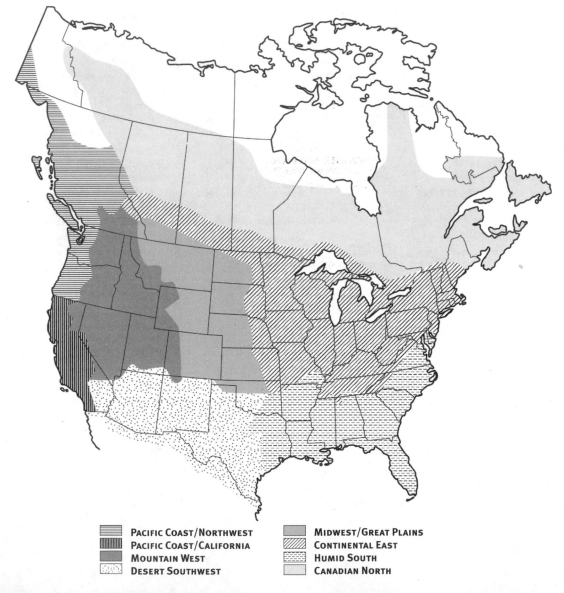

PACIFIC COAST/NORTHWEST

PACIFIC COAST/CALIFORNIA

MOUNTAIN WEST

DESERT SOUTHWEST

MIDWEST/GREAT PLAINS

CONTINENTAL EAST

HUMID SOUTH

CANADIAN NORTH